GOODBYE FLEET STREET

GOODBYE FLEET STREET

Robert Edwards

To Vic

A fellow

sinner

with love

Bob

JONATHAN CAPE
THIRTY-TWO BEDFORD SQUARE LONDON

First published 1988
Copyright © 1988 by Robert Edwards
Jonathan Cape Ltd, 32 Bedford Square, London WC1B 3EL

British Library Cataloguing in Publication Data

Edwards, Robert
Goodbye Fleet Street.
1. Newspaper publishing – England – London
I. Title
338.4′707212   PN5129.L/

ISBN 0-224-02457-4

Typeset by Computape (Pickering) Ltd, Pickering, North Yorkshire
Printed in Great Britain by Butler & Tanner Ltd
Frome and London

for Brigid

CONTENTS

Acknowledgments   xi

1   The Birthday Present   1

2   Family Affairs   7

3   'At Reading today . . .'   20

4   Tribune   32

5   Investigative Journalist   40

6   Evening Standard   54

7   JJ   64

8   Walking with the Lord   73

9   La Capponcina   88

10 Cutting Roses   97

11 'Study my answers please.'   114

12 League of Friends   128

13 After Beaverbrook   150

14 Sunday Editor   157

15 Royal Love Train   169

16 Strictly Libel   184

17 Decline and Fall   196

18 Cap'n Bob   215

19 Playing the Game   231

20 Farewell   248

Index   255

ILLUSTRATIONS

between pages 68 and 69

1 At home in Bracknell
2 Milkmen at Edwards & Sons
3 Beaverbrook
4 Aneurin Bevan
5 Max Aitken
6 Sir John Junor
7 John Knight, Cecil King and Lord Ryder
8 Working by day
9 Working by night

between pages 164 and 165

10 Princess Anne
11 Marje Proops and Hugh Cudlipp
12 Bob Maxwell
13 Lord Snowdon
14 Mrs Thatcher, Richard Stott and Joe Haines
15 The CBE

ACKNOWLEDGMENTS

My thanks to Graham C. Greene for suggesting the book and for all his encouragement, to Jenny Cottom for her editing, and to all the other splendid staff at Jonathan Cape. I would also like to thank the distinguished historian, A. J. P. (Alan) Taylor, former director of the Beaverbrook Library and author of *Beaverbrook*, for permission to use the exchange of memos and correspondence between Lord Beaverbrook and myself; Katharine Bligh, Assistant Archivist at the House of Lords Record Office, for making them available to me and for all the other help she gave; and the staff of the British Library at Colindale for so willingly providing a copy of every paper I edited. I am also grateful to Bernard Donoughue for his enthusiasm – he bears no responsibility for my words; to my former secretary and now established journalist, Sheridan Stevens; to Karen Smart who put the words on computer; to Lydia Segrave who did the index; and to all my friends and enemies in Fleet Street, whose forgiveness for any errors or omissions I crave, knowing that they will understand.

I gratefully acknowledge permission to reproduce the following photographs: 2, *Unigate News*; 3, *Daily Express* (Harry Benson); 4, Camera Press Ltd (Jitendra Arya); 5, 6, 7, 8, 9, 11, 12, 13, 14 (Mike Maloney) and 15, Mirror Pictures; 10, Kent Press Pictures.

I

THE BIRTHDAY PRESENT

It was the editor of the *Sunday Express*, John (later Sir John) Junor, who said to me at the start of a week in 1957, 'It's the Old Man's birthday on Sunday. You must buy him a present.' I had worked for two years for Lord Beaverbrook on the London *Evening Standard*. Now I was managing editor of the *Sunday Express*, a grand title which on that paper meant deputy editor. I said, 'Why should I buy him a present, John? He's worth millions. I can scarcely afford my season ticket.' 'You must,' said John. 'There's no question about it.'

The following day after lunch John called me in again. 'I want to show you something,' he said. He opened his bottom right-hand drawer and took out a pair of binoculars in a leather case. 'That's real leather,' he said. 'Smell it.' I did. Everyone obeyed JJ. 'It's my present to the Old Man. What do you think?' They were very expensive. How was I going to match that? That was my thought, but I said, 'They're wonderful, John. The Old Man will love them for his boat.' There was nothing else to talk about. My duties on the *Sunday Express* were light. John ran everything. A nice man called Victor Patrick brought the paper out under his direction.

On Friday afternoon the buzzer summoned me once more to the editor. Again we were not discussing the actual paper. 'A strange thing happened this morning,' said John. He explained that Tom Blackburn, joint chairman with Max Aitken, had asked him down to his office. 'He raised some footling issue,' said John. 'But I knew there was something else on his mind. Finally, he said he could not think of anything to buy the Old Man for his birthday. Had I any ideas?'

'And . . .?' I said, showing genuine interest. 'So I suggested,' said Junor, 'he should buy the Old Man a pair of binoculars. I'm keeping the ones I got him for my boat. Look what I'm giving him instead.' From the same bottom drawer he produced a small leather box containing a sheepdog whistle, the kind that is inaudible to human beings. 'Do you think he'll get the joke?' asked John. 'He's the shepherd, we're the sheep?' I thought he would not, but said nothing.

Next morning, my nerve cracked at last. With John's permission I borrowed the office driver, bought a plastic birthday card for two shillings that played a mediocre version of 'The London I Love' and after adding a devoted message from my wife Laura and myself, dropped it into Lord Beaverbrook's flat at Arlington House behind the Ritz. I did not send a present.

He was on the phone on Monday. 'Would you like to go walking with an old man?' There was the usual breakneck drive from my home in Hemel Hempstead, and when I arrived at Arlington House he was still opening presents from the previous day. A perplexed look came over his face, which I had observed before. It was usually accompanied by a flickering of his right eye. 'Junor sent me a whistle,' he said, 'that didn't blow.' I could have explained, but sensing that my chances of taking over the paper had measurably increased I treacherously did not. After a moment or two's thought, he added, 'The pea must have fallen out.'

A letter came from Lord Beaverbrook thanking me for 'your most original birthday card. I shall play it again and again. And with all good wishes, B.' I had advanced from Beaverbrook to B. John Junor buzzed me later that week. He raised some other issue that I knew was not the purpose of the summons. Then he said casually, 'By the way, did the Old Man ever thank you for his birthday card?' 'No,' I said, tactfully. 'He didn't thank me either,' said John, relieved.

A first meeting with Beaverbrook was something one does not forget. How this lucky break came about for me is important to the story. He was as fond of Michael Foot as Michael was of him, and therefore the Old Man's loyal and ambitious staff knew that he would be pleased to be told of any interesting articles in *Tribune*. 'Did you by any chance, Sir, read that amusing piece by a chap called Bob Edwards attacking George Gale in *Tribune* today?' someone no doubt said. 'No, I didn't. Please let me have it right away,' he would have replied. Gale, a young star on the *Manchester Guardian*, had written a book, *No Flies in China*, in which with commendable honesty he referred to getting drunk on two or three occasions. Since the *Guardian* was violently anti-*Tribune*, I exploited this confession by its star contributor, and this had the effect of drawing Beaverbrook's attention to both of us. George was soon on the *Express*, much favoured by the Old Man, but it was John Junor who was finally to tip the balance in my favour.

Churchill retired, uncharacteristically, in the middle of a strike. It had caused a total shutdown of national newspapers. BBC radio had the idea of asking editors deprived of their own platforms to say what they thought of Anthony Eden as his successor, and although we were not shut down I was invited as editor of *Tribune* to be Mr Nasty with a left-wing slant. John Junor and I were at each other's throats throughout an otherwise tedious programme, and it was I who later turned out to be right about Eden. Afterwards Junor recommended me to Beaverbrook. JJ took me to lunch at the Reform Club. He was plagued by a real or imagined ulcer at the time and said: 'I'm having melon and Dover sole, how about you?' For several years afterwards John invariably ordered melon and Dover sole. 'How would you like to work for the Old Man?' he said, as he prodded the familiar fish.

Whatever my reply, it was meant to indicate that I thought that was a very sound idea. Eventually Beaverbrook wrote a brief letter saying that he would like to continue the discussion where John Junor and I had left off. It was a letter a few thousand journalists would have given their right arms to receive.

I have never met anyone who impressed me as much as Lord Beaverbrook. Not prime ministers. Whenever I was invited to No. 10, they generally appeared harassed and bad-tempered, giving the correct impression that they were not on top of their jobs. Harold Wilson and Mrs Thatcher were the exceptions. Nor archbishops; who struck me as being as far removed from their products as chief executives of popular newspapers. Lord Beaverbrook was something else altogether. He was enormously attractive. I can quite understand why A. J. P. Taylor in his fine book, *Beaverbrook*, said he loved him more than any other person, though I would not go that far. Radicals like Michael Foot and Ian (no relation) Aitken of the *Guardian* remain under his spell as I do, and looking back on my nine years' relationship with him I think I treated him pretty badly at times. He was kind, brutal, considerate, selfish, honest, eccentric and a bit mad, but utterly sane in his judgment of newspapers. Above all, he had a presence that no actor who has played him in films or TV series has succeeded in putting across. I sat waiting for my first meeting rather nervously on a vast sofa, facing a large painting of a horse by Stubbs, in the drawing-room at Cherkley, his country home near Leatherhead, Surrey. Outside the weather was suitably foreboding, dark clouds and the threat of thunder. I realised it was sinful of me to be there: I, a Socialist, offering myself to a Tory Press Baron, whose *Daily Express* had printed the infamous headline SOCIALIST GESTAPO in the 1945 election. I was in the presence of Mammon all right.

The great door opened. Beaverbrook stood there. He was, as others have commented, not as short as the Low and Vicky cartoons of him suggested. His right fist was clenched in a curious fashion. 'You must be Mr Edwards,' he said in a gentle voice. He advanced towards me, and then came the surprise. 'I would like to shake you by the hand, but I can't. My hand is full of worms' – he unclenched his fist dramatically to show them to me – 'to feed the fish Churchill gave me.' His other hand touched my arm. 'Would you like to see them?'

There was an ornamental pond outside the library. Large fish swam about in it lazily. Beaverbrook was no longer interested. That game was over. He threw the worms into the pond and walked on to a lawn. 'You must excuse me, Mr Edwards,' he said. 'I am an old man. I must make water.' This he did, on the lawn, in full view of the house. It seemed to me that working for Beaverbrook, if he offered me a job, could be amusing.

The next thing I recall about that day is being asked to stay to dinner. No doubt Beaverbrook had made several phone calls to his editors to impress me, treating them kindly to show me what a nice fellow he was, his legs wide apart, waistcoat over rather large belly, eyebrows raised, that famous smile and every now and then a loud 'ha!' as something was said that interested him. (Try saying 'ha!' with a Canadian accent, and there you have it.) Also, no doubt, as he went through memos and letters invariably piled up in front of him, he sent several messages on his dictaphone, which were as much to impress his visitor as to guide their recipients. Beaverbrook liked showing off. He liked watching himself do it and had mirrors carefully placed for the purpose. There is no doubt that what gave Beaverbrook the most pleasure in life was Beaverbrook. He hugely and literally enjoyed himself.

Before dinner, back in the drawing-room, I had my first taste of Beaverbrook's cocktail. He made it with a machine someone had given him that ground the ice cubes into powder, to which he added a concoction that had been prepared under orders by the butler, Mr Mead. It was tart and far too cold, but Beaverbrook liked his toy and even his most intimate friends felt bound to say, as he searched their eyes for a reaction, that it was the finest they had ever tasted. (There was no such problem with Robert Maxwell. I introduced him to Buck's Fizz years ago, as he frequently acknowledged during the brief honeymoon period after he took over the Mirror.)

Another thing I remember about that first dinner with Beaver-brook was the presence of finger-bowls. He was at the head of the table and had put me on his right-hand side. 'What are these for?' I asked, and he explained without being the least shocked at my ignorance. Among the guests was Beverley Baxter, a Tory MP. He was the other half of Brendan and Beverley, one of Michael Foot's famous Yellow Books published by Victor Gollancz in the middle 1940s, a good dramatic critic and one of the best commentators on that annual seaside show, the Labour Party conference. He had also been a rather poor editor of the *Daily Express* in Beaverbrook's early days. As I will never forget, he had with him his two adolescent daughters, who at that stage in their lives, though exceedingly nice, were rather plain and dumpy. There were several other guests.

Throughout the dinner Beaverbrook constantly praised the faith-ful Baxter in a way that everyone else knew verged on the cruel. 'Just look at Beverley, Bob,' he said loudly, extending an upturned palm towards him while looking at me. 'Consider the wonderful gifts the Good Lord has bestowed on him. He was a b-r-i-l-l-i-a-n-t' (he said slowly) 'editor of the *Daily Express*. There is no finer dramatic critic. And, of course, he is a fine politician. But the greatest of all the gifts the Good Lord has given him are his two beautiful daugh-ters' – almost shouting now – 'don't you think so, Bob?'

It was, as he intended, difficult not to laugh, and the theme of the dinner was the 'two beautiful daughters'. After soup, chicken and whatever merited finger-bowls Beaverbrook invited us to his private cinema. 'You go ahead,' he said to Baxter, 'and sit in the stalls. I'll sit in the royal circle with Mr Edwards.' He held me back with a slight touch on the arm. 'Nice fellow, Beverley,' he said. 'Pity about his daughters.'

Sure enough, as legend said it would be, the film was his favourite 'Destry Rides Again' with Marlene Dietrich. After exclamations of joy at the beginning, he soon fell asleep, slumped at my side. I felt very warmly towards him. Possibly this had something to do with losing my father when I was twelve. I also felt highly complimented. From the *Reading Mercury* to being the honoured guest of the great Lord Beaverbrook was not bad. He asked me to stay the night and the following morning saw me personally to my car, a Bonnie and Clyde style pre-war Chrysler I had used as Labour candidate for Merton and Morden in the recent general election. Years later I discovered that Bob Maxwell also accompanies people he wishes to please to their motor cars.

To my disappointment, Beaverbrook did not offer me a job that weekend. There was a ritual to go through first. I had recommended another former *Tribune* writer, Ian Aitken, to him (he was working on *Reynolds News*, a typically dreadful Labour Sunday newspaper). We were both invited to lunch at Arlington House, with the great Arthur Christiansen, editor of the *Daily Express*, as the fourth member of the party. As Ian and I learned years later, Beaverbrook had arranged that at a signal from him Christiansen would nod if he approved of the choice of Ian and nod again if he approved of me. Predictably, as anyone who knew Chris would have expected, he dutifully signalled to the Old Man that, as ever, his judgment was as sound as a bell. Ian became a top-class foreign correspondent. Beaverbrook offered me a leader-writer's job on the *Evening Standard*, 'a path well trodden by socialists,' he said wickedly. With great humour, he added, 'I think Bob will make a good yellow journalist, don't you, Chris?' Chris concurred. On the way back to Fleet Street in his Jaguar, where he dropped me off at the *Tribune* office opposite the Law Courts, I said ecstatically about the job I had coveted since I was fourteen, 'It must be great fun being the editor of the *Daily Express*.' The one word reply has stayed with me ever since. 'Fun?' he said. I decided it must be his fault if it wasn't.

2

FAMILY AFFAIRS

It must have been the surprise of her life for the attractive woman I came to know as Auntie Winifred. She was, in fact, my half-sister. Her father was a well-off director of United Dairies. He had sold his business, which included three farms and several dairy shops, to them rather than face the overwhelming competition. He was also my father. But I did not know of her existence, nor she of mine or my two brothers' or my sister's as she drove by chance down a quiet country lane near our home in Berkshire. My father, and hers, had a new American car every year. This one was a Chevrolet, a very nice car indeed, as now seen in gangster movies. When he was not playing at the East Berks Golf Club, which he did most of the weekends he invariably spent with us at Bracknell, he would take us for little drives. We enjoyed them a lot, taking our teddy bears and our Sealyham, Jan, with us, and it was while our entire large family was on one such trip that Winifred, driving a new Vauxhall Ten her father had given her, happened to pass the unmistakable Chevrolet in a lane that goes by a pub named The Who'd 'a Thought It. She had a brief but positive glance at him and all of us, and no doubt as she continued her journey, more stunned than she had ever been, all sorts of thoughts that had vaguely troubled her down the years fell neatly into place.

For example, she must have thought it odd that her father was such a golf enthusiast, and such a devotee of one particular club, that he spent not just occasional weekends in the country, starting on Fridays and ending on Monday mornings when he drove direct to the office, but every single one. Again, such was the trust between father and daughter, she never really pressed the point about where her father actually stayed. Nor did her mother because she did not know either, and was possibly prevented from enquiring further by some sound instinct of self-preservation. It was even more of a man's world then. For my part, with equal vagueness, I noted that my father had no friends who visited him at our home except for a solicitor who, like my father, smoked a pipe. Perhaps, as far as Winifred's family were concerned, her father stayed with him, or at some hotel which did not exist attached to the golf club. Another thing I noted with greater clarity than my pleasant and kindly father's lack of friends, was his unfailing absence on Christmas Day. He would play a round of golf on Christmas Eve, and after one of my mother's plain but well cooked lunches kiss each of us briefly with his prickly moustache and return without explanation to London. Shortly afterwards at least one of our three delightful maiden aunts who lived in a nice modern house in Lewisham would arrive on the steam train from Waterloo and spend Christmas with us. Once I asked my mother, 'Why isn't Dad here on Christmas Day?' She answered instantly, as if prepared for such a question, 'He has to attend an office dinner.' It was the first time I had heard of this phenomenon. I immediately felt sorry for all the other children at United Dairies who were similarly deprived of their fathers on Christmas Day. Naturally, I believed my mother totally.

So far as I can judge, Winifred showed great discretion over her chance discovery that her father had two entirely separate families, because the balloon did not go up and he continued to drive the 27 miles every Friday for his weekend golf. It seems inconceivable that she did not tell him and possibly her brother or brothers. She must have had at least one brother because her, and my, father's firm (though this detail was kept from us in occasional proud briefings on his eminence as a dairyman) was known before the merger as Edwards & Sons.

Winifred entered our lives only after he died. She appeared mysteriously and walked up and down the large lawn in our garden talking earnestly to my mother. I was consumed with curiosity. 'This is your Aunt Winifred,' said my mother. 'She has very kindly given me a cheque for £100.' My mother always believed in telling as much of the truth as possible. Winifred was very kind to us and to the woman she could have thought had been responsible for taking her father away every weekend for fourteen years. She was fond of me, and let me drive her Vauxhall though I was only twelve. Its engine was so quiet I tried to start it while it was running. She did not mind.

There were clues which, if children were given to distrusting their parents, might have prompted me to wonder why our lives were different from other children's. We had all the apparent stability of a middle-class family, church on Sundays and tea quite often with the rector, who had an ancient open Trojan car with solid tyres, a dickey and coconut matting on the floor. We had a gardener called Joe who was paid ten shillings for his day's work ('Bobby don't like new potatoes, do he?' he liked to tease), a nanny, a maid and a cleaning-lady called Mrs King, who became a close friend of my mother's. But we were told when he was aged only six that my older brother Bill was being sent to a boarding school called Balmore at Caversham, near Reading. Bill is wiser in many ways than I am, and my mother painted such an attractive picture of the school for his benefit that I insisted on going too. There was very little resistance to this idea, I noted, and at five years old I was sent away from home presumably so that my father could have quieter evenings at home after golf and less disturbed mornings. He listened to 'In Town Tonight' at 7.30 on Saturday evenings and 'Music Hall' at 8 o'clock and probably had as fine a collection of classical music as any director of United Dairies. The records were played on a radiogram with fibre needles that needed constant sharpening, and my father would listen to whole symphonies while sipping whisky and soda and occasionally allowing us to sit on his knee. He probably had at least as good a collection at the other home in London we did not know about. The whisky with two bottles of lager, a soda siphon and an opener was kept discreetly between a tall-boy and the fireplace, hidden by the large armchair that was reserved for him at weekends. When we grew old enough he played Monopoly with us. I noted that he was much older than most fathers and ran in a funny, shuffling way on the rare occasions when we played cricket. The dining-room drawer held many gold-plated teaspoons he had won at the East Berks Golf Club. There were no trophies despite his undoubted skill at the game. Perhaps they were taken to his home in London in the boot of the Chevrolet, and previously the Chryslers, as proof of his obsession with the game.

My mother did not accompany us on our first journey to boarding school. We were taken in a large fawn Austin with a driver I can still remember from Drake and Mount's garage, which specialised in corn and seed delivered in marvellously painted carts drawn by dray horses in pairs. Bill and I each had our teddy bears but our arrival at Balmore, after the kindly chauffeur had handed us over to Mrs Gwatkin, the headmaster's wife, was daunting. The school was for a few boys, most of whose parents had to live abroad and not 11 miles away, up to the preparatory school age of seven, and girls up to the age of eighteen. I found some of the girls so frightening irreparable damage might have been done to me. One of my clearest early childhood memories is when I had the first of many sneezing fits that have since afflicted me, and also my friends. It was my first breakfast

at Balmore. Outside it was pitch dark. The school was still lit by
old-fashioned direct lighting, which gave the cheerless appearance
of a reformatory. I was surrounded by large, terrifying girls aged
about ten. An enormous bowl of lumpy porridge just beneath my
nose was not at all like the Quick Quaker Oats we had at home.
Suddenly, without warning, I sneezed. More porridge, cold milk and
brown sugar than seemed possible distributed itself over the fearsome girls of Balmore School for Young Ladies, Caversham. 'You
horrid little boy,' spat one of them. These are the first actual words I
remember.

   Mrs Gwatkin wore pince-nez, or as Bill and I called them motor-
bike glasses. She may have been kindly but she looked severe. Her
husband was a reverend and wore a dog-collar. He was not at all like
the jolly rector of Easthampstead at home. Bill and I would wander
around the school and its grounds playing together. One day, possibly from one of the other boys, he made an interesting discovery.
The school hall had a sprung parquet floor on which the ghastly girls
took ballroom dancing lessons, and all round it under intricately
patterned iron grilles were large central heating pipes. Bill's discovery was that by the simple device of making water on them a
realistic smell of burning cakes filled the air. He suggested that I
should try, and as I did so Mrs Gwatkin entered. I have forgotten
what happened to Bill but I was taken upstairs and laid face down on
the Gwatkins' double bed, which had been turned back for the
purpose, so that I could be slippered by Mr Gwatkin. I was so scared
by a punishment the severity of which I no longer recall, or possibly
in anticipation of it, that I made water again on their bed. Serve
them right, I consoled myself afterwards in a quite adult manner. It
is a memory I treasure. I can still vividly recall the soft bed and the
fear.

   At the age of seven my brother was sent to Marlborough House, a
prep school in Reading. As a special indulgence, I was allowed to go
too. The school was for day, weekly and full boarders. We were full
boarders, though we often came home at the weekend. My mother,
despite her humble background of a good elementary school followed by a shorthand-typing college, went to inspect it, making
some excuse that my father was too busy distributing milk to come
along. As with her three well-brought-up spinster sisters (two of
them working for United Dairies, the third keeping house) nothing
about her betrayed her working class origins. She had a strong-
willed Scottish mother and a rather ineffectual sickly father. They
had often lived in considerable poverty, but such was the quality of

primary education and the degree of encouragement from her parents at home that my mother was totally literate and wrote us both, and later my youngest brother Peter, very good letters. I recall only one from my father. He had very small handwriting.

The headmaster, Mr H. E. Makins, all in all was a kindly man. He sent his daughter Anne to Dartington, the then newly founded school for self-expression and anything goes (where I sent one of my sons), but he used the cane regularly. For boarders, as at Balmore, the punishment was administered in his bedroom after school hours, usually on bare bottoms. It happened to me only once. I think he was aware that I was very much against that kind of thing. He did not tell me to lower my pyjamas. I was aware of his breathing as I lay, for the second time in my life, on a headmaster's bed, this time bent over it. One or two of the masters were paederasts. At evening prep in the school hall, three boys teased one of them, a muscular, square-shouldered young man prematurely balding, by talking in loud voices about his large blue thing. He slippered each of them in front of all the boarders, a bold action I was shrewd enough even at that age to judge, but it shut them up and he survived. I was not sure what he could have done, but it was something very wrong, that I was sure.

The headmaster had one leg. The other was blown off in the First World War, and we grew so accustomed to hearing him creaking along the corridors with his cumbersome artificial leg we could not conceive of having a headmaster with two legs. None of us, probably, had ever seen our parents naked, and it was a shock at first to see Mr Makins and the other masters plunging with nothing on into the swimming-pool as part of the school's advanced thinking. Mrs Makins may have thought it rather odd, or quite pleasing. She looked after us all like a good surrogate mum. I remember her lighting a large sheet of brown paper over the WC that divided the two large baths we shared because one of the boys had produced an unspeakable smell. She gave each of us two teaspoons of California Syrup of Figs every Thursday night and regularly bought me 2s. 11d. Siro shockproof pocket watches from Marks and Spencer. She would hold each new one in its wrapper against my ear at school dinners, a thrill we shared. One of the nastier boys, whose father was a famous war correspondent in the Spanish civil war, strongly disputed that they were shockproof, and to prove they were I dropped a new one from the top of the school down the staircase well to the stone floor at the bottom. I learned that whatever shockproof meant, it was not what I had imagined. I accidentally dropped another, with a picture of a railway engine on it, between my thighs while sitting on the lavatory. I did not like to fish it out.

The money to buy the watches usually came from cheques sent by our remarkably few relatives and a retired homosexual judge who lived, appropriately, at Camp Cottage, Bracknell, near our home. He was very fond of me and, to encourage visits, sent my mother presents of plates and other crockery. He always seemed to me to be stroking the private parts of his cat. In fact I was mistaken about their position, and he was not. 'Let me place my hand on you,' he once said. I knew what he meant, replied politely, 'No, thank you,' and moved away. He was no trouble really and the cheques continued to arrive about once a term. I hoped he had been a merciful judge since I knew he was a quite considerable sinner himself.

The school food was often dreadful. To this day my older brother cannot eat onions. We were expected to eat large, whole soggy ones served with a pretence of stew, overcooked wet cabbage and potatoes in their jackets that were sometimes mouldy with dead bugs in them. We were also served jelly with sliced bananas magically embedded in it, which we liked, and had orangeade made out of powder on Sundays. The school library had a billiard table, on which I played for many hours, often alone. It also had bound volumes of *Punch* and the *Illustrated London News* back to the turn of the century. I marvelled at the graphic drawings by G. H. Davis in the *Illustrated London News*, especially of naval battles in the First World War. There was little else to read except Sapper's Bulldog Drummond and Henty, and I read all their books. On the marble mantelpiece above the gas fire there was a collection box for the Bible Society in the shape of a Bible. It contained a few pennies, goodness knows who had put them in it, and on one occasion, which weighed heavily on me for years afterwards, I shook it and managed to extract four pennies for a large tub of ice cream.

I regularly broke school rules and ran a mile through the Reading outskirts to a sweet shop, pretending to be a train, where I invariably bought dolly mixture. The school tuckshop, a cupboard, was opened on Sundays and the aged scoutmaster, Mr Haigh, a terror in geography class with the habit of hitting the inattentive or stupid on the knuckles with a pointer at least eight feet long, beamed with bonhomie. I favoured Mars Bars and Nuttall's Mintoes. The school had an excellent annual magazine, with one of the pictures in colour. It was remarkably frank about some of the boys, considering their parents paid good money to send them there ('One Edwards is bad enough, but THREE ...'), and pulled the leg of the metalwork and carpentry master, whose name I have forgotten. He was a leading Reading communist, committed to destroying us. At the time I thought how liberal-minded it was of Mr Makins to have him there. My fellow pupils and I noted that he broke wind in a very evil, furtive manner.

The greatest triumph of the year was the stage production in the school gymnasium. I was the dormouse in the 'Mad Hatter's Tea Party'. One year we did an adaptation of '1066 And All That', which was retitled 'Omnibus' to avoid, as a master explained, paying copyright fees. The centre-piece was a replica of the headmaster's Ford V8 shooting-brake. My father never came, I observed, to the school play. A sadistic master put smaller boys in the boxing ring with older ones, and rather than put up with this I hid once in one of the dormitories. My brother Peter was so miserable and homesick on his first night at the school that he lay on the dormitory floor crying so hard I thought he was having a fit. I did not think of looking for Matron and instead persuaded him to come into my bed. There was a sensational thunderstorm one night, preceded by distant rumbling like guns on the approaches to a city, and another just like it the following night. Nobody came into our dormitories to see if we were afraid. There was a lack of love in our lives.

On holidays I overcame this by spending countless happy hours with Mr Alf Youens and his assistant, Stan, in the back of his bicycle shop in Bracknell High Street. Mr Youens had a large tub full of water to detect the punctures that were his chief source of income. He sold carbide for gas bicycle lamps, and paraffin for the oil versions that released black smoke if the wick was too high, or blew out. My father bought Bill and me two new bicycles one Christmas. They were £3 17s. 6d. each and he insisted, through my mother, on a reduction to £3 15s. 0d. for bulk purchase. I thought that was very mean of him. Mr Youens was one of the most decent men I have ever known, without a single unredeeming feature, and therefore one of the greatest.

Many further hours were spent on Bracknell railway station, watching the shunting engine built before the turn of the century arrive shortly after lunchtime, followed by the magnificent goods train on its way to Feltham sidings. The engine hauled as many as one hundred trucks, carefully counted by me. It reversed its huge load into our sidings to allow a passenger train to pass, picked up the trucks assembled for it by the shunting engine by a simple manoeuvre, and with immense style, steam and noise, climbed the gradient towards Ascot, where its water supply was replenished.

Twice only I was lifted on to the footplate. Nobody minded my being on the platform. I came from a respectable family.

Trains were an important part of my life. We caught the 7.50 a.m. to Reading on Monday mornings when we had spent the weekend at home. Travelling alone once in thick fog, with explosive signalling devices on the line, I thought we were going the wrong way and screamed in fear out of the window. Looking back, I realise I was often as lonely as the boy portrayed in Dennis Potter's brilliant TV series 'The Singing Detective'. Like him, I spent hours on top of a tall tree. Mine was an elm, by the garden gate. Sometimes, when I grew a little older, I cycled as far as Hyde Park Corner, 24 miles, again pretending to be a train, and walked for miles with Toc, the dog I was given after the maid Betty and I had taken the Sealyham, Jan, to be humanely and noisily killed a few moments after we had handed him over. Betty jumped when we heard the shot. I thought, mother sent me because she did not think I cared about Jan, but I did, except that he had bad breath.

Very strong convictions were forming in my mind as I observed life around me. There was a workhouse half a mile away at the top of the road by Easthampstead church. Men called tramps would call at the back door for water for their billy-cans, but probably in the hope of something better. In those days, there was no fear when strangers knocked at the door. I felt sorry they were so poor. One summer afternoon two men in their early thirties knocked at the front door with a camera and tripod and, showing examples of their work, suggested they should photograph me. My mother politely said no, and I pleaded with her. She relented and I still have the picture that eventually arrived through the post. I recall the incident only because, when my mother was out of earshot, one of the men said to me in a heartfelt voice, 'Thanks, son.' I felt something was wrong when a grown-up person should feel so grateful to a spoilt boy.

The maid kept her bicycle, bought on instalments of 2s. 6d. a week, in the scullery. As she was about to cycle home in the dark one night, my mother lifted the flap of her large saddle-bag. It contained sugar, flour, tea and other packets stolen from our well-stocked larder. Although she persistently trod on my Hornby train set, I was sorry for her. So, I imagine, was my mother, because she stayed. At the end of an often muddy path between hedges dividing two fields, a short distance from the railway embankment, an old woman called Mrs Beezer lived alone in an old semi-detached house tarred at her end to fight the damp. She befriended me, the posh little boy from Crowthorne Road with M.H. for Marlborough House on his blazer, and I loved her despite her humble circumstances and the marmalade she once had on her dress. She would stand at the bottom of her garden and wave a handkerchief at me across the narrow field as we went slowly by in the train on Monday mornings. On my eleventh birthday my father bought me an astonishing present, a hand-built, Bassett Lowke working model steam traction engine that cost seventeen guineas. This was because I was supposed to be suffering some kind of nervous breakdown. Mrs Beezer bought me a single Hornby railway signal that cost 1s. 11d., and since I was steeped in biblical stories and knew all about the widow's mite I thought this was the more valuable present.

The 'breakdown' was something I concocted to get away from Marlborough House and stay at home. I invented stories about being bullied by an unfortunate master called Mr Nicholson. I affected to be so haunted by his awful presence that I pretended I could see him standing at the door of my bedroom at home. When the nice, alcoholic Dr Hicks came to see me I threw a toy at him to demonstrate that I was not well. I also walked with a pretend limp. I triumphed and was taken away from Marlborough House. For six months I was tutored by the headmaster of the local elementary school, Mr Peyman, earning a few extra shillings a week. He wore a bright check suit. I thought he was very dull, not at all like some of the masters at Marlborough House who had driven us around in their Morris Minors and beetle-shaped Rileys. I was not allowed to talk to council-school children, though both my father and mother had been to council schools, and had no friends. I would wander around the house when I was bored crying, 'I don't know what *to* do,' 'I don't know what *to* do,' varied by 'Nobody loves me,' 'Nobody loves me,' thinking that is what all little boys did. My mother took me to a phrenologist at Reading, who felt my bumps and said that when I grew up I should not go into anything heavy, like the furniture trade.

Dr Hicks sent me to a Harley Street specialist, presumably a psychiatrist, who prescribed a prep school called Hildersham House at Broadstairs run by a friend of his, Mr A. O. S. Snowdon. The journey was much longer by a steam train from Reading that had started hours earlier in Birkenhead. Mr Snowdon was a harmless old buffer whose last recorded act after he retired was to send a letter of protest to the *Kent Messenger* because the paper, reporting the scores in cricket matches between Gentlemen and Players, had dropped the prefix 'Mr' before the names of the gentlemen. It was a better class of school than Marlborough House, where most of the boys went on to Leighton Park, Michael Foot's old school, Radley or, worst of all, Dauntsey. At Hildersham we played games against a school, St Peter's, most of whose pupils went on to Eton. Broadstairs was stiff with prep schools. 'The sea air is bracing,' the specialist told my mother, implying it would have some therapeutic effect on my troubled soul.

Hildersham, recalled by Ted Heath when he was a council-school boy, is now a housing estate. It had a chapel with its own pipe organ which the headmaster's large wife played atrociously at evensong on Sundays and the music master superbly at matins. I sometimes wandered round the school at dead of night, stealing sugar orange slices from the kitchen, and had an almost overwhelming desire to climb the narrow, iron, spiral staircase to the quarters of the friendly maids. Obviously I was searching for the warmth and affection that the psychiatrist failed to observe was missing from my life. There were other pleasing undertones that prompted my interest in the maids. A couple of years earlier at the Reading school I had been driven by the sister of a rich boy called Spratt to and from their riverside home at Shiplake. The car was an open Railton sports with impressive rivets along its bonnet and leather straps, but what attracted me even more was the sister's long, slender legs and tiny shoes as I sat next to her. I was filled with an inexplicable longing.

The headmaster at Hildersham sent for me one morning. He shut the door of the small study where he caned fewer of his pupils than Mr Makins. I could see he was embarrassed. He was a simple man. After we had learned the Collect on Sundays, a dreadful imposition, he read a chapter or two from the Bulldog Drummond books I had enjoyed at Marlborough House. 'Your father,' he said. 'I am afraid he is ill. He is very ill indeed.' I guessed, and asked the appropriate question, assuming what I imagined was the correct grave expression. 'How ill, sir?' 'I am sorry to say, Edwards, your father is dead.' There was a perceptible silence, and I thought some comment from me was called for. 'Sir,' I said, 'what will happen to my father's car?' 'I will ask your mother and let you know,' he replied kindly. He did not, of course, and we never saw the car again. Although, compared with most sons and fathers, I scarcely knew him, he was in my dreams for years to come.

My mother misguidedly, but selflessly, kept me at the school for another couple of terms despite her appalling change of circumstances. The school doctor decided that a hernia I had had from birth should be operated on, and since we could no longer afford private treatment the headmaster said I would have to go into a general ward at the local hospital. Because of an epidemic at the school, I had to stay with the matron and her husband, the caretaker, until the period of quarantine was over. Mr Snowdon was apologetic on both counts, especially the second. 'I hope you don't mind,' he said, meaning their house was humble and not what I had been accustomed to. It struck me forcibly how odd it was that a headmaster should feel that what was considered adequate for two grown-up people, both employed by him, was not good enough for a twelve-year-old prep school boy. At the hospital a young man of nineteen who had crashed his motor-bike befriended me. He moaned pitifully at night when his pain seemed to be at its worst. A male visitor from Toc H kissed me on the lips. I did not like that. I noticed Mrs Snowdon staring at my rather grubby sheets when she came on a visit. She looked warily around the large ward. I felt it was her first time in one. Britain was two nations all right. I did not need a Disraeli to tell me.

After my father's friend the solicitor gave my mother some good advice, she took my brother, to his great relief, away from his public school. He went to work for a business valuer in Reading and became a highly successful estate agent. I was sent to the local grammar school, now a comprehensive, at a fee of £5 per term, which enabled me to by-pass the entrance exam. I met several of the boys I was not allowed to speak to when they were at elementary school but best of all there were girls and I fell in love with four of them simultaneously, Hazel Sargeant, Rose Smith, Betty Mitchell and Pat Egan. Unfortunately, such was my upbringing, I was unable to communicate with them. Pat Egan was stunningly beautiful, with hair almost down to her waist. I cycled regularly to a crossroads I hoped she would pass on her way home. She seldom did, and even then all I could manage was a shy 'hello' as if I was there purely by chance. To my dismay, later she married an American army sergeant and became a G.I. war bride. The nearest I got to an intimate relationship was with the girls who appeared as 'artistic studies' in the monthly *London Opinion*. There were two in each issue, and they were referred to as such on the contents page in a discreet little box making them easy to find. They were far more mystical than today's centrefolds and I can remember one of them vividly.

The war broke out shortly after my first term at Ranelagh began. I recalled Mr Snowdon saying at Hildersham House six months earlier that he thought war would not be declared because 'Herr Hitler' had sent a letter of condolence to the King on the accidental sinking of the submarine *Thetis*, a foolish remark I thought at the time. The

London School of Building was evacuated and took over Ranelagh every afternoon, which made it even better. My mother, with a remarkable stroke of inspiration unprompted by me, bought me a good Remington portable typewriter. Almost every afternoon I hammered out a scandal sheet about the school, with several columns to a page, sensational headlines and crusading editorials. For want of good copy, it was mostly fictitious and I showed it to no one.

I was editor, of course, and although I had never met a journalist, not even the war correspondent father of the Marlborough House bully, I knew exactly what I wanted to do. I fixed firmly in my mind that I would be editor of the *Daily Express*, but anyone looking over my shoulder would have thought the *Daily Mirror* more likely. The headmaster, a churchwarden who knew my mother, advised me against journalism and suggested working in a bank as a secure profession. I won a prize for a short story I wrote for the school magazine about a killer who escaped from Broadmoor, the local criminal lunatic asylum as it was called in those days. Almost the entire long opening paragraph was lifted from a Bulldog Drummond book. Nobody, to my relief, noticed.

It was not long before I was working on the *Reading Mercury*, as much a vocation for me as being called to the Church. I decided that the first paper I edited would have the biblical slogan, 'Ye shall know the truth, and the truth shall make you free' beneath the masthead, and was both miffed and pleased when looking at newspapers in Reading library opposite the office that the *Christian Science Monitor* already did so.

One night without preamble or any kind of warning my mother came into my bedroom and with a haunted face said: 'Your father and I were not married.' My brother, who had been called up and was applying for a commission, had asked for his birth certificate. It had the wrong name on it and he had to be told. I was shocked, utterly amazed. Everything about our upbringing had been the quintessence of respectability, prayers every night kneeling by the bed, church every Sunday, and we were a family looked up to and admired by the shopkeepers and neighbours. Mr Henry Brooke, one of the neighbours, who later became Home Secretary, even talked of getting me a job on *Time and Tide*, assuming that from such a seemingly normal and stable background I was bound to be a Conservative.

Now, as with Winifred when she passed The Who'd a' Thought It and my father in his car, everything fell into place. I instantly recalled his absences at Christmas, the brief periods he spent with us on holiday when we rented a house each year at Hayling Island, the fact that he never punished us, his age and how, when he became ill before he eventually died, he was in London somewhere and my mother went through the french windows into the conservatory with tears in her eyes and looking so alone. The strain of his death on her must have been colossal. Nobody so far as I am aware, except my father's solicitor friend, had known our secret, or, if they had, showed the true Christian charity preached at us on Sundays; and then his death notice which our neighbours would have looked for must have appeared in the *Daily Telegraph* (or *Morning Post* as he preferred to call it) with an entirely different grieving widow and family from those known in Bracknell. And where did my mother tell the neighbours to send their flowers? Did she say the funeral was private, no flowers by request? My father even had his name, fortunately common, in our local telephone book.

Several years later, after I had returned from the RAF, my mother again came into my bedroom late at night. 'I can't stand it,' she said. 'I don't know what to do.' Eventually she sank into schizophrenia and almost died, a pathetic bundle lying on a low bed in a side room at a huge hospital in Southall. Many years later, after several remissions and long periods in different hospitals, she recovered sufficiently to live without pills and was no longer troubled by voices. But she was never happy again. My father had died after catching pneumonia playing in a golf tournament on a wet day at the East Berks Golf Club.

3
'AT READING TODAY . . .'

Those were the days, of course. There were no misprints in the *Reading Mercury* (established 1723). Major Foran, the reviser, made sure of that. He had a curious hole in his left cheek, skin-covered like a drum. When he was excited, it blew up as a frog does under stress. Major Foran – for some reason we never called him 'the major' – had retired from what he claimed were amazing adventures before the Second World War. He boasted that he had been in thirteen different wars and was wounded thirteen times. We liked him far too much to ask which wars and what his injuries were, apart from the obvious wound on his face. He also claimed to have been a reporter on a Chicago paper which once (he said) carried a headline about King George V: K5 NO BIGAMIST, SAYS FORAN

Whatever the truth about his exploits, Major Foran was a great spotter of 'literals', and fielded any that crept past the devoted proof-readers, 'Baldy' Le Seuer and Jim, to whom all galley proofs were sent by tube, complete with copy, in their eyrie at the top of the rickety, mostly wooden, building in Valpy Street, Reading.

Baldy and Jim were enthusiastic members of the local Temperance Band, Baldy on cornet. Like most newspaper people, he drank like a fish. As a good Labour man, he led the band in Colonel Bogey when the candidate arrived at a Tory fête. Their little room was smoke-filled, but not as foul as their language. I was told that their drawers were filled with pornography. They corrected the proofs, exactly as taught in the manuals, and between them and the printers there were few faults for Major Foran to find on his final inspection in the reviser's office next door. Reference books were constantly consulted, and arguments raged over the correct use of the language. The idea of offering £1 to any *Reading Mercury* reader who could spot a literal, as did the pre-war *Daily Mirror*, proud of its own performance, was unthinkable. There were no misprints.

The great editor, Mr Frank Neale, bald head gleaming behind the roll-top desk in his large office, his heavily-bejewelled wife forever

20

beside him, was able to concentrate on other matters. We had not the vaguest idea what, but assumed them to be questions of high policy. Mr Frank Luckett, both news editor and chief sub-editor, had problems of style with the teenage reporters. We were devotees of *Time* magazine, as well as of Glenn Miller, and had the habit of writing sentences backwards and saying 'quoth he' when reporting some mayor's pedestrian comments. If these attempts to update the *Mercury* got past Mr Luckett, whose mind was often on dog-racing or his freemason's lodge, they were expertly fielded by the proof-readers, who knew how to switch words into their correct order with a lightning squiggle, by the book.

I have had scores of letters over the years from parents and would be journalists about how to get into the profession. At the Mirror, with its tradition of being a caring company, we sent a brochure listing all the training schemes and I would always enclose a personal letter of encouragement. But I got in by a simpler device. I asked my mother to write to the editor. This she must have done splendidly. From my first and only interview, when I was fifteen, Mr Neale and his snobbish wife treated me with a slight diffidence that the un-privileged in this country sometimes accord the public school edu-cated. 'We like public school boys on the *Reading Mercury*,' boomed Mrs Neale one day after I had persuaded her husband to give me an extra five shillings a week. The editor smiled at this in a rather sickly manner, I thought. I felt it unwise to put the record straight, not least because the misunderstanding must have arisen over something my mother had written in that letter. Whatever accent I had acquired at my prep schools had come in very handy.

Max Aitken once rebuked me for running up the stairs in the Express building. 'Editors don't run up stairs,' he said in his simple, clipped way. Mr Neale was most people's idea, certainly Max Aitken's, of a proper editor of an English paper, in contrast to the perpetually angry, frenetic editors of American papers we had seen at the pictures (we imagined the editors of *Time* magazine to be a different breed, deceptively effete in appearance, lying on couches composing their inspired sentences).

Mr Neale not only did not run up the narrow stairs. It was an event to see him on them. He was large, distinguished, and wore smart grey suits, except on Saturday mornings when more casual wear was in order. He did not visit the composing room. That was the domain of the formidable head printer, Mr Bill Cleare, who was a proper head printer, totally in command. Mr Cleare's bald head matched Mr Neale's. It was covered at all times in sweat, as was his face, indicating hard toil and responsibility. He shared an interest in dog racing with Mr Luckett the news editor, and (I suspected) free-masonry, and they ran the show under the great editor with one other member of the team, the chief reporter.

All of us Fleet Street practitioners of the black art who were trained on the *Reading Mercury* and its sister paper, the tabloid *Berkshire Chronicle*, have undimmed affection for Mr 'Gus' Elmer. He had shaggy, greying hair and was a large, slightly lewd, father figure who sat at the head of the reporters' table in another smoke-filled room. His rank was denoted, as if that was necessary, by a small roll-top device on the table, behind which, when his head was bowed, he was invisible. He was invariably invisible after he had visited Elm Park, headquarters of Reading football club, on Thurs-days. Once a month, wearing his best suit, Gus went to Oxford to cover the Oxfordshire Education Committee. It was an outing he much enjoyed, though he referred to it in respectful tones, as if he were reporting a key debate in the House of Lords. I suspect now that there were added attractions, such as a pleasant bar in an ancient tavern and someone warm and friendly behind it. Perhaps he also enjoyed the train journey throughout the Thames Valley, turning right at Didcot.

When Gus was at Oxford, one of us would sometimes sit almost out of sight in his place behind the roll-top. He was one of those colourful people who it is easy to mimic. I was thus installed on the only visit I can recall the editor making to the reporters' room, when I had returned to the paper after the war. The other occupant, very visible, was the startlingly good-looking, teenage Drusilla Beyfus, who later married the fortunate Milton Shulman. She was said to be related to the famous QC, a public schoolgirl, and altogether well qualified to work on the *Reading Mercury*. Since I was improperly in the chief reporter's chair, I bowed my head instantly as I saw Mr Neale's large frame at the door. But he had eyes only for Drusilla, and thinking she was alone not only expressed a solicitous interest in how her career was progressing, but commented at some length in a strange tone of voice on her singular beauty. I think he called her 'Drusie' or some such term of endearment and I was glad when he felt the fearsome pull of his wife who must have begun to wonder why he was taking longer than was required to go to the lavatory. The incomparable Drusilla and I were highly amused that our for-midable editor was altogether more human than we had imagined.

Nobody was bullied on the *Reading Mercury*. We had a charmed life. Gus Elmer supplemented his income and ours on what we suspected was not quite the fifty-fifty basis he claimed, by sending endless reports to the London evening newspapers the *Star* and the *Evening News*, plus the Exchange Telegraph news agency. (Frank Pettingell, editor of the *Reading Standard* next door – he was a shirt-sleeves editor not a proper one like Mr Neale – had collared the London *Evening Standard* and Press Association linage.) Gus had no literary pretensions. His first call when I joined the *Mercury* in 1941 was invariably to the *Star* because it was a red-hot paper that did not like to be beaten on the news. He would transfer the telephone charge in the time-honoured manner, speak to the news desk so that they would order the story, which meant that he would be paid whether or not it was used, and then invariably begin his report when he had been put through to the copy-takers (or tele-phone reporters, as they are now): 'At Reading today, comma . . .' After a short interval, to give the more demanding and better-paying *Star* the edge, he would call the *Evening News* in the same way, beginning his report with the same words, uttered in the hoarse voice we affectionately imitated, 'At Reading today,' but varying the rest of the report significantly so that the *Evening News* would believe he was working exclusively for them. A few minutes later he would phone the Exchange Telegraph with a further slight variation of the same report, also beginning 'At Reading today,' and when the editors of the *Star* and the *Evening News* saw that their man in Reading had yet again beaten the agency by a clear twenty minutes (the *Star*) and ten minutes (the *Evening News*) they felt they had possibly the best news gathering service in the entire world. Mr Elmer, who scorned motor cars and rode an ancient black bicycle, knew how to maximise his earnings, a word Major Foran would have struck out at once.

In the 1940s and 1950s, and before the war, newspaper readers had a far better news service than they do now. Today magistrates' courts, divorce courts, inquests and even assizes are frequently not covered and all kinds of good stories are missed. Some courts might as well be secret for all the attention they attract, whereas in the *Reading Mercury*'s circulation area you had only to be fined 2*s*. 6*d*. for riding a bicycle without a red rear light for your misdeed to be recorded. If your excuse was sufficiently amusing, alert sixteen-year-old would-be editors of the *Daily Express* could be depended upon to add it to their report. I well remember telephoning my first report to the *Star*, announcing myself as Elmer of Reading, and beginning, of course, 'At Reading today . . .' It was a bit frightening, but when I had said, 'Goodbye, old man,' in my young voice to the copy-taker who had said the same to me, I felt I was positively on my way to the top.

You need luck as well as some ability to succeed in journalism. Mr Neale noted from my mother's letter that I had the General School Certificate at what he inexplicably imagined was my public school. In fact, I would have failed to pass in sufficient subjects but for a lucky break. The rather quaint English lady from London University who took my French oral exam had some difficulty in conveying to me in French that she wished to know if I had chosen a career. Finally, she said it in English, and I replied, 'Un journalist.' Her eyes lit up and she told me, happily still in English, that her husband was editor of the *Continental Daily Mail*. As I recall it, the rest of the conversation remained in English and I no longer laboriously had to attempt to describe the crowded farmyard scene she had earlier placed in front of me. I passed, and she pressed me to seek a job from her husband the moment his paper resumed publication after the war.

My next bit of luck occurred on my second day on the *Reading Mercury*. Mr Neale had appointed me as office boy to a man with a withered arm, Mr 'Mickey' Tull, who had the grand title of literary editor. He was a depressing little person who was totally unlike any journalist I have met since. The first task he set me was to get him some lemonade. He was a skilled scissors and paste operator, who, to my amazement, cut out leaders from *The Times*, altered them here and there, and put them in the *Reading Mercury* in his other role as the paper's leader-writer. He did the same as book critic, lifting whole reviews, abbreviated and slightly disguised, from *The Times Literary Supplement* and elsewhere. Mr Tull fancied himself as a man of deep religious principle and compiled the vast list of church services that appeared each week in our sister paper the *Berkshire Chronicle*.

Because we were so short of money, I cycled the 11 miles to Reading each day (48 minutes with a following wind), and on my second day a sight befell me that was to free me instantly from the tedious Mr Tull. Passing a farm I saw a small boy driving a tractor on his father's farm. He was eight years old and I wrote a nice little report about his war effort. Mr Luckett, the news editor, showed it to Mr Neale. It went unaltered on the front page, complete with a picture taken by Mr Bossom, the fattest photographer I have known. The editor, his snobbish wife clucking with approval, transferred me there and then to the care and guidance of the splendid Mr Gus Elmer as a junior reporter. Office boy for one day, I thought with some satisfaction.

Soon we were joined by other young reporters, such as Alan Jenkins, who was by far the most capable and covered major trials at Reading Assizes at the age of seventeen. He was to become Northern Editor of the *Daily Mail* and editor of the *Glasgow Herald*, a first class paper until he fell out with the proprietor and left. He now works on *The Times*. Alan's grandfather, 'Pop' Cawston, owned two river steamers and we all spent many happy hours going up and down the Thames. Pop smoked his Woodbines and advised us, as he blasted his hooter to warn lock-keepers of his approach, 'It doesn't matter what you do as long as you have a good time.'

I persuaded the editor to let me take over my own village of Bracknell, plus Ascot, Wokingham and adjoining areas, as well as working from the office. I tried to get a column of news from each of the principal villages and this sometimes involved a degree of slight hyperbole. The arrangement also gave me a lot of freedom to go to the pictures in the afternoon, with free passes gouged out of cinema managers, and even at Reading I recall leaving the office as if on some important mission and treacherously taking the trolley bus to the Granby at the far end of the town. A favourite spot for the young reporters was Sally's Coffee House in an arcade. It had been opened just before the war by Jack Buchanan and we were served by pretty girls who liked the jolly gang from the three newspapers. 'Just going to Sally's,' we would say to Gus. 'All right,' he would reply hoarsely. But we never failed to be in the office on Friday afternoons to collect our pay in small envelopes from Mr Charlie Smallbone, the chief cashier, who was hairless, wore a winged collar, black coat and striped trousers and was reputed to be ninety. He collected the firm's entire payroll alone from the bank in a black Gladstone bag.

The search for news in the villages led me to all manner of people, such as Mr Frank Newing, who ran the British Legion at Bracknell and just about everything else. 'I don't do all this just to get my name in the paper,' he liked saying to me. 'Frank Newing's the name.' My regular contacts included undertakers – no obituary was ever spiked – and I remember one at Wokingham who played the part as if from central casting. Just once, standing by the grandfather clock in his hall, he allowed the suspicion of a gleam to come into his mournful eyes during a flu epidemic. The rector of St Paul's in the same town, unusually for vicars, did not like young men. Each week I sought out instead his deaf, bent-backed and ancient gravedigger, Mr Eamer. Especially on cold days he liked to smoke inside the graves he had dug, and was thus nowhere to be seen. Through cupped hands I would cry in a very loud voice, 'Mr Eamer!' until his head emerged from his chosen grave.

This pleasing way of learning our trade is described by elderly journalists, contemptuous of the graduates now frequently chosen by editors, as 'going through the mill'. I spent a month or two being taught Pitman's shorthand in a class of disappointingly plain girls at a night school, but did not complete the course on the grounds that if talent was properly rewarded in this world I would soon be an editor and others would do the shorthand. I was sorry to hear many years later that Mr Neale had committed suicide by cutting his throat in the bath. The theory by former members of his staff was that he could not stand the boiled fish his wife gave him every evening. 'Mr Neale likes boiled fish,' she would say, as if he was not there, in the habit of some wives. He was a proper editor and, of course, they don't make them like that any more.

My first two years on the *Reading Mercury*, wondering how I could get from there to an evening newspaper, but preferably to a national paper whose editor would soon move over for me, were interrupted by my call-up papers. I had not given a thought to a service career, only to newspapers, and when I was asked by some lucky recruiting officer at Reading, who was as well away from the war as anyone, I opted for the Royal Air Force. This seemed the least disagreeable prospect. Pen poised, he asked me what I wished to be and I replied with the only job I could think of on the spur of the moment: 'Pilot.'

In 1943, you had to be accepted for aircrew to get into the RAF unless you were medically unfit, over thirty-five, or a volunteer member of the junior Air Training Corps. The ATC thus attracted a considerable proportion of far-seeing young men who wished to avoid bayonet charges and the other extremes of war. We did not all wish to die, as Enoch Powell has confessed he did. Some of the cadets, however, were actually keen on flying rather than having cushy jobs in ground crew. I met one, impressively with sergeant's stripes, when I attended the aircrew selection board at the Endsleigh Hotel in London. 'Not in the ATC?' he said, glancing at my long hair. 'Too busy,' I said, 'I'm a reporter.' I told him I wanted to be a pilot. 'Well,' said the boy sergeant, 'they may offer you air gunner just to test if you're really keen and if you agree they will let you be a pilot. Of course, air gunners don't last longer than six months at the outside.'

I had taken several aptitude and intelligence tests, at which I always do badly, including Morse aptitude, and when I appeared before the Air Commodore and two other officers they were extremely polite. 'I'm afraid you had one or two prangs on your simulated flying test,' said the Air Commodore, 'and it's not a question of intelligence or anything like that but your Morse aptitude wasn't too promising.' I knew what was coming next and I thought I detected a slight look of concern in his friendly eyes. 'Would you like to be an air gunner?' he asked. I had an immediate vision of the ATC sergeant bringing his smouldering Wellington home on a wing and a prayer and one crew member, his rear gunner, gone. Such is pride, I answered, 'Yes, but I still think I would make a good pilot.' To the future benefit, or otherwise, of Fleet Street, they exchanged glances like magistrates in court. The Air Commodore said, 'It is very good of you, Edwards, but we have all these chaps as keen as mustard in the ATC and so we are very sorry but we think we should give them priority.' This, surprisingly, is how against all the rules I entered the ground crew of the RAF. A man with a single propeller on his arm, the equivalent of an army lance corporal, stopped me in the corridor and said, 'The guvnors say you can join the ground crew if you want to. OK, mate?' Indeed it was, and I was soon in front of a bored Flight Lieutenant who said, glancing at my papers, 'Your Morse aptitude is very good. Would you like to be a wireless operator?' They thought they were short of 'wops' at the time, but after several months' training I did not once operate a wireless set during my four years in the RAF except to tune in to the Hit Parade on the American Forces Network. In fact, I was never on operations of any kind.

On a Morse slip-reading course at RAF, Compton Bassett, I ran an unofficial paper called 'The MSR Express', for which a boy called Jock Pollock from the Glasgow slums proved he was a born writer. (Where is he now?). We used RAF paper, copying equipment and typewriters and no one seemed to mind. It was a weird place in a deserted part of the White Horse hills, where we learned high-speed operating that we never used, and the CO made us cut the grass outside our huts with our eating knives. Otherwise he was harmless enough. The famous RAF Skyrockets Big Band came down once. They were almost as good as Glenn Miller. The shyer ones among us were deeply impressed by the two randy cockneys in our hut who made love to their WAAF girl friends in our presence after lights out.

Eventually I had the good fortune to be posted to RAF, West Drayton, where I joined 140 other wireless operators who had not a single wireless set to operate. A few of us worked under the kindest

of men, Corporal Strong, in the 'discip. hut'. We had dart and shove
ha'penny boards and whiled away the endless days. Each morning I
would go to West Drayton on an RAF bike to collect cheese rolls for
the hut from the Two Sisters café. I joined the Windsor Divisional
Labour Party and was made editor when we started our own
monthly paper called *Progress*. Several teachers from Windsor
Grammar School wrote for it. There was a marvellous, witty,
gossipy column by a 21-year-old ex-Wellington schoolboy and
ex-army Captain, John Stock, who scourged the upper classes. He
later became a *Daily Telegraph* reporter. It was a good little paper,
full of fun as well as earnestness. We sent a copy each month to
Bernard Shaw. There was no response until after the third issue, in
which one of the clever teachers had quoted Shaw. 'Why don't you
print something interesting in every edition?' GBS wrote on one of
his famous postcards. Naturally, I reproduced it on the front page.

One of the regular contributors, who needed quite a lot of
subbing, was Ascot's deputy postmaster, Mr Harold Lane. He had
Labour Party notices on a board outside his front garden in the High
Street, a provocative act in that part of the world, and he provided
me with one of my best scoops, shortly after I returned to the
Reading Mercury. In 1947 it was reported that Lieutenant Philip
Mountbatten and Princess Elizabeth, shortly to be married, would
take over an empty house in Windsor Great Park called Sunninghill
Park which had several former RAF huts in its grounds. The huts, of
course, would have to come down, which incensed Harold. He said
to me when I visited him on my Triumph Speed Twin motor cycle
(my first company vehicle), 'I'll never let it happen. It's an outrage.'
So far, not much of a story. 'How will you stop it, Harold?' I asked.
'The homeless will march on it. The huts will be occupied,' he
announced. 'They are enraged.'

This story was altogether too hot for dear old Gus Elmer. Three
locally renowned freelances had returned from the war, one of
whom, Henry Maule, was everyone's idea of a great reporter. He
became for many years London correspondent of the *New York
Daily News*, had an Alvis car with three carburettors and wore an
Alan Ladd raincoat which came almost down to his ankles. Another
partner was a flamboyantly dressed communist, Fred Radford, who
wore a monocle. But the one I phoned was the senior partner, a cool
character called Bob Black, who seemed to have the phones to every
police station in the area tapped and lived in some luxury at Pang-
bourne on Thames. 'A good story, Bob,' he told me, checking the
spelling of Lane, which I thought was highly professional.

The story, sold exclusively in the first instance to the *Evening Standard*, greatly excited Fleet Street, obsessed almost as now by Royalty. All the best reporters came down and stayed in the Royal Ascot Hotel, the Berystede and – the losers – at the Royal Foresters. They had a wonderful time entertaining each other on expenses and succeeded in interviewing unnamed homeless mothers who were prepared to march into Windsor Park when the crusading deputy postmaster gave the word. Bob Black, who had sent a further string of exclusive reports, rang me up. 'Quite marvellous,' he said, 'I'm giving you £100.' Harold went too far and announced the day of the march. Pathé and Movietone News were at the gates on the appointed day plus the whole gang of reporters after a joyous week away from the office. So was Harold Lane. Not a single homeless person was in sight. I felt rather depressed, until one presumably homeless mother or possibly sightseer arrived with her baby in a pram. Her presence was obviously a surprise as far as Harold was concerned. 'Now, now,' he said, 'I told everyone not to march today. The whole thing is postponed. I'm expecting a settlement.' The newsreels recorded the scene. The story was over. Nobody complained. Some weeks later Bob Black phoned me after midnight. 'You're missing a good story,' said the freelance, who also knew all the fire chiefs. 'Sunninghill Park is burning down.' I did not believe that Harold Lane could do anything so extreme. He later joined the Conservative Party and was awarded the MBE. Nobody moved into the RAF huts. I did not meet a single homeless person, except the lady with a pram. No spoil-sports from Fleet Street exposed the story. Investigative reporters and 'Insight' had yet to be invented.

We were a jolly gang, not all of us reporters. We would visit a pub at Cheapside, Ascot, that has since become fashionable, drinking rough cider so cheap it was almost free, and go home late to one of our homes to listen to Glenn Miller's first recording of 'String of Pearls' or, for the umpteenth time, Benny Goodman's fabulous concert at Carnegie Hall. Perkins, son of an Ealing gas worker, stayed in the area after being evacuated with the London School of Building. Gary Tyrwhitt-Walker, our only intellectual, had a family tree that went back to William the Conqueror. His brother played saxophone in the local dance band, and his gentle aristocratic father after several job failures had become the local rat-catcher. For reasons not difficult to fathom, Gary became a communist. He had a bust of Karl Marx by his bedside and told us, in deep confidence, that he ran the Ascot cell. (We were sure that no one else was in it.)

John and Jim Mossman were also friends. Jim became a *Daily Telegraph* foreign correspondent and later a famous BBC/TV presenter until, sadly, he ended his life. John also became a Fleet Street reporter. They had friendly relations with a much older and extremely interesting lady called Mrs Glass, and we were deeply awestruck. Richard Beeston was the son of a delightful woman who had fallen on hard times and taught cookery at Ranelagh School as well as running a café that was open house to us all, next to Mr Hall the undertaker on the terrace at Wokingham. Richard, who worked on the despised *Reading Standard*, later went with John Mossman 600 miles across the desert in a taxi from Beirut to scoop the world over a revolution in Damascus, John for the *Daily Herald* and Dick for the *News Chronicle*. Neither paper had had such a scoop for years. Dick has languidly ducked a large number of bullets, according to legend with a gin and tonic in his hand. When the deadly duo of a bad proprietor and weak editor led to his once great paper's death, Dick said while others wailed, 'What is the problem? I haven't lost an arm or a leg.' He spent several years in Beirut and Moscow for the *Daily Telegraph* and became their paper's distinguished Washington correspondent. He was disgracefully pushed out on a miserable pension by the new régime at the *Daily Telegraph* in 1986 and was immediately taken on as Washington correspondent by the *Daily Mail*, whose editor, Sir David English, is himself a first-class reporter.

Another person I got to know when I took him on as a contributor to *Progress* was a young engineering fitter called Bill McCarthy. His well-informed articles from the shop floor helped him on to Ruskin College, Oxford, and after relatively few years he became Lord McCarthy, the man who was trusted by both sides to resolve disputes in the railway industry, which he did with great skill by invariably and properly recognising the strength of the railwaymen's case. A fellow *Reading Mercury* reporter, Mike Newberry, who became a member of Sir John Junor's financial staff on the *Sunday Express*, and I met two attractive Swiss au pair girls in one of our pub haunts. I spent nearly all Christmas with one of them, mostly, as I recall, in the bath at her employer's flat while they were away.

Ruth was sexually skilled, unlike me, and so good-looking we foolishly became engaged. For some mad reason I paid a deposit on a bedroom suite at Maples, though we had nowhere to put it and very little money. We made love all over the place, and one summer's evening after being badly bitten by mosquitos I persuaded her to let me slip into her bed for the night, though her employer was in the flat in a grand Georgian house at Bracknell. He was an elderly Jewish refugee with a slight foreign accent who owned an iron-monger's shop at Reading. His wife seemed to be a permanent invalid in hospital. While I lay in Ruth's bed, she made him some cocoa and I heard him wish her 'goodnight, Rusee' in a tone that convinced me he yearned for her desperately. Later, on a glorious moonlit night, I opened the window gently to get rid of some of the weak beer the Labour Government had imposed on the nation because of a world shortage of grain. There was a sound like a roll of drums. I stopped and looked out. There was a conservatory under-neath. 'You can't go to ze lavatory,' said Ruth. 'He vill 'ear you.' The crisis ended when I persuaded her to get an empty hot-water-bottle from the kitchen. Next morning her respectable but frustrated employer expressed concern as she prepared his breakfast. 'You were very restless in the night, Rusee,' he said, 'and you had a terrible cough.' Ruth became pregnant despite my enormous expen-diture at Flower's, the men's hairdresser, and hurried home for an abortion with £40 from me. We later decided that marriage was not what interested us. Maples gallantly returned the deposit. I remem-ber Ruth fondly, as I do a Land Army girl called Jane Layman, who had introduced me to sex at the late age of twenty-one. I was mad about her, but she was rather rough and not good looking like Ruth. Cravenly I did detours on my motor-bike to avoid being seen with her in my village.

All this was 'going through the mill', in the old fashioned way, to achieve the impossible dream, a job in Fleet Street.

4
TRIBUNE

On 9 January 1948, Ian Mikardo sent a letter to me that I kept because I thought it might be the start of something. 'I don't know whether you are now fully occupied, and completely satisfied with the work you are doing,' he wrote, 'but there is a vacancy on the staff of *Tribune* for a bright bloke to do some writing and sub-editing.' He suggested ('without any commitment to either side') that I should drop in on Michael Foot at 222, The Strand.

This turned out to be a delightful office on the third floor of an old building which has a right-of-way for judges and lawyers going to and from the Law Courts. The lift was activated by tugging a rope thick enough to tow a galleon. To stop the lift's erratic ascent and alarmingly precipitate descent when (as it was explained to me by an elderly porter) water pressure was high, it was necessary to grasp the rope again at a carefully calculated moment. Since the rope was stationary, this had the effect of chafing one's hands unless gloves were worn. Presumably the lift had some fail-safe device for the faint-hearted though that phrase had not been invented when it was built in the previous century.

Michael Foot, incredibly, was then only thirty-three. He seemed much older to me, probably because he had achieved so much and was already a legend. He suffered from three complaints that I supposed were psychosomatic; eczema, insomnia and asthma, and he would scratch his painfully blistered wrists, yawn and apply a puffer device to his mouth almost simultaneously. This had the effect of making him even more endearing. All three complaints vanished after his terrible car crash years later.

Michael was indecisive about taking me on, which was not surprising since my prime role as journalist was as a district man on the *Reading Mercury* and, unlike most writers on the weeklies, my education was sketchy and I had shown precious little promise. The literary editor, Tosco Fyvel, was a marvellous person with origins somewhere in eastern Europe and a pleasant stutter. 'You m-must

32

make up your mind, M-Michael,' he told him, so he reported to me later. Rather sadly, because I liked him, I gave in my notice to Mr Neale on the *Reading Mercury*. His wife was in the room. 'Edwards,' she said, 'you are going from a giant to a pygmy.' I was so nervous on my first day that I walked up and down the pavement outside the Law Courts unable to enter. And there was Fleet Street, a few yards away.

It was a delight to work at *Tribune*. At that time there were few divisions in the Labour Party. MPs sang the 'Red Flag' when the mines were nationalised. The New Jerusalem was on its way. The joint editor of *Tribune* with Michael Foot was Evelyn Anderson. Her roots were also in eastern Europe, as had been those of the previous editor, Jon Kimche. She was obsessed, if that is the right word, with the perfidy of the Russian communists and the treachery of their dupes in the occupied countries, and was an authority on the Oder-Neisse line and similar matters on which I was woefully ignorant. In fact, on a radio Brains Trust, mercifully broadcast only to the Far East, I was asked my views on the Oder-Neisse line and was totally stumped. Robert (later Lord) Boothby came to my rescue by saying it was impossible for a socialist like me to be an empiricist, after I had fatuously said I was sure the problem could be solved with good will on all sides. Evelyn Anderson's bible was a publication with pages as big as the *Independent*'s called *For a Lasting Peace and a People's Democracy*, produced by dissidents and for all I knew Trotskyites. She pored over it for hours, smoking incessantly, producing from it what she thought were nuggets for a column called 'What's Happening' that should have cured even poor Michael of his insomnia.

Her full-blown editorials on eastern Europe were, fortunately, matched by Michael Foot's witty and passionate dissertations on wicked press barons and other infidels closer to home. He received nothing for his work at *Tribune*, earning probably quite a modest living as an MP and leader-writer on the *Daily Herald*. In that job he alternated with Douglas Jay, the economist, who became First Secretary to the Treasury. The difference in their styles was startling.

I met Attlee once. It was at one of those awful Labour Party dances at which Herbert Morrison excelled. Michael Foot, for some inexplicable reason, was also there, and asked if I would like to meet the unlikely figure who had thrashed Churchill at the election, and I was introduced. The band was taking a break. Attlee and I stood alone on the dance floor. He was smoking his pipe. His look was friendly, but since he did not waste words he said nothing. The following was the entire conversation:

'Which papers do you read, Prime Minister?'
'*Times.*' Pause. Puff.
'And on Sunday?'
'*Observer.*' Pause. Puff.

I noticed that he had made no reference to the Labour papers, the *Daily Herald* and *Reynolds News*. I pressed on:

'Why the *Observer*?'
'Crossword. Ximines.' Pause.
'How long does it take you to do it, sir?'
'Five minutes.'
'It would take most people longer than that simply to write down the answers.'
'Do it in my head.'

We stood, liking each other, I felt. 'Good luck,' said the leader of the great post-war revolution, gripping my arm.

It does not make very good journalism to support the government. Our literary pages under Tosco and later Richard Findlater, who became a leading authority on the theatre, were excellent. Evelyn waged her one-woman war in eastern Europe. To help keep the paper going the Labour Party at Transport House took over our two centre pages for awesomely dull propaganda. Budding talents, like that of Michael Cummings, the cartoonist, were encouraged. He did one of the best cartoons I have ever seen on Harry Truman's unexpected presidential election victory in 1948. Michael hit all round the wicket, except at the Labour Party.

I wrote articles about other people's jobs, post-war housing that was far better than the disastrous high-rise developments that were to follow, profiles of unknown trade union leaders, particularly in the quaint craft unions, including undertakers, and similar reporting. At the age of twenty-four, at the invitation of someone who had read my articles, I was adopted as prospective Labour candidate for the Horsham division, where I met my first wife, Laura, and had a happy time campaigning in the countryside, staying with the typically agreeable people who were the backbone of the Labour Party, at least in those days. At my suggestion, the Tory candidate, Col. Gough, and I had a debate in a village hall, which attracted the expected large audience. We agreed to meet for a drink in the local pub afterwards. He went to the public bar, expecting to find me there, and I went to the saloon bar as a gesture to him. The climax to all our fun in this Tory heartland was a procession with flaming torches in Horsham itself, which must have scared the life out of most of the locals.

I stood down before the election in order to work full-time for Sam Campbell at the *People* and a year later, at Michael Foot's suggestion, returned to *Tribune* as editor. This, fortunately for me, almost coincided (while Attlee was in hospital) with the sensational resignations of Nye Bevan, Harold Wilson and John Freeman over the first Health Service charges on teeth and spectacles and general fury with the Chancellor Hugh Gaitskell. I visited the House of Commons and thought Wilson made a notably better speech than Nye. Overnight the word 'Bevanite' went into the language, as well as 'Nyedolater', for his wildly enthusiastic followers, and *Tribune* as the only Bevanite organ instantly became 'must' reading for every political correspondent and commentator. Saatchi and Saatchi could not have done a better job for the paper. Messengers from all the newspapers and news agencies waited every Thursday morning for the first copies to arrive at 222, The Strand in our little red van.

Whatever we said on the monumental battle with the insufferable Gaitskell and the trade union moguls who wielded their block votes on his behalf was quoted as if it had been personally concocted by Nye and his fellow plotters in some smoke-filled cellar. There were grounds for this suspicion, except that the scheming was more likely to have been done in Nye's grand house off Eaton Square or at the best table at the White Tower restaurant in Greek Street (which I could later afford when I went to work for Beaverbrook and afterwards the Mirror group). The cost of our cuttings service, as we were quoted not only by every Fleet Street paper but in the large number of morning and evening papers that existed throughout the country, became so great we had to cancel it. At the Labour conference in Scarborough in 1953, when his former friend Desmond Donnelly stood sensationally in the centre aisle pointing his finger at Bevan and crying, 'I accuse,' it was I who led the 'We want Nye' chant in the visitors' gallery that enveloped the hall as we demanded the right of reply for our hero from the infamous charges Donnelly had hurled at him.

The Labour Party was far more exciting split than when those we admired most were in government. *Tribune* brains trusts all over the country were a huge success – in sharp contrast to the Maxwell flop thirty years later when he went on the road, or rather the railway,

with the Mirror stars. Ian Mikardo was the best chairman, Michael
Foot the greatest star. The messianic figure of Nye Bevan never
appeared. Revivalist meetings that would not have disgraced Billy
Graham were for him, where his magic oratory and wit made up for
what was, on reflection, an often disappointing obscurity or thinness
of content. Most Labour Party workers were genuinely shocked by
the health charges, and the traditional pacifist leaning against
increased arms expenditure was real. But for all our protestations,
personalities rather than policies were the major issue. Attlee was
obviously going. We wanted Nye as leader, not as we saw him the
rather stuffy, earnest Gaitskell. Bevan's promised land would be a
lot sunnier.

The fight for possession grew heavy at times. After Michael had
written an editorial, instantly quoted everywhere, attacking the
right-wing trade union caucus that favoured German rearmament,
two of its members, Arthur Deakin, leader of the transport workers,
and Sir William Lawther of the miners, rang me on the afternoon it
appeared, threatening fearful consequences. My recollection, which
seems barely credible, is that Lawther said, 'We will get you, have
no fear.' Perhaps they had had a good lunch. Years later these two
key unions at the Labour Party conference swung left. The diatribes
against the undemocratic bloc vote ceased miraculously, only to be
revived again by its previous beneficiaries, the extreme right.
Bevanism lost its glamour after Gaitskell had been finally elected
because the real issue had been decided. Nye's acceptance of office
as Shadow Foreign Secretary was a clear recognition of that, as was
the famous speech in which he distressed his followers by pleading
against resolutions for unilateral nuclear disarmament that would
have sent him 'naked into the conference chamber'. It was a piece of
pragmatism, I thought. The battle was over. He had lost. It was far
better that he was opposing the Foreign Secretary than someone
else, and he had to bite that particular bullet or be ruled out. I
comforted myself with a similar rationale when I became editor of
the *Daily Express*, although a warm admirer of Wilson at the time.

Nye was a grand patriarchal figure for those of us who toiled at
Tribune. We scarcely saw him. Someone I had always thought was
an uncritical admirer and intimate of Nye's said to me recently, 'He
only enjoyed the company of millionaires.' Certainly he had several
very rich friends including Howard Samuel, the publisher and reluctant property millionaire who committed suicide by walking into the
sea, a tragic replica of a comedy scene in the film 'Dead of Night' in
which Basil Radford did the same after losing at golf in a wager with

Naunton Wayne over a girl. Howard, who helped *Tribune* survive, was a troubled but dull man. He arranged for me to live with my wife and our first baby at a reasonable rent in a basement semi-slum he owned in Great Titchfield Street and occasionally took me to lunch at the Savoy. I reciprocated by taking him to the Gay Hussar, then, as now, the restaurant of the discerning Left and journalists of all persuasions. Nye's friendship could only be, I felt, because Howard was rich. There were far more entertaining people in the Parliamentary Labour Party who did not have a bean. I was only once invited to eat at Bevan's house during my eight years' association with *Tribune*. Laura and I went to Sunday lunch at his farm with several other guests. Not yet having met Beaverbrook, it was the most impressive meal I had attended, providing me with my first sight of a whole, fresh salmon, as distinct from the tinned variety. It was a gift of Nye's millionaire socialist friends in Scotland, the Mackies. Seeking to please the great man as I enjoyed this new culinary experience and his rare hospitality I said to Nye, 'What marvellous salmon.' His reply was disconcerting. 'T-too dry,' he stuttered.

If a note of sourness is detected in these recollections, it is not intended. My admiration for him has not faded. But sometimes both he and Jennie Lee shocked me a little. In the Bevanite period we published a series of *Tribune* pamphlets. I wrote one on the Cresswell pit disaster called 'Dirty Coal'. Gathering material for it, I experienced for the first time the warmth and friendship of miners in a small community. I stayed at a Trust House country hotel some miles from the village. It had a grand staircase leading to sumptuous bedrooms. I went first to the Miners' Institute, formerly built by the coal-owner, and then to the Comrades' Club owned by the miners. Overjoyed to be in such good company, I eventually passed out. Next morning I awoke in my hotel. A group of miners had taken me back, up the grand staircase, and put me to bed.

I liked what I had written. At Michael Foot's suggestion I took it along to Nye and Jennie for their approval. It was their subject after all. This was the first and last time I saw the house off Eaton Square before they moved to the farm. Coal fires blazed in two vast rooms. Nye sat in an armchair and Jennie on a long settee reading the galley proofs. They did not seem at all enthusiastic. Eventually Jennie uttered the most inexplicable sentence I ever recall hearing. 'Only the scum are left in the mines,' she said moodily. What did Jennie mean? I am sure she did not mean it literally. I reeled out into the opulence of Belgravia, stunned with disbelief and deeply disappointed at their response to my efforts. What did she mean? Perhaps the miners' leaders had done something to cause Nye pain, as they frequently did. Perhaps it was Will Lawther again. The pamphlet was well received.

J. P. W. ('Curly') Mallalieu, one of the good crop of new Labour MPs in the first post-war Parliament and author of the best-seller *Very Ordinary Seaman* on his wartime naval experiences, organised a *Tribune* cricket match at his riverside home near Hampton Court. Jitendra Arya, an Indian photographer friend of mine, took a highly marketable set of pictures of Bevan playing in his braces. Since he was the bogey of every Fleet Street newspaper, we thought they would be helpful, but Jennie vetoed them because they would be bad for his image. They were released years later, to the delight of Nye's friends.

I had one monumental row with the Bevans during the battle with Gaitskell. At that time nuclear disarmament was not a major issue. In fact, I could lay some claim to being the original unilateralist. Dick Crossman, one of Bevan's principal lieutenants, and George Wigg MP wrote an immensely long thesis in the *New Statesman* arguing for Britain's manufacture of the H-bomb on the grounds that it would reduce the need for conventional weapons and free resources for all manner of good works. Also, they reasoned brightly, it was a totally dependable deterrent since the other side would not dare use their weapon so long as we had our own. In a weekly column carefully called 'Speaking for Myself', and headed DICK CROSSMAN'S BOMBSHELL, I derided their arguments. 'What line should the fashionable socialist take towards the manufacture by Great Britain of the H-bomb?' I began offensively, outlining their arguments. My views notably resembled Neil Kinnock's thirty years later (at least up to this moment of writing). 'America and Russia have enough H-bombs to destroy civilisation,' I mocked. 'That is the maximum that our statesmen can hope to achieve at the moment.' I put the then unconventional case for conventional weapons. 'They enabled us, at colossal sacrifice it is true, to defeat a filthy evil and in the end to start building a fine new world – now imperilled by our pig-headed, lunatic rulers.' In case anyone had failed to get the message, I added a final bitter paragraph: 'And no one need worry. The Americans are not telling us to manufacture the H-bomb or get out of NATO. And there will be plenty of H-bombs available without ours to kill every man, woman and child in all the cities of the earth.' If I had looked into a crystal ball I could not have more neatly encapsulated Labour's defence policy in the 1980s, which made no sense unless with NATO's support America had the bomb.

I was pleased to have poked one in Wykehamist Dick Crossman's face. I met him by chance at the House of Commons in my year as a *People* reporter and he had said disdainfully, 'I suppose we are colleagues.' Nye Bevan was far from pleased. He was ill in bed with flu. Crossman drove down to Asheridge Farm, ran up the stairs despite Jennie's attempts to dissuade him, burst into the sickroom and launched a violent assault on Bevan for what he was sure was an attack Nye had personally inspired. That was the version given to me before an emergency meeting of the *Tribune* board called to discuss the crisis I had caused. I was asked to attend, rather like a court martial, though I was not a director.

'What you did', spat Jennie, jabbing her fingers towards me three times, 'was damnable, damnable, damnable.' I was like a small boy caught doing something unmentionable. Everyone looked unhappy except Jennie, whose face registered black fury. Up spoke the still, small voice of Michael Foot, no doubt scratching his wrists. 'Well, he *is* the editor,' he said, putting the liberal case, as he could always be expected to do on such matters. Four years later, as deputy editor of the *Daily Express*, I was sitting alone on a sunny Easter Monday in a window at the Savoy Restaurant. The waiters all knew me. I did not even have to sign the bill. I was eating salmon from a delightful dish surrounded by a circle of mashed potatoes. The traffic along the Embankment ceased and after an interval large numbers of my friends went by in one of the first Aldermaston marches, led by Michael. 'I put them up to that,' I told my friend the carver, who had stopped to watch.

5
INVESTIGATIVE JOURNALIST

In 1951 Curly Mallalieu decided it was time I supplemented my income of £12 a week on *Tribune*. He had a word with Sam Campbell, legendary editor of the *People*, who gave me a double shift on Saturdays worth £9. Sam had the title of managing editor. Harry Ainsworth, a spiritualist eccentric, retained the title of editor though he had long since given up control. His salary was linked to the paper's circulation. This was less than 400,000 when he took over in the 1920s. It was now over 5 million. He was reputed to earn more than anyone in Fleet Street and naturally he did not want to give up. Sam accepted this annoyance philosophically, as did John Junor on the *Sunday Express*, who had to put up with having John Gordon as editor-in-chief. Gordon's column alone, secretly written in his last few years by John Junor before 'JJ' took it over in his own name, was worth his salary and Lord Beaverbrook further rewarded him with a second-hand Rolls-Royce. There is a limit to the generosity of proprietors. In my experience they always paid about the market rate, proving that Karl Marx knew a thing or two.

Sam Campbell, who always seemed to wear the same brown suit, had the good fortune to edit the *Sunday Pictorial* as caretaker for Hugh Cudlipp, while he edited army newspapers, rising to the rank of colonel. When Cudlipp was demobbed, so was Sam, and walked straight into the editorship of the rival *People*. My opinion of Sam was pretty low following an incident in Reading in 1943. A British restaurant was bombed. Sam sent down the *Sunday Pictorial*'s ace writer, the cynical Rex North, who wrote a moving but fictitious account of what happened. This enraged the journalists on the Reading papers. A resolution was passed by the local National Union of Journalists' branch and sent to Sam. His reply was that since the censor only allowed reference to 'a Home Counties town', the report was not necessarily about the Reading incident at all. He appeared to be saying that since Rex North did not say it was Reading, what harm was done? Sam was clearly perplexed by our rage.

He turned out to be a pleasant, tolerant man to work for, who regarded truth as dispensable if he could improve a quote or a story and get away with it. I was lucky again. My first job was to go to Bradford and cover the story of someone the daily newspapers called Syncopating Sandy. He was not much of a pianist, but by that weekend he had played for nearly a fortnight without stopping. He failed, alas, to break a world record and was taken to hospital. Harry Ainsworth, his familiar packet of sandwiches beside him, was sitting as usual next to Sam on the big table (the heart of the newspaper on Saturdays) when he read my report. He told Sam he liked it. Sam, pleased that his predecessor had confirmed his judgment, offered me a full-time job. On my first Saturday as a casual, that must be something of a record. '£18 a week all right?' said Sam, and we shook hands. As I started working for the *People* for a year before going back to *Tribune* as editor, Cyril Kersh, a Damon Runyon character who later became editor of *Reveille*, warned that when I got my first pay packet I would discover that Sam was paying me less. To my surprise, he was right. It was £15. 'Sorry, old man,' said Sam, '£18 was it?' Cyril explained that this was not Sam's way of testing the character of a new employee. He was simply mean.

Editors who look after their budgets tend to last longer, so long as they also sell the paper. Sam took me to The Ivy for lunch, then one of London's most fashionable restaurants. He went there almost daily, we presumed because it was within walking distance and he could save the taxi fare. His voice broke through my eager study of the menu. 'What'll you have, old man? Steak and kidney and a light ale?' Sam must have been the only person who ordered light ale at The Ivy, but they liked having him as a customer. He brought in a lot of famous people whose confessions he was seeking. Gilbert Harding was one of his discoveries. So was Jimmy Savile. He recognised their potential from their earliest broadcasts. That is a double any editor of a popular paper would have been proud of.

Harding took over the 'Man of the People' column, formerly 'Man o' the People', which every Sunday exposed wicked folk whose misdeeds had been dredged from every part of the country. In fact, most of the column under Harding's name was written by Sam's secretary, Mrs Kate Wadleigh, and re-written by Sam. Kate kept a bottle of whisky in her desk. She ended her career on *Nursery World*. Harding would come into the office once or twice a week to see what he was supposed to have written. 'You shouldn't be on a paper like this,' he said to me once. 'Let me take you to the south of

France to meet Somerset Maugham. If he places his hand on your knee, do not recoil as you do with me.'

It is well known that many journalists in key positions on Tory newspapers are Labour sympathisers. Conversely, though this is not well known, some of those who run Labour papers are Tories. Dick Dinsdale, appointed by Hugh Cudlipp to edit his new creation the (ill-fated) *Sun*, was regarded by his staff as one. His right-wing views caused much amusement among politically committed writers on the paper with a sense of humour, and distress to those without one. Reg Payne, another Cudlipp favourite, was never suspected of being a fully paid-up member of the Labour Party when he edited the *Sunday Mirror*. Lee Howard, for years the highly capable editor of the *Daily Mirror*, showed no interest in politics and left the whole political direction of the paper to the brilliant Cudlipp on the ninth floor. He had no choice anyway. Likewise the *People*, as the then *Daily Herald*'s sister paper, was thought to be a Labour paper, but Sam was a Tory. Since there was no Cudlipp on the ninth floor before Cecil King and the Mirror Group took over the company, Sam ran a skilfully neutral line in the key 1951 election when Attlee's now acclaimed post-war Labour Government was finally defeated, followed by the return of Churchill and thirteen years of Tory rule.

I wrote the main election article each week on a subject chosen by Sam that steered clear of any political issues. This considerable feat was achieved (eleven days before polling) by selecting bright young candidates in all the parties, including an unknown 'very attractive' twenty-five-year-old Margaret Roberts, later to become better known as Mrs Thatcher, and (four days before polling) analysing the career backgrounds of the candidates. This showed that, as now, lawyers and journalists had a much better chance of being selected even in the Labour Party than manual workers, but Sam's editorial above, which bemoaned these findings, steered clear of any sugges- tion about how the readers should vote. Wordsmith Sam knew how to make the paper sound radical, which many readers wanted, without actually offending Tory readers. To him, circulation was the thing, quite apart from his personal belief that life would be better under the Tories. He successfully broke the rule that papers without a strong political line fail.

The election over, Sam said: 'You can forget about politics now, old man, and write something the readers want to read. Ask George Formby for his life story.' Sam looked shocked when I asked how much he was willing to pay. 'He'll do it for nothing, Bob. These stars like the publicity.' I went with Formby's agent, Torrington Douglas, to see him and Beryl in their apartment at the Dorchester Hotel. When asked, I said that Sam assumed no payment would be required. 'Can't really do that,' said George. 'The *Empire News* paid me £2000 for my life story before the war. I couldn't accept any less than that.' Back at the office I told Sam the deal was off. 'Why's that, old man?' 'He won't do it for less than £2000.' 'Well done, old man,' said Sam. 'Sign him up.'

I discovered that the editor's meanness was matched by Formby's. When he took a cigarette with his own name on it from a gold box, then shut it, Torrington Douglas said, 'We also smoke, George.' Writing this series was something of a struggle. Formby had little sense of humour and no powers of recollection. 'When it's all over, I'll buy you an overcoat,' said Torrington Douglas, glad of his 10 per cent. I remained cravenly silent, the only time I failed to refuse a bribe. Aided by the pre-war *Empire News* articles, other cuttings and a considerable imagination, I managed a 'tell all' story that reads well even today. It ran for five weeks as the 'great new series' at the start of 1952. Sam had a bargain: I did not get the overcoat. Formby fooled us all. I made a feature of his great love for Beryl, like Reagan and Nancy, and all the time his real love was a Sunday School teacher in Blackpool, whom he later married.

Sam ran a formula paper. His imprint is still on it today. Each week he sought to protect his readers from evil men who were seeking to cheat or corrupt them. 'Far from wishing to abolish identity cards,' wrote pre-Gilbert Harding 'Man o' the People' in June 1951, 'I should like to see them more detailed and complete – to the benefit of decent citizens and the undoing of rogues, vaga-bonds, spies, deserters, and all the "lunatic fringe" that scums the rim of our community pool.' The tone was almost fascist.

In the same typical issue there were the weekly 'Lines of Comfort' from Jean Morton. She may or may not have existed, and her job was to rival Patience Strong in the *Sunday Pictorial* (now *Sunday Mirror*):

God be with you as He
will, through Life's vales
and up Life's hill,
through Life's tumult
and its calm, shielding
you Within His Arm.

all in ital., reverse indent, as we say in the trade. MOTHER, Mrs Rose

Buckner, took her readers into yet another happy, humble home, and the famous 'Follow Me Around' columnist Arthur Helliwell, complete with his 'titfer' (hat), affected to be shocked by blue jokes from the Beverley Sisters at a London Palladium show also starring Danny Kaye: 'When I went to hear them last week I was, quite frankly, shocked and disgusted. After their act I didn't even wait to see Danny. I walked straight out of the theatre in search of some fresh air.' Colleagues assumed that the reason Helliwell did not stay to see Danny Kaye, and needed fresh air, was because he was drunk, and had rather neatly saved his face.

On page one of the same issue Duncan Webb played his role in the Campbell formula with yet another 'dossier', a favourite word of the editor's, on the 'evil traffic' in prostitution. The dossier, as usual, was being passed 'urgently' to the Home Office, which clearly did not want it. Only the last sentence was reproduced from a letter sent by the Home Office to Webb who had made his customary request for a public inquiry: 'Meanwhile, the Secretary of State will be pleased to consider any representation you may wish to make on the need for the appointment of such a committee.' Next to the photograph of this single sentence from the letter, Sam wrote: '*People* reporter, Duncan Webb, whose exposures of organised vice in London caused a nation-wide outcry, has been asked by the Home Office for further evidence.' The following week Sam further embroidered the Home Office's formal, single, publishable sentence: 'Now our investigator, Duncan Webb, has been asked by the Home Secretary for evidence that will help him decide whether a full-scale inquiry should be held. Webb has accepted.'

This solemn, official style appealed to the readers. With suitable gravity, Campbell wrote, as if the pros and cons had been carefully and responsibly weighed up: 'Webb has decided to make his report public.' This was not surprising if, as the paper claimed, Webb, three reporters and three 'former detective officers' had been working on the story for a year. Sam liked to attach the label 'after months of inquiry' even to reports that had taken little more than a week.

Duncan 'Tommy' Webb was one of Sam's greatest creations, as indeed was Helliwell, a hitherto undistinguished reporter and war correspondent whom Sam had pointed into a semi-fictitious immediate post-war world of minor Soho spivs and crooks. Webb, too, might have remained an unknown reporter if Sam had not had the happy thought of getting him to expose prostitution, immortalised by his (or Sam's) words: 'I made an excuse and left.' Police contacts, bribed lavishly by Sam's standards, told Webb about the Messina brothers, four ponces, one of whom rather shamelessly employed his own wife as a prostitute. Thus appeared in 1950 the famous (in Fleet Street) *People* headline ARREST THESE FOUR MEN! complete with pictures of the evil quartet. 'They are the emperors of a vice gang in the heart of London,' wrote Sam Campbell, ecstatically. 'The Messina gang exposed.' They were, week after week, in one of the best-selling post-war stories, rivalled only by the Duke of Windsor's memoirs published at vast cost in the *Sunday Express*. Eventually even the corrupt vice squad had to take notice. One of the brothers was sentenced to two years' imprisonment for running a disorderly house. The rest, as Sam put it, 'escaped' to Italy, where they were pursued for several weeks by Webb, who had the misfortune to arrive at several hotels just after they had left, until at last the story ran out of steam. It was a notable triumph, though the award-winning investigative reporters who inherited Webb's mantle would have filled the gap in his reports. Why had the police failed for so long to act against these small-time brothel keepers? Did they not notice, or were they paid off by the Messinas? Duncan Webb once took me back to his flat, where he lived alone. There were eight locks on the door. 'You can't be too careful,' said the great investigator, who once when the Messina series was flagging claimed he had been beaten up. He was not too seriously injured.

Another part of Sam's successful formula was to cater for hypochondriacs. He invented a family called the Ne'erwells, later to become the Neverwells, one of whose members every week was stricken with one illness or another. They were cared for by the ever-patient, kindly Dr Goodenough, with such skill that none of them ever died, despite such extreme vulnerability to germs that they would now be suspected AIDS victims. So successful was this feature, Sam eventually gave Dr Goodenough a column of his own, where he wrote in straightforward terms about illnesses while a worthy but anonymous NHS doctor took over the Neverwells, a soap opera that ran for many years.

Sam sensibly believed in readership research, which showed how sound his instincts were as an editor. He knew that 'warm, human' stories, as the researchers categorise them, are sure-fire winners, that more men almost invariably read the back sports page than the front, that more women read the stars than anything else in the paper, and that a city column is strictly for the birds, so he reduced it to three paragraphs. A large, impressive, bearded man called Ross Shepherd was the theatre critic. He was usually confined to a single paragraph, but his adeptly truncated words of praise adorned almost every theatre in London.

One day Sam called me into his office to join his deputy, Nat Rothman, who was a good libel lawyer as well as a first-class honest journalist, and the art editor Eric Nudd. 'I thought you'd like to see how a paper is planned,' said Sam. He turned to Nat and Eric, 'The trouble with next Sunday's paper is that it's all doom and gloom. What it needs is a bit of 'ope. Get me a nice baby picture, Eric. I'll find a way of putting it in.' Later that week I took him an article he had asked me to write attacking an author named Cook who was a follower of Malthus and prophesied the early demise of the human race through over-population. 'That's no good,' said Sam, genially. 'First you must scare the living daylights out of the readers. Then you say it's all balls. You don't knock it from the start.' The article (eventually) quoted an optimistic Lord Boyd Orr and an equally buoyant Professor J. B. S. Haldane. Despite Sam Campbell's advice not to knock the book in the first paragraph, the headline he wrote WAS BABY CAN SAY BOO TO CALAMITY COOK plus a large baby picture provided by the art editor.

Thanks to Michael Foot, Sam had one of the best Sunday paper political scoops for many years, Aneurin Bevan's resignation. Nye and the Bevanites decided that the will-he won't-he? speculation was harmful. It suggested that careful calculations rather than deep convictions were involved. So Michael phoned me ahead of Nye's official letter of resignation; and that's how you beat the opposition. Sam used a technique much practised in those days. He 'led' the paper with another story in the first edition that went to Plymouth, remote areas of Wales, half Lincolnshire and the Suffolk coast. These areas were often deprived of the best reports and had to be content with page one stories that seemed to have been blown up out of all proportion to their real worth. A nightly ritual among national newspapers is the exchange of rival first editions. They are the first off the presses and within minutes they are being examined, usually with much scorn and derision, by competing editors and their assistants. No one ever enquires who pays for these stolen copies, or whether those who provide the service pay income tax.

A lesser exclusive I passed on to Sam before Labour's election defeat was about a forthcoming *Tribune* pamphlet 'Going Our Way', a moderately written statement of policy by the Bevanites. This appeared with, as we call it, an end-of-the-world size headline BEVAN BOMBSHELL FOR ATTLEE: ALL-OUT ATTACK ON CABINET. Beneath it there was a wildly distorted account of Bevanite plottings pegged to the news of the pamphlet. 'It's so untrue,' I told Charlie Rowe, the news editor, 'we might as well be working for *Beano*.' Charles told Sam, who called me across to the big table, an amused Harry Ainsworth watching. Sam picked up his pencil: 'OK, Bob, let's go through it line by line.' 'Well,' I said, 'Ian Mikardo is not at a secret meeting in Cardiff. He's not even in Wales.' Sam struck it out and everything else which I thought was over the top. 'All right, Bob?' he said with his twisted but friendly smile. 'Well,' I said again, 'there's the headline.' Sam put down his pencil. 'Listen,' said the editor determined to sell his paper, 'I'll change anything except the headline.'

Another end-of-the-world headline that year was DALTON'S MIN- ISTRY GETS INTO A BLACK MARKET DEAL. Hugh Dalton, fired for giving budget secrets to a journalist, had worked his penance and was back in a humble role as Minister of Town and Country Planning. Unknown to him, the general public and the press, the only way to get steel for building in those days was to pay above the state regulated prices on the black market. Ministry officials gave per- mission to St Pancras borough council to do that rather than fall down on a housing project, and an aggrieved small-time black marketeer told us about it. He was aggrieved because another Ministry was prosecuting him for selling over the odds.

The story took off. I became a sort of *agent provocateur* detective, setting up crimes, and sold substantial quantities of steel rods that did not exist to major companies. Unknown to me, one of them had built our offices, which we shared with the *Daily Herald*, and they were on good terms with our bosses. Sam overcame this little hitch by getting me to say in my report: 'At this stage I will not disclose the names of the firms concerned, as I see no reason to single them out when the whole of the building industry is buying steel at over the controlled prices and the merchants themselves are up to their necks in these transactions.' What we lacked was a colourful rogue. The informer obliged with a lady who owned a dress shop and dealt in black market steel part-time. Sam had no hesitation about naming her and she became, predictably, the Queen of the Black Market.

After my triumphant return to the office, complete with her order for £2000 worth of steel, Sam said, 'Now, old man, you have to go back to her and say who you really are. That'll make a good story.' My witness was an elderly reporter called Stanley Buchanan. He took white alkaline powder to combat nervous indigestion and his lips were regularly flaked with it. Every investigative story filled him with foreboding. When Sam told him to expose the lack of security at RAF stations by posing as a chimney sweep, which he succeeded in doing, he looked as if he would rather be safely locked up in a cell at Sing Sing. 'Don't go back,' pleaded Stanley as we got into his ancient Morris. 'There are a lot of nasty people there. Say you went back and I'll say you did.' The Queen of the Black Market's response was unexpected, when I confronted her as instructed. 'Ooh,' she said, 'that's disgraceful,' as I told her I was a 'special investigator' from the *People*. 'You came here under false pretences. You lied to me. I shall tell the *News of the World!*' She was not joking. Elated, I stormed into Sam to pass on this wonderful quote. He was not impressed. 'Don't mention it, old man. Never advertise a rival.' The *Sunday Times* or the *Observer* would, of course, have loved it. The lady was fined £700, and after the Tories won the election they sensibly dropped steel price controls.

My experience of newspaper informers, even those who were not paid, is that they were invariably tawdry, as indeed were many investigative reporters I have known. A tall, white-faced, youngish man with a starched collar and black suit materialised behind the counter in our newsroom, which was like a crowded detectives' office in a New York precinct. It turned out that he had been sacked by the People's Dispensary for Sick Animals, a charity with clinics throughout southern England, and looking at him I was not surprised. His revenge was to tell us that this highly respected charity was illegally imposing charges on people who brought in their pets for treatment instead of leaving them to make a donation if they wished. 'How do I prove this?' I asked him. 'It is simple,' he said. 'Take a cat.'

Thus in a Bayswater basement flat a large, furry cat was handed to me in a basket by an elderly lady friend of the informant. The cat looked surprised and, I thought, very fit. 'Tell them the cat is constipated,' said the informer. 'How would I know that?' I asked. He replied: 'You would if you were a cat lover. Say he paces up and down restlessly and has a regular sort of foam on his mouth.' The vets would spot these as symptoms of cat flu, he explained. I set off with Laura Ellwood, before she became my first wife, on what seemed to be both a promising assignment at PDSA clinics along the south coast and a nice day out together. At the first clinic the vet, taking the magnificent and placid cat out of his basket, listened sympathetically to our rehearsed story, as the apparent owners. His practised eyes seemed to me to convince him that there was nothing much wrong with the cat. He decided to placate Laura and myself by taking the cat's temperature with a large thermometer inserted in its rectum. Next he pressed the sides of the cat's face and dropped a small pill down its throat. 'I think you'll find he's all right now,' he said. He placed the cat back in the basket and seemed to expect us to leave. 'What is the charge, please?' I asked, my hopes sinking. 'No charge,' he said, smiling. 'You can drop something into the collection box if you like.'

There was a similar disappointment at every other PDSA clinic we visited. At each one I described how the cat was constipated, often foamed at the mouth, and paced up and down. At each one his temperature was taken anally, his mouth prised open and a small pill inserted. No charge was imposed. The charity had emerged, unfortunately, without a stain on its character. Ever conscientious, I decided to try one more PDSA clinic at Lewisham on our way home that evening. The cat still looked well, though a little tired. 'He is badly constipated,' I said, like an actor tired of his lines, as the vet opened the basket. 'Well, he isn't now,' said the vet, and very kindly cleaned out the basket for us. Once again no charge was imposed and because no story emerged I kept my expenses to the minimum. It was quite a day for the cat.

Harry Ainsworth, with Sam's permission, called me into his office on a story that came close to ending with me in the box on a contempt of court charge. He had some spiritualist friends who wanted to expose an alleged phoney medium called Bertie Basham, who operated at Notting Hill Gate. The genuine spiritualists were seven in all, and because they were all male and uniformly small became known in the office as the Seven Dwarfs. I was to accompany them to a seance conducted by Mr Basham. They said that because he had not met me he might have a word beforehand. I took Laura along for the fun, and we were soon in the kitchen with Mr Basham and two young male assistants. Both were effeminate and clearly devoted to him. I presumed that whatever else they did they also provided the sound and other effects I had been warned to expect. Having taken my fee, Mr Basham solicitously asked why I was there. I told him I had lost my Uncle Henry, of whom I was extremely fond, and hoped to have some contact with him. 'Uncle Henry?' repeated Mr Basham, and we went upstairs to the large Victorian drawing-room filled with others seeking their loved ones, mostly widows, plus the Seven Dwarfs.

I was surprised when they told me that the procedure was the same as at 'genuine' seances. Two luminous plaques lay on the carpet in front of Mr Basham's armchair. They were to illuminate the face of Mr Hassan, Bertie's spirit guide whose portrait was on the wall. He was an Egyptian. The plaques, conveniently, had handles. We were to sing loudly hymns like 'Onward Christian Soldiers', and when we had exhausted these, popular songs like 'Dearly Beloved' and 'She'll be Coming Round the Mountain'. I presumed this was to drown the noise of Mr Basham and his assistants clumping about. The curtains had been pulled, the lights put out and Mr Basham supposedly was in a trance in his armchair. Cold water was flicked on my face, a strange smell filled the room accompanied by a cold wind, and Mr Hassan's bearded face appeared in front of me illuminated by the two plaques. The long since departed Egyptian, I noticed, bore a marked resemblance to Mr Basham, despite the beard. Mr Hassan, or Basham, gave me a brief reassuring message from Uncle Henry and disappeared. I hugged Laura with delight, and then the plaques illuminated the unconscious Mr Basham himself as ectoplasm appeared to emerge in a large quantity from his mouth. At this moment, as arranged, the Seven Dwarfs turned on all the lights dotted about the room. A fight broke out between them and Mr Basham's supporters, and two of the dwarfs tugged at a length of muslin cloth to which Mr Basham firmly clung, groaning loudly, while still apparently unconscious.

'Stop the fight!' I cried, after a suitable interval. If it had gone on much longer, the police might have been called with disastrous results to my exclusive story. We went out of the front door and down the steps to the pavement, where our photographer took a flash picture as Bertie and his angry assistants followed. The photographer meekly handed over an old-fashioned plate when the young men seized him, but I need not have worried. He had kept the one with the picture on it. We went to a pub to interview the Seven Dwarfs. Each had a lemonade, and Sam had a good page one, right-hand second lead, as it's called in the trade.

Bertie Basham was arrested that weekend. On Tuesday we had to put in suggestions to the editor. Mine was that we should pay Basham to confess. 'Good idea,' was Sam's response. I saw Mr Basham by appointment, disturbingly in the presence of his mother, and said, 'I know you're guilty. You know you're guilty. You're bound to go to prison. We will pay you £1000 to confess your guilt after the case and at least you will have done some good by warning others.' To my surprise, he insisted vigorously that he was totally innocent and told me to leave. Two detectives arrived a day later at the *People* and asked for me. They said a complaint had been made by Mr Basham's solicitor that I had sought to influence his client to plead guilty and that was contempt of court. Apparently the solicitor was hidden in a cupboard when I went to see Basham. Duncan Webb, who was somewhat dramatically protected at his desk by bullet-proof glass, intervened at this moment. 'Say nothing, Bob. Leave this to me.' He went out of the building with the detectives and two days later said I was to go to our local pub, The Enterprise, stand apart from him and watch what happened. To my intense shock he carefully handed over a roll of pound notes to one of the detectives so that I would witness the transaction. Nothing more was heard of the complaint against me. I was not called as a witness, which may have been the deal, Mr Basham claimed the muslin was planted on him and the West London stipendiary magistrate found him not guilty, though the magistrate added wearily that he hoped no one would say he had confirmed that the dead could be contacted at seances. I have been an authority on the subject of contempt of court ever since.

Another character on Sam Campbell's staff was the celebrated Hannen Swaffer. He was a guest at a Royal Garden Party shortly before King George VI died. 'He's slipping you know, Bob,' said Swaffer afterwards, gripping me by the arm to make sure I was paying attention. I looked up from my typewriter. 'Who's slipping, Swaff?' 'The King. Didn't even recognise me.'

When the King died, Swaffer was asked to go to Sandringham where the King's body lay in the parish church for the weekend. On second thoughts I was sent to back him up, and walking with Laura from the lovely station early on the Saturday morning met Swaffer being driven in the opposite direction in a hired Rolls-Royce. Hilde Marchant, one of Britain's best reporters, was with him. He opened the door. 'G-good to see you, Bob. Larst night the c-chief c-con-stable called a press conference and said, "Sorry, you're not allowed into the church tomorrow. Only the Press Association court reporter and estate workers. Any questions?" So I said, "W-what time is the first train back to London tomorrow?" G-goodbye, Bob.' Sure enough, two plain-clothes detectives stood outside the gates to the church, which is inside the walls of Sandringham. An elderly *Sunday Express* reporter came across to me. He jumped up and down in a rage. 'Fuck, fuck,' he shouted. 'We're not allowed in.' I knew a dangerously good *News of the World* reporter would be on this story and when the *Sunday Express* reporter had moved on I said to Laura, 'Go and talk nicely to those detectives and see if they will let you in.' She was a good looking girl and I wandered into the woods while the infamous deed was done.

Shortly after a pleasant lunch at a good hotel, I telephoned my report:

As the bright sun of a brilliant winter's day faded over this garden paradise this evening, I walked quietly and alone along the 50 yards drive to Sandringham Church to pay my silent tribute to King George VI ...

The altar stood, shining and silver, like a vision, only 30 feet from the church door. Two tall white candles flickered on it ...

I stepped into the wooden pew where King George himself prayed only last Sunday. There I knelt for a few moments in this House of God undisturbed by the turmoil of the world ...

Laura and I went on for an idyllic walk somewhere and when we got back to the hotel there was an urgent message to ring the news editor. 'Christ, Bob, where have you been?' asked Charlie Rowe, 'The Press Association report says the "Darling Papa" card with the flowers from Elizabeth and Philip was signed "Lilibet and Philip" and you said "Elizabeth and Philip". Who is right?' 'Those damned copy-takers,' I replied instantly, 'they can't get anything right.' This report was about the naughtiest thing I have done in my career, which I don't think is too bad. I was right to be worried about the *News of the World* reporter. Although he did not pretend to have entered the church, his story was better than mine.

The story I was proudest of in my year as a *People* reporter followed a somewhat bizarre and undoubtedly illegal trip to Hull. A Windsor councillor and friend of mine, James Stewart Cook, who had written years earlier for our local Labour paper *Progress*, had somehow become acquainted with a 'mole' inside the offices of the Distant Water Trawler Owners' Federation. The Federation ran a price-fixing ring that would today have resulted in prison sentences and heavy fines. But outside the Ministry of Agriculture and Fisheries and the headquarters of the White Fish Authority, which was at Harrogate, the furthest point from the sea in England, no one knew the cartel existed. Jim Cook promised that if I went with him to Hull I would find out all about it. As soon as contacts travel under a newspaper's auspices they like to live it up, which can cause sharp words between news editors and reporters when the story is disappointing. By the time we reached Hull I had never seen so many empty beer bottles on one table in a train. In those days, wine was not in vogue. After an expensive dinner at the best hotel, we met our mole in a dismal pub. He was as shady looking as all such informants, however much of a public service they perform. We went in his car to the Federation's offices, which he entered, switching on the lights and returning in a few minutes with what I assumed was a stolen document in his pocket. This was a copy of the monopoly agreement signed by all the Federation's members. Under it they would return to harbour with only three-quarters of the holds filled, when necessary send catches at giveaway prices to fish meal factories to maintain agreed shop prices, lay-up vessels for the same purpose and impose heavy fines on anyone who broke the agreement. The losers were the fishermen and their skippers, because commissions were cut, but most of all the customers. Our revelations caused a great fuss in Parliament and outside, but the monopoly was not effectively broken until many years later by Edward Heath's legislation against resale price maintenance and Common Market regulations. Sam Campbell was delighted when I showed him the stolen document, but he uttered an immediate caution. 'Whatever you do, Bob,' he said, 'don't use the word "ramp". It automatically results in a libel action.' In fact, I had no thought of doing so. RAMP is only used by sub-editors when RACKET is too long for 144 point headlines. That Saturday evening I waited eagerly to see the proof of page one and how prominently Sam had projected the scoop and my by-line. The headline was right across the text size page: GREAT FISH RAMP EXPOSED. Thus I learned one of many important lessons from the legendary Sam, whose hand still guides editors of the *People* today. When the story is good enough, always yield to temptation. Jim was paid a modest sum for his time and trouble and lived very comfortably for a few days while I followed up the story.

6
EVENING STANDARD

Journalists who worked on the *Evening Standard* in the 1950s still meet occasionally at nostalgic tea-parties at the Howard Hotel, presided over by Anne Sharpley. She was understandably admired by Beaverbrook, who sent her flowers, and he, as ever, is the principal subject of discussion over the smoked salmon sandwiches and meringues.

My luck held as far as the editor was concerned. Once again I was working for the most considerate of men. Percy Elland had replaced Bert Gunn, a wild, dynamic character, more like a screen editor than one in real life. Egged on by Beaverbrook he had gone over the top in a smear story about the socialist scare figure of the time, John Strachey. He wrote the outrageously defamatory headline FUCHS AND STRACHEY SENSATION in a story that attempted to link the ex-Labour Minister with the celebrated Russian spy. It was one of those periodic blunders in Fleet Street, like the *Daily Mail*'s publication of the forged British Leyland slush fund letter and, to a lesser degree, my publication in the *Daily Express* of a phoney picture of prisoners in chains in Ghana. Though he had been swept into this madness by his lack of political knowledge and desire to please Beaverbrook, Gunn was doomed. On the day he was sacked, in a still famous event, he threw an ink bottle at the portrait of Beaverbrook that peered ominously at *Evening Standard* editors. Years later, when Bert Gunn became seriously ill, I suggested to Max Aitken that we run a sympathetic paragraph in the *Daily Express* William Hickey column. 'Don't do that,' he said, horrified. 'He threw an inkpot at my father's picture.' That evening I mentioned his illness to Beaverbrook when he telephoned for the news. 'Say something nice about him in Hickey,' said the Old Man immediately, without any prompting from me.

Percy was a quiet Yorkshireman. His shoes were always clean and his desk clear and he hid all the tensions of editing and working for the tyrannical Lord Beaverbrook behind the calmest of exteriors. His deputy was Charles Wintour, unjustly known in those days as 'ice-cold Charlie', who must have added to Percy's stresses since he was a Beaverbrook confidant and well equipped to edit the paper, which he later did with distinction for twenty years. The third man on the paper, Dave Williams, was not destined to be an editor but was one of the greatest professionals I have known. I never saw him with a coat on in the office. He brought out the paper, edition after edition, always on time and with none of the misprints and 'pie-ups' that disgraced management, printers and journalists in Fleet Street's final years. His belly inside his invariable white shirt rested against the composing room stone as he scanned every page, spotting errors that lesser mortals had missed, reading page one splashes at breakneck speed from the actual type, upside down and reversed as in a mirror. He would point to where paragraphs could be cut without bothering to mark proofs, to save seconds, and when some erring sub-editor's headline 'bust' simply tell the printer the alternative version, which he would scurry off and get set without any nonsense about house agreements and working to rule. If a sub-editor was making heavy weather of editing a difficult story, he would pull up a chair next to him and scribble his way through it at awesome speed. Walking one morning with Lord Beaverbrook I rhapsodised over Dave's un-acknowledged skills. A day or two later he was surprised to receive a 'You are the greatest' letter from Beaverbrook that must have baffled as well as delighted him. When he retired, he continued to live within a few yards of Fleet Street. He would not have been at home anywhere else.

I had expected Beaverbrook to appoint me to the *Daily Express*, after Arthur Christiansen had nodded his approval of me at Arlington House. Or to the *Sunday Express*, since it was John Junor who had recommended me to him. Instead he made me a leader-writer on the *Evening Standard* at a salary of £50 a week ('and you can have what proportion of that you like in expenses.'). This job was a little difficult for my friends to understand since a few months earlier in 1955 I had been the Labour candidate for Merton and Morden, Surrey, in the general election. I justified my perfidy, if that is what it was, because I had served a total of seven years on *Tribune*, neither the *Daily Herald*, *Reynolds News* or the *News Chronicle* had shown any interest in me, the Tories were safely in for another Parliament, and I wanted to be a national newspaper editor. Also Michael Foot had beaten exactly the same path years earlier, via *Tribune* and *Standard* leader-writing to the top. In fact, most of the political leaders were written in time for the main editions by the chief leader-writer, the young, studious, Rudolph Klein. Jack Waterman, who became a stylish sports writer, and I struggled with first edition leaders on a wide variety of London topics. They were usually melted down by 1.00 p.m., especially when Beaverbrook was in town. Percy Elland favoured on-the-spot leaders, which were a great relief from sitting in the office. When the millionth Morris Minor was built, the model that is still a cult car, I suggested a trip to Cowley to discover the secret of its popularity. The chief design engineer there explained that because the four wheels were in each far corner the car was unusually stable and people felt safe driving it. To prove the point he took the chief public relations officer, a large bowler-hatted man with a brief-case and a black labrador, and myself at a stunning pace down the lanes to Abingdon airfield. He announced that he would drive us along the runway and turn the steering wheel right round at 50 m.p.h. 'Most cars would turn over,' he said. 'This one won't.' He was right. He asked me if I would like to do the same. I agreed, at which the public relations man said he would do a lot for the company but this was too much. He stepped out of the car on to the runway with his bowler, briefcase and labrador. The sight of him in the rear mirror as we hurtled off is a memory I treasure, such were the simple pleasures of leader-writing on the *Evening Standard*.

Beaverbrook left me alone for most of my first few months and Percy filled in my idle hours by encouraging me to write series. One that I did on teddy-boys, who were then scaring people of nervous disposition, I found heavy going, but it reads quite well today. The opening two paragraphs of the much publicised series began:

> Among the heavy, ugly blocks of council flats in Cherry Gardens Street, Rotherhithe, I searched for the home of Joseph Fell, bus conductor. At the greengrocers, they knew him.
> Warming her hands over a brazier outside the shop, a woman assistant said: "Jim Fell, you mean? The one that got it from the Teddy Boys? That's him across the street."

I wrote another on London's mental hospitals, inspired by my mother's long periods in one of them, a secret I kept to myself. At Warlingham Park in Surrey, the highly respected medical super-intendent, Dr Rees Williams, had stunned the old guard by abolishing padded cells, opening up all the wards and installing public telephones in the centre of the Victorian complex. This led to some interesting outgoing telephone calls, and I was amused to read a letter in *The Times* one morning signed Col. (retd), Warlingham Park, Surrey. The Colonel, if indeed he was one, did not live in quite the circumstances or the sort of residence imagined by the letters editor of *The Times*, I felt. I was shown round the hospital by a journalist patient in the alcoholics ward. He edited the *Warlingham War Cry* during his regular returns to the hospital via Fleet Street and Skid Row and asked me what I thought of a formidable lady in a large hat who complained to me, when I watched her making a basket in the work therapy room, that she was now totally sane and wrongly kept there. 'Well,' I said, 'I presume she is still mad, but I would not have guessed it.' 'Notice the hat?' said my escort. 'She even wears it in the bath to keep out the atomic rays.' I asked a psychiatrist on duty that day what he thought of his patients, after I had attended a group therapy session in which they talked eagerly about their problems. 'I hate zem,' he said unexpectedly in an appropriately foreign accent, as we walked across a vast lawn and passed a man endlessly crying 'fuck, fuck, fuck.'

I saw Dr Williams again at the end of my visit. It seemed to me he was guided more by commonsense and humanity than the teachings of either Freud or Jung. 'It is difficult to decide whether the schizophrenics are fit to go home,' he said. 'If they are men I usually have them in here, give them a cigar and casually ask in the middle of the conversation, "How are the voices?" They almost always give it away if they are still hearing them.' At another hospital the medical superintendent, as they were known then, made the obvious statement that a woman weeping and muttering in the admission ward was depressed. Showing off, I thought, he gave her electric shock treatment in front of me in a side room. She convulsed and stopped breathing. He applied artificial respiration and fortunately she recovered. I made a mental note not to let things get me down. For lunch we were served chicken and claret by two trusty patients, which seemed odd. Later the doctor was a patient in his own hospital. Gathering copy for this series I was given an electro-encephalograph test at the Middlesex Hospital, which involved attaching a multitude of wires to my head. The specialist paused while looking at the read out, which appeared to me like a seismograph of the San Francisco earthquake, murmured 'that's interesting,' and then, recalling that I was not an actual patient, added 'Oh, it's nothing really.' I did not put this in my report and wondered about it every now and then for several years.

My brief period of non-proprietorial interference ended after Randolph Churchill had written a number of articles in the paper sniping at the Prime Minister, Anthony Eden. On 13 March 1956, his latest diatribe was headlined WHY I ATTACK SIR ANTHONY. IT IS NOT A VENDETTA. It was of course. 'From the earliest days I never thought that he would make a good Prime Minister,' he wrote. 'When he reached this office nine months ago I publicly explained in these columns why I did not think so, but added that I might likely be wrong, since people often grow into a bigger job. I don't think he has.' Beaverbrook was embarrassed by these attacks and I have since heard that Winston Churchill asked him to take the heat off his protégé and chosen successor. Thus I was invited alone to lunch at Arlington House. It was a warm, intimate occasion and I was highly complimented at being so honoured. Over brandy he said to Mead the butler, 'Get Mr Edwards a big cigar.' It was enormous, and I soon recognised that as a sure sign that he was up to no good. 'Bob,' he said, 'it is good journalism to say the opposite of everyone else. Why don't you write a defence of Eden in the *Evening Standard*?'

I did not bother to argue the merits of the case, since that was clearly irrelevant, but said that I could not possibly do it since I had come to his attention through attacking Eden on the radio. Besides, I had so recently been editor of *Tribune*. Still it was a good idea, Randolph Churchill and A. N. Other slogging it out over Eden in the *Evening Standard*. Through a cloud of expensive cigar smoke I recklessly put forward a suggestion that was to cause a ten-day-wonder in Fleet Street. 'I will write it for you under a pseudonym,' I said. 'Everyone will know you are responsible and it will cause a sensation.' Beaverbrook was delighted. He was not so vulgar as to reward me with a handful of cigars, but he would have given me the box if I had asked.

Neither of us could think of a pseudonym. Later that day a memo arrived: 'How about Richard Strong?' I agreed. It had just the right phoney ring. I was hidden with a typewriter in a room in the *Evening Standard* basement and only Percy Elland and Charles Wintour were supposed to know that I was the author. At great speed I wrote two ludicrous articles, parodying Beaverbrook's style, in defence of Eden. They appeared with great prominence on successive days. The first was headlined EDEN IS A <u>GOOD</u> PRIME MINISTER and signed Richard Strong, as if he was a famous and respected contributor. Beaverbrook read through the drafts in a state of high excitement, though they were probably the oddest articles in defence of a Prime Minister ever written. 'It's a wonderful thing,' he said, 'defending the indefensible,' and did not alter a word. It seemed to me that he was more concerned to cause mischief than help Eden. Here are extracts:

> There is mutiny in the Tory ranks. In the smoking-room of the House of Commons, in West End clubs, the rumbles against Sir Anthony Eden grow louder. It is said that he is a weak Prime Minister, that under his administration the fortunes of Britain go sadly into decline . . .

> No Prime Minister has ever suffered so cruelly at the hands of his party within so short a period of office. Upon this every commentator agrees . . .

> Outside the House of Commons all is portrayed as bright and beautiful. Only within is there ferment and intrigue . . .

> Why does Randolph Churchill lambast Eden? What are his complaints? I detect one above all. That Eden is no Churchill (Sir Winston).

> That is true. Churchill is that rarity in British politics. A genius. Eden is not . . .

> No one has ever heard the whole of a speech by Sir Anthony. That is perfectly true. He drawls. His delivery is poor. He has to be read, and the clichés removed, to get the significance, if there is any . . .

Next morning Peterborough in the *Daily Telegraph* reported: 'A powerful new force has emerged in Fleet Street. His name is Lord Richard Strong.' And Randolph Churchill joined him in the fun. In his regular Thursday article he wrote: 'Within a very few days of Beaverbrook's return he has given new proof to Fleet Street and Westminster that he is still firmly in the saddle by discovering and establishing an outstanding new political journalist, a Mr Richard Strong. This brilliant young writer, whose talents have so far been overlooked by all the editors in Fleet Street, and whose name cannot be found in any work of reference, was singled out with lightning and unerring intuition by Beaverbrook himself.' Henry Fairlie in the *Spectator* revealed that I was the amanuensis. I looked up the word in the dictionary. It was all right.

Richard Strong made several more appearances. In one he defended Bulganin and Kruschev's visit to London at Eden's invitation. Randolph Churchill had been sniping at the trip and he had another go after Strong's article: 'It is to be hoped that the British public will behave in a cool and dignified way and keep a decent distance; and, above all, not allow their innocent children to be pawed by these blood-thirsty murderers.' I was in total agreement with Strong and Lord Beaverbrook, who did not regard even Stalin as a murderer but the saviour of Russia and a personal friend.

In another article Strong attacked the U.S. Secretary of State, John Foster Dulles, for undermining Britain and Eden in favour of Egypt. This had words that were so unmistakably Beaverbrook's I must have written them verbatim in my notebook, probably in a sunny corner of his garden at Cherkley: 'As he strides confidently into his second year of power, he (Eden) can be sure of this: the dissidents will not stir against him again. They are exhausted, like the bee that has stung once and cannot strike evermore. The enemy has scattered as the night.' Vintage Beaverbrook, as was this slightly mad paragraph: 'For the sake of every one of us, for our livelihood, the cry must go out: Support our side. Uphold the cause. Help our leader.' Beaverbrook knew only four or five quotations. He used them repeatedly. 'We know what builder laid that keel' was a favourite. He used it in this article about Churchill's role in the Anglo-American alliance. Beaverbrook the myth-creator gave the impression that he had read many books, including Shakespeare and the classics. I suspected that his reading had largely been confined to books of quotations. Once, in a rather sycophantic moment, I asked him to define genius. The following day he sent me a note. 'The capacity to take great pains.' He had looked it up. He disliked long books. When I showed important ones to him that had been sent for review, he would say, 'Put it on the weighing machine. Tell them it's too heavy.' Richard Strong's support for Eden led a Tory MP, Sir Thomas Moore, to write to the *Evening Standard*: 'In your commendable efforts to give proper support for Sir Anthony Eden, you use so many contradictory arguments and make so many dogmatic statements your support becomes positively harmful.' I did not believe Beaverbrook cared much either way so long as the *Evening Standard* was the paper people talked about. The only politician and possibly the only person he looked up to, as we looked up to him, was Churchill.

As Joe Haines probably found, writing under the name Charles Wilberforce for Robert Maxwell in the *Daily Mirror*, the thrill of ghosting articles for the boss soon wears off, despite the initial excitement. Robert J. Edwards returned from an apparent holiday with a powerfully projected article DON'T LET NATO FOOL YOU. 'Before we committed the criminal folly of attempting to rearm the Germans,' it argued, 'there was not even a sham defence system against the Russians. And yet they did not march. How much less likely are they to march now, with Stalin, the madman, dead and with both sides possessing weapons that would destroy capitalism, Communism and us all.' It was not surprising that Tory politicians like Oliver Poole complained to Max Aitken that his father had let a dangerous person loose in his papers. Publication of this attack on German rearmament and the belief that Russia wanted peace in Europe was another example of the curious accord between Beaverbrook and *Tribune*, just as during the war Bevan, Beaverbrook, and Michael Foot, editor of the *Evening Standard*, spoke at mass rallies in favour of a Second Front, and against the mass bombing of Germany as a waste of resources. The article on NATO evoked an amusing response from Randolph Churchill: 'If none of the foregoing has any effect on Mr Edwards I suggest that he ask his colleague Mr Richard Strong to arrange an interview with the latter's great hero Sir Anthony Eden. Sir Anthony was one of the architects of NATO which he and thinking politicians of all parties still regard as the foundation of British foreign policy.' Both 'Mr Edwards' and Richard Strong had become well known, but I wish I had not written the following, which appeared under my own name after Krushchev's speech denouncing Stalin in the Twentieth Congress of the Communist Party:

> It has been said by the Russians that Stalin was a coward who ran away from Moscow as the German armies swept forward . . .
>
> If this does not stand up, the rest of the story is in doubt. It does not stand up.
> At the very time he was supposed to have run away, he was spending night after night with Lord Beaverbrook and Mr Averell Harriman in Moscow discussing the exchange of vital raw materials – this while the Germans were almost pounding against the city gates.

At the time this seemed to me a fatal flaw in Krushchev's case against Stalin. Beaverbrook's loyalty to the old despot was remarkable. So was mine to him.

Then came the Suez war. I was as opposed to this as I was to President Reagan's bombing of Tripoli in 1986. Happily I had developed a cold and stayed at home. The country was deeply divided with the majority backing Eden. The *Daily Mirror*, the *Guardian* and the *Observer* bravely lost sales taking the minority view. At the end of my first day off Charles Wintour rang. 'How are you?' he said. 'If you are at all well enough, could you come in tomorrow?' I said I would and at 8.00 a.m. went into his office. He

pressed a switch on his intercom, said laconically, 'he's here,' and we
walked across the big room into Percy Elland's office. There was
nothing on his desk and his shoes gleamed, as usual. He shuffled
uncomfortably and said, 'Thank you for coming in, Bob. We would
like you to do all our leaders on Suez.' Charles Wintour was sitting in
the leather armchair traditionally reserved for deputy editors in most
offices. It is placed on the right of the editor's desk so that he as well
as the editor face the other executives at morning conference and he
can, if he is so disposed, exchange cynical glances with those of them
who share his view that the editor's days are rightly numbered. The
disloyal deputy's chair is what I have called it from time to time. I
began to tell Percy that unfortunately I was so opposed to Eden's
invasion that I could not possibly write leaders in support of him,
and Charles got up and left. It all seemed dramatic stuff and I
wrongly concluded that Charles had suggested to Beaverbrook that I
should write the leaders knowing that I would refuse, and thus
knock me out as a rival for the next editorship. The true explanation,
as I heard at one of Anne Sharpley's tea parties thirty years later, is
that Rudolph Klein, the chief leader-writer, had also refused to
support Eden. Presumably Beaverbrook suggested that I should do
them, because Percy said when I was alone with him, 'I'll have to tell
the Old Man.'

It seemed to me my career was in some jeopardy. The Express
newspapers backed Eden against his enemies in Britain with all the
outrageous vituperation of which they were capable. For several
days I was in the dog-house. There were no calls from Beaverbrook.
I had nothing to do, not even first edition leaders on the need for an
underpass at Tolworth junction on the A3 near Leatherhead, a
Beaverbrook favourite. I wrote him a letter appealing to be put back
to work and pointing out that before he took me on I had said that as
a socialist there were bound to be times when I took an opposite
view, to which he had said, 'Don't worry. There is always someone
else who will do it.' He replied promptly to my letter, with some
irony in his second paragraph:

Dear Bob,

    I have received your letter.

    I have written to Mr Elland. I am sure he will make more and more
use of your extraordinary abilities. Before long you will be a pillar in
the temple. It was Dean Inge when he was attacked as a pillar of the
Evening Standard who replied that he was no pillar; he was two
columns.

As good a put down as I have ever received. A few weeks later he made me deputy editor of the *Sunday Express*. You never can tell in this business.

7
JJ

I would not say he was the editor I most enjoyed working for, but he was the best. During his astonishing thirty-four years as editor of the *Sunday Express* John Junor was in total command. Woe betide anyone on his staff who had any other impression. Of course there was Beaverbrook to worry about, but nobody among the journalists handled him better. In discussions at Cherkley or on the roof garden at Arlington House, lesser mortals would trample over each other to agree with whatever point the Old Man was making. Then he would turn expectantly to JJ, eyebrows raised under the familiar straw hat, 'What do you say, John?' And John, more often than not, would reply, 'I am sorry to say I have to disagree.' For all his independence, he must have paid a high price, I suspect, to succeed John Gordon on the *Sunday Express*. He lived for some years in a sort of grace and favour house on the Cherkley estate, which meant that he was constantly on call to Beaverbrook when he would rather have been with his family, and he was plagued with stomach troubles until he was firmly installed as editor. However, there was no doubt on the *Sunday Express* who was regarded as boss of the paper. It was JJ, whereas on the *Daily Express* Beaverbrook's presence was felt in the remotest corners of the office where malingerers and scrimshankers spent uneasy days drinking in pubs unfrequented by the editor and writing articles that were sure to be spiked.

Probably nobody in Fleet Street has produced a more eccentric, quirkish but successful paper than JJ's *Sunday Express*. How many shipwrecks of long ago were salvaged in series of vast length under his editorship? How many airmen bobbing about in liferafts had their bravery recalled in every detail over 40 years later? How many drawings have *Sunday Express* artists done for JJ of those in peril on the sea? His formula was as rigid, though different, as that of the odd, but hugely successful, *Sunday Post* in Scotland, starting with a leader page stiff with every prejudice and emotion that gets right to the heart of Tory Britain, superbly written. John was also cost-conscious, an aptitude possessed by few editors, and I suspected that his preference for maritime tales was not simply because they responded to an instinctive British fascination for the sea. They were also cheap. His interest in the day's news was minimal. John Junor was not the man to let cataclysmic events interfere unduly with the formula that took his paper to a sale of over 4 million.

Just as the *Sunday Express* seemed to be the same every week, our lives were the same. We lunched each Saturday at the Cheshire Cheese, now a principal attraction to American tourists. And about ten of us headed by the editor dined after the first edition at The Wellington, a favourite Fleet Street restaurant, where unaccountably the more gentlemanly-looking group from the *News of the World*, led by the editor Stafford Somerfield who later became a supremely good columnist on the *Dog World*, had linen napkins while we had to be content with paper ones. One pleasant summer evening, Edward Westropp, our city editor, raised with John the appalling cost of educating children at public school. Douglas Clark, the political editor, joined in and I thought it was all rather élitist. I realise now they were simply applying pressure for higher salaries: John was careful about such matters. He made what I thought was a devastatingly good point in favour of state education. 'How many of us went to public schools?' he said. 'Raise your hands those who did.' Nobody did. This would have been a surprise for *Sunday Express* readers, who had been skilfully led to believe that we and they were a cut above the others. John said to me after one of us had written, under his careful direction, the usual warm, human editorial about children returning to boarding school following the summer holidays, 'In case you're wondering, I know perfectly well that many *Sunday Express* readers live in council houses and send their children to state schools. But they like to feel we think they live in much grander houses and can afford school fees.'

Several of us wrote the *Sunday Express* editorials after discussing subjects with John over lunch. They were masterpieces of style, economy and puerility, if you like, and we wrote three times as many as were required. The late Robert Pitman, a former school teacher discovered by *Tribune*, was best at it. It was a matter for pride to get them past John without alteration, which I seldom did. Years later on the *Sunday Mirror* I indulged myself with leaders of great length which I wrote myself. Harold Evans, when he was editor of *The Times*, told me they were the first thing he turned to in the Sunday papers. Four people taught me to write leaders: Michael Foot, John Junor, Hugh Cudlipp, and Lord Beaverbrook. After dinner one

Saturday at the *Sunday Express*, one of JJ's cronies brought him the news that the bandleader Oscar Rabin had died. We were sitting on the backbench with the rest of the paper's chiefs. John turned to me. 'You must write a leader,' he said, solemnly. 'He may not have been a Paganini but he brought pleasure to millions.' I wrote exactly what he had suggested. 'Brilliant,' he said. 'Now, altogether, one ... two ... three.' And the entire backbench hummed 'Dancing Time' the signature tune of the once famous big band.

John inspired great loyalty, not entirely compounded of fear, and his staff stayed with him. Arthur Brenard, air correspondent and deputy news editor, told me a story against himself of how, deeply troubled, he went to John because his wife, Stella King, was paid a higher salary as a journalist on the same paper. I felt Brenard had rehearsed his tale to me in several taverns: 'Well, John was very considerate, as you would expect. He asked me to sit down when I said there was something on my mind, and I told him I did not really object to Stella being paid more than me, and in a way I was GLAD, but this humiliating situation had forced me to ask myself a simple question, "Am I a man or a mouse?" ' 'And what did John say?' I asked, after Brenard had paused dramatically. 'He said, "a mouse" .'

Though an expert on city matters and a pleasing person, Edward Westropp was a simple, earnest soul concerned to impress his editor whenever possible. In fact, I have been struck by what simple souls most city editors are. JJ had just shown me the binoculars he had bought for Lord Beaverbrook when Westropp came in, craving a moment of his time to listen to an idea. It was a tedious one and as Ted droned on, John, unable to staunch the flow, raised the binoculars to his eyes and gazing through them out of the window interrupted his devoted colleague, 'Do you know, Ted, with these binoculars I can see the pigeon shit on the roof of St Bride's church?' It was before my time there that John had to make his famous apology at the Bar of the House of Commons for insulting Labour MPs in a manner that was held to be in contempt of Parliament. He told me that Beaverbrook did not once speak to him or give him any support as he fought his way through that crisis to emerge with great dignity and respect. My pay as his deputy was £70 per week, including £20 fixed expenses.

On the Saturday before my first period in charge of a national newspaper, John handed me, as if it was contaminated, an article Lord Beaverbrook had sent him by a former Prime Minister of Canada. 'It's terrible,' said John, 'I'm not publishing it, so I'm handing it over to you.' He left at 6.00 p.m. for Port Hamble and his annual voyage in his yacht to northern France. Feeling rather important, I read the article and sharing John's judgment decided not to print it the following week either. This was not the idea at all. The editor had assumed I would not be so crass as to reject an article from Beaverbrook on my first week in charge and had thus told him that, alas, there was no room in the current issue but there would be in the next. Max Aitken later described to JJ the spectacle of his father searching the *Sunday Express* confidently expecting to see, prominently displayed, the article that would delight his friend the former Prime Minister. 'He went all through the paper as far as the middle,' said young Max, as we called him, 'then back to page one to do the same again. Still he couldn't find it, and went past the centre pages to the sports pages, which he has never seen before.'

That was not the only offence I committed in my first issue of the *Sunday Express*. On Saturday the paper flowed past me like a river in flood and it was more than I could do to control it. Happily there are always professionals to protect the editor if he is drunk, incompetent, or both, and when Victor Patrick, the number three, said we had a fine page one splash reporting that Russian planes had landed in Kashmir, I was deeply relieved and fonder of him than ever. He himself had a Russian family background, drank copiously and ate magnificently. He put the headline 'RUSSIANS IN KASHMIR' in end-of-the-world type across page one, with a dramatic report from an unnamed *Sunday Express* correspondent, quoting Pakistan's foreign minister quoted by Reuter. I should have been alerted by the use of single quotes around the headline. 'Why those, Victor?' I should have said, but I was probably desperately trying to get the leaders to match up to John Junor's high standards of rhetoric or warmth, depending on the subject. When the rival papers came in there was no reference in them to the world-shattering events in Kashmir. It was not followed up by the BBC. Not a paragraph about it appeared in the papers on Monday. The correct interpretation of the story was that Russian planes had not landed in Kashmir. No one with any knowledge would have countenanced for a second the foreign minister of Pakistan's absurd claim. Beaverbrook did not refer to this blunder. He waited until my three weeks in charge were over and sent me a warm letter of congratulations.

One thing more slipped past me on the *Sunday Express* the next time JJ was away. The Ephraim Hardcastle gossip column was edited by the deceptively good-looking Peter Baker, whom I later called Dorian Gray because of his wicked ways. Though he could

have appeared on the cover of a romantic novel, and was much liked
for several years by Beaverbrook until he lied to him about his
salary, his cool and pleasing manner disguised one of the wildest,
most ruthless journalists I have known. I had learned to read
everything that was due to appear in the paper with great care,
especially a minefield like Hardcastle. On this occasion there was
nothing to worry about in the page proof for the first edition, but
during the night Baker changed the page without consulting me, for
which grievous crime JJ would have had him garrotted. He slipped
in a paragraph, all in black, so lethal that it was the final spark that
ignited the great Bank Rate scandal. It appeared to be innocent
enough, referring to the good fortune of Lazard's Bank in having
such a politically well-placed and knowledgeable adviser on its board
as Mr (later Lord) Oliver Poole, chairman of the Tory Party. For
several days hysteria had swept Fleet Street over rumours that
Lazards had cashed in on an increase in Bank Rate because someone
on high had criminally tipped off the company. There were such
hilarious stories as a civil servant being overheard discussing the
forthcoming increase on Watford railway station while waiting for
his train to emerge from the tunnel. Almost every newspaper vied to
put the pieces of the non-existent jigsaw together. The paper with
the most authoritative sounding report, which virtually accused
Lazards and A. N. Other of conspiracy on a grand scale, was the
Daily Express on the Thursday of that week. That, plus the reference to Oliver Poole in the *Sunday Express*, was all the ammunition
Labour MPs like George Wigg needed to demand the setting up of a
Bank Rate Tribunal, which they were instantly granted.

I had the misfortune to be a principal witness on the grounds that
no editor would have published such a paragraph without satisfying
himself that it was soundly based. To have admitted that I had not
read it until I almost choked over breakfast the following day would,
I felt, have condemned me as unfit to run a newspaper. Harold
Evans was unfairly derided throughout Fleet Street years later
because he said he had not read an unfortunate caption in the
Sunday Times colour magazine. The mockers included daily editors
who, to my certain knowledge, frequently did not read a single word
that appeared in their papers until they recovered from their hang-
overs the following morning. Possibly because of inexperience I had
no qualms about appearing before the Tribunal, which had all the
powers of the High Court, and thought it might be extremely
interesting. So it was. Frederick Ellis, the *Daily Express* city editor
who had written the report in his paper, was cross-examined for

1 At home in Bracknell, Berkshire in 1938, with faithful companion Toc, and elder brother Bill.

2 Loyal employees of the family firm in south London before my father sold out to United Dairies.

3 My favourite boss. Beaverbrook in the garden at Cherkley in 1964.

4 *Above* Nye Bevan clean-bowled in his braces.

5 *Above right* Max Aitken at ease with wary *Daily Express* editor.

6 *Below* Sir John Junor, for 32 years editor of the *Sunday Express*.

7 *Below right* Journalist John Knight (left) and myself with Cecil King and Lord (Don) Ryder.

8 and 9 Reading an illustrious rival, and bringing out the *People* in a power strike.

hours by the fearsome Mr Roger Winn, QC, brother of Godfrey Winn. Mr Winn had a physical deformity that caused him to appear less tall as he stood up than when he was seated. This made him more daunting than ever, and as I watched his brilliant performance I thought how well he would have been played by Charles Laughton. Fred Ellis, sweating copiously, as he often did anyway after a good lunch at Shekey's in the city, was no match. Eventually, rather than face possible imprisonment for refusing to name his source, he was reduced to saying he was someone he had met in a pub, but he had completely forgotten who it was. Mr Winn expressed his disbelief in an Oscar-winning interrogation, and Ellis staggered from the witness box apparently on the edge of a breakdown. He was quickly restored to his normal blustering self by loyal colleagues who congratulated him over several large gin and tonics for so courageously protecting his source. Fleet Street generously wished to believe that he did indeed have one that justified his great world exclusive.

My problem was obvious: to explain our diary paragraph on Oliver Poole's incomparable value to Lazard's Bank if it was not deliberately linked with our sister paper's sensational report, and meant to imply that Mr Poole was, in fact, a crook who had betrayed his country for personal gain. That was how the Labour MPs and everyone else had read it. I asked Douglas Clark, our shrewd political editor, what I should say when they asked why I published the paragraph. He replied immediately, 'Say it was a tribute.' That is what I did. Mr Poole was present. He emitted a loud and long incredulous 'ooh', as frequently heard in matrimonial cases when one spouse gives evidence against another. Happily for me, Mr Winn was resting after his mauling of Fred Ellis, and I was let off lightly by his junior. The Tribunal report justifiably expressed grave disbelief about my evidence. Mr Poole, Lazard's Bank, the Tory Government and everyone else except Fleet Street were declared guiltless. It was The Scandal That Never Was.

Looking back, my days on the *Sunday Express* were happy enough. It is good to have an editor the staff feel is fully in charge, just as sailors like to have a skipper they can respect. I have found some curious phrases in articles I wrote for the leader page of the *Sunday Express* at that period, later kindly described as 'brilliant' by a writer in *World's Press News*.

'Better by far to be destroyed in defending our own than suffer a slow, painful death through starvation, with traitor's hands upon our throats.' (This, if our 'enemies' seized Kuwait and our oil, clearly inspired by Beaverbrook.)

'For all the problems of keeping the Tory party together, Mr Macmillan is in high spirits. He is, as ever, buoyant and beaming. Wherever he goes, there is a dance in his step.' (Either suggested by JJ, or a good imitation of him.)

This article continued:

'That is not so surprising. He makes his appeal with gaiety as Mr Baldwin did with his pipe, Mr Chamberlain with his umbrella, and Mr Churchill with his V-sign.' (Beaverbrook without a doubt.)

Another example (again successive paragraphs):

'President Eisenhower walked off the 18th tee at the Georgia golf course and gave the command as unconcernedly as most people would order a round of drinks.' (JJ or imitation.)

'SIXTH FLEET, SAIL! CALL THE RUSSIAN BLUFF! DARE THEM TO PICK UP THE GAUNTLET' (Beaverbrook, with All Caps, as we say in the trade.)

Reading these articles, which I had totally forgotten, they seem to have been written by a spritely, jolly old man steeped in knowledge of the first half of the century. When I was on the *Evening Standard* readers did not have this impression since my picture appeared on most of my articles. This was for two reasons. Sycophantic layout people thought I was a Beaverbrook favourite and wanted to please him. And a photo of the author helped the art editor to overcome the difficulty of finding a half-tone illustration for an article he personally found too utterly tedious to read (most layout people hate reading anyway). Newspapers frequently make the mistake, purely for layout reasons, of publishing journalists' pictures which have the effect, so gauche and youthful they usually appear, of reducing the credibility of the articles almost to zero. Beaverbrook put a stop to it in my case. 'Mr Elland,' he said in a note to the editor of the *Evening Standard*, 'Edwards does not photograph well. You may make his name bigger if you wish.' This caused a protest from Randolph Churchill that my name was bigger than his. I was Robert J. Edwards on the *Evening Standard*, as on *Tribune*. The J is for John, because my parents lacked imagination. In my teens I considered using the impressive signature Robert Jefferson Edwards (this would have been a bad mistake. I should have realised that, for obvious typographical reasons, the longer the by-line the smaller the type). On *Progress*, the Windsor Divisional Labour Party paper, I called myself Robert Jefferson when I had written too many articles under my own name. Just about the first words John Junor said to me on the *Sunday Express* castrated me further: 'I think we should drop the J.' We did, but such are the long memories in Fleet Street even quite young journalists still call me Robert J. Edwards.

Robert Edwards, minus the J, wrote an article on 16 June 1957, with the simple theme HOW TO SAVE BRITAIN. The message, of course, was to exploit the Empire, by which I meant the Commonwealth, as also did Harold Wilson in his years of opposition to the Common Market. It began characteristically:

> How to save Britain? 'What a question!' said my friend. 'Things were never so good.'
>
> 'ARE THEY?'

Nobody else could have got away with an opening paragraph like that. I can imagine Beaverbrook saying it, the last four buttons of his waistcoat undone, legs wide apart. I was learning all the time and highly complimented by his belief in me. The only reason that some people thought I was a turncoat was that, unlike many journalists, I had known opinions in the first place. Not once had I sought to advance the fortunes of the Tory Party against Labour and I had been billed on the *Evening Standard*, straight from Beaverbrook's mouth – who was possibly angry that I had been given the assignment – as 'a socialist with instructions to deal with the news and his sincere and honest interpretation of the news,' when I was sent to cover a by-election. Until I went through back numbers of the *Evening Standard* I had forgotten that I had been allowed to write a 'personal commentary' on the outcome of the abortive Suez talks before Eden's invasion. 'The views he expresses are his own and not those of the *Evening Standard*,' said the paper. The article totally opposed war and supported sanctions, the exact opposite of Beaverbrook's later backing of Eden. Not bad for someone who had left school at fifteen and only nine years earlier had served four years as an aircraftman second class.

John Junor did me many favours, apart from recommending me to Beaverbrook in the first place. He said one morning, 'As a deputy editor you should have a car. Apply to me immediately.' Fleet Street was just entering the era of company cars. Each company now has scores, with horrendous parking problems. The standard of cars on the Beaverbrook newspapers were better than intended, all because the transport manager had misheard instructions from Max Aitken. 'Get Pickering a car,' said 'young Max' in his best squadron manner. 'What kind?' asked the urbane and gentlemanly manager, son of E. J. Robertson, for years Beaverbrook's trusted managing director. 'Oh, give him a Zephyr,' said Max, but such is the awe in which editors are held, even by members of the Royal Yacht Squadron like John Robertson, he thought Max had said 'Sapphire,' an altogether grander car made by the now lamentably deceased Armstrong-Siddeley company. Pick's good fortune had a ricocheting effect down the line, so that the Ford Consul I was prescribed had been converted into a shooting-brake by a firm in Farnham, Surrey, and cost more than a Zephyr with every possible extra. Cars became important currency in Fleet Street. Whenever someone who mattered had his nose put out of joint by a younger man's promotion, he could usually be soothed with the offer of a new car, with double wing-mirrors, a sun-roof and a rear windscreen-wiper. The smell of leather upholstery worked therapeutic wonders. E. B. Raybould, a perpetual number three or number two on the *Daily Express*, was driven around in a Humber Super Snipe that looked as if it was the flagship of the Godfrey Davis fleet. He smoked his Manikins in it as if they were Havana Havanas. He was, like many journalists, a simple, rather dull man with an instinctive knowledge of his craft and was most at home in the composing room.

Charles Wintour fulfilled his destiny when Percy Elland died, and became editor of the *Evening Standard*. I was appointed managing editor, which again meant deputy editor, of the *Daily Express* in place of Charles. This was probably the greatest moment of my professional life. I was now number two on what Fleet Street, at any rate, regarded as the best popular newspaper in the world, printed in three cities with some of the finest writers in Britain, plus cartoonists Osbert Lancaster and Giles, the best sub-editors, 60 photographers, and foreign correspondents everywhere. The black Express building in Fleet Street, an architectural marvel, gleamed as if it had been polished every day. Beaverbrook never went there, except once with me when I had left something behind in the office, but everyone from Max Aitken to the man who compiled the crosswords and the commissionaires was aware of his presence. And I was his choice.

8
WALKING WITH THE LORD

Beaverbrook was a most attentive listener. This, I believe, is a hallmark of greatness, and I wish I had the same ability. Even with important people like prime ministers, my mind tends to wander and I have to force myself to pay attention. Yet I can remember whole conversations with clarity, particularly with Beaverbrook. 'Don't you think so, Bob?' he would say, jolting me out of any inattention. 'What have you got to say about that?' he would ask, on a subject that would normally have been of no interest to me. I would do my best to answer sensibly, and he would listen closely to every word. He did not have to. He seldom did anything that did not please him. So his interest was genuine, but it also showed his personal liking for the person whose inadequacies on the subject under discussion would have been only too obvious to anyone else.

I was struck by how seldom he met some of the greatest stars among his staff. He would send warm, personally written notes of praise to Carl Giles, and was immensely proud that he employed this genius who got closer to the homes and hearts of Britain than any other cartoonist. But the two men seldom met. Perhaps Beaverbrook sensed that Giles was a talent best left alone. He will put his drawings on the train from Ipswich. He will offer you no choice. They will be incomparable, and indeed Giles is one of the principal reasons the *Daily Express* did not entirely lose its magic despite years of bad editing and hopeless leadership after Beaverbrook's death. Giles would not challenge his sacred cows, but he would joke about them. They kept apart, with mutual respect, and Beaverbrook's far less intuitive, though warm-hearted, son Max Aitken foolishly decided one day to draw Carl closer into the family circle. Next morning Max said to me (it was after a small dinner he gave each year in the private basement room at L'Écu de France to mark the opening of the flat racing season): 'I took Carl to a night club. He was impossible and temperamental and kept threatening to resign.' Max was perplexed and a little hurt, but I said, as any *Daily Express* editor would have done, 'That's Carl. He's great, but he needs a lot of reassurance like most people. We have all had that experience. He is a terrific chap, and the best possible company most of the time. Think nothing of it.' A year later at the same venue the then Duke of Norfolk was the chief guest. Max Aitken, doing his best to be friendly to me, said to him after the meal, 'Would you like to meet the editor of the *Daily Express*?' 'Must I?' said the Duke.

Beaverbrook scarcely ever met J. B. Morton, writer of the famous Beachcomber column, which others tried nobly to copy and failed. I saw him once or twice out of a sense of duty. He was melancholy and seemingly a rather depressing person, and it is to my shame that for some time I thought his column should be dropped. I even dropped it for a two-week period over one Christmas to see if anyone protested. No one did. Beaverbrook, I suspected, had never understood the appeal of this daily column, always on the leader page and always fitted in somehow, whatever splendid dispatches from René McColl, Giles cartoons and little pieces about 'the Principal Reader's' art gallery at Fredericton, New Brunswick, had to be accommodated. I wrongly thought it had had its day, probably because I seldom read it. Sitting on the roof garden at Arlington House on one of the sunny days that invariably seemed to accompany Beaverbrook, we discussed Beachcomber's future. 'Bring the *Express* with you when we go walking,' said the Old Man. 'Then you can read today's column to me.' So in one of London's parks that morning a young man was to be seen doing his best to walk beside Lord Beaverbrook while reading to him his longest established and least favourite column. It turned out to be extremely funny and difficult to read out loud without laughing. Beaverbrook did not laugh much, but he knew immediately that dropping the column was a notion best forgotten. So did I. We did not discuss it again. There are some things you do not tamper with in good newspapers, if you have any sense.

Beaverbrook preferred most of all the company of young men who clearly admired him. There were, of course, the key people like George Malcolm Thomson, his outstanding chief leader-writer, who transcribed Beaverbrook's thoughts on affairs. There was a warm if, from George's point of view, slightly wary relationship here. But shaping the characters and minds of young discoveries occupied a considerable amount of his time. 'There is nothing like it,' he once said to me in God-like fashion, 'making men.' It was a megalomaniac remark which disturbed me at the time. He made it after one of his favoured young men, Peter Baker, had left Arlington House ahead of me. Baker had edited the William Hickey column, headed the New York bureau, and full of promise had worked for several months as editor of the *Glasgow Evening Citizen*. His handsome face showed slight traces of a dissolute life not untypical of English journalists working in the city. 'You've grown up a lot,' said Beaverbrook, peering at him approvingly. Richard Killian, Christopher Dobson, Ian Aitken, and, in their day on his newspapers, Michael Foot, Frank Owen and Tom Driberg. We were the favoured ones. Other invaluable members of his staff such as William Barkley, Osbert Lancaster, Tom Delmer, Percy Hoskins, Chapman Pincher and Trevor Evans were treated with due deference but were far less likely to be seen walking with him or eating at his dinner table. Beaverbrook's liking for young men was greatly to my advantage. I once wrote to him in New York, genuinely, but aware that a degree of sycophancy was involved, saying how much I enjoyed walking with him. On his return to London he rang each working day for a fortnight inviting me to join him on his daily exercise. I could not decide whether this was simply to please me, or himself, or to provoke his errant son Max, who in his father's view was far too devoted to yachting (pronounced 'yatting') and the high seas.

It was quite a feat finding enough to talk about on these walks. It was also quite a feat walking, because there was the danger of crashing into objects while paying close attention to Beaverbrook. Unless he had something specific he wished to discuss, which was usually jotted down on a piece of paper, he expected his chosen escort to produce a series of topics to while away the one hour spent actually walking, and however long it took to get to and from the chosen place. 'Next!' he would occasionally say, almost irritably, when a subject had petered out. There was never a moment for strolling silently together, as with normal mortals, and the skilful journalist would steer clear of subjects that might lead to actual work, such as the suggestion of an article of little or no interest to the public, or a strangely obscure 'paragraph' (meaning three or four paragraphs) in the London *Evening Standard* diary. Bonar Law was a good ploy. It had become almost impossible even for Beaverbrook to find an excuse to mention yet again in his papers the long since forgotten prime minister, whom he seemed personally to have created. 'What was Bonar Law really like, sir?' was a safe bet for a good few hundred yards. H. G. Wells, Walpole and Rudyard Kipling, all of whom he knew, were useful for the same reason. It was unwise to mention those he disliked, like Bernard Shaw and

Noel Coward. A reference to any of these would ensure a long gap before the next walk.

I had many demanding but pleasant hours with Beaverbrook escaping office duties, though too frequently he summoned me, knowingly I felt, on my day off. If I wanted a close relationship I had to pay the price, seemed to be the message. A regular walk, because it was convenient to Arlington House, was in Green Park and St James's Park, though they were too small for the distances he liked to cover at a steady pace. There his obsession with the Royal Family sometimes emerged. We were standing outside Buckingham Palace one sunny morning, looking at it rather moodily as far as he was concerned. 'Now, Mr Edwards,' he said, 'why don't you suggest in your paper that they build a stadium in front of this place, and earn some currency from it? They could do two shows a day and three on Saturdays.' Sometime later René McColl wrote an article saying that the Palace should be open to the public, like the White House in Washington. Beaverbrook's hostility never interfered with the *Daily Express*, in particular, exploiting the public's unquenchable thirst for stories about the Royal Family. The *Express* invariably covered Royal weddings and indeed Royal funerals better than anyone. The artist, Robb, because of his friendship with the equally camp dress designer Norman Hartnell, knocked rivals almost senseless by exclusive drawings of wedding dresses several days before the event, as if by Royal Command. The *Daily Express* associate editor, Harold Keeble (never mind who was the editor, no one could match his layout abilities) put them in the paper with breathtaking flair. Possibly because Lord Beaverbrook did not seek to ingratiate himself with the Royal Family, quite the opposite, there was often an edge to royal reporting then lacking in the other papers whose proprietors like the occasional invitation to the Palace. It was done without malice. Many people still remember Donald Edgar's incomparable report from the robing room of the House of Lords when Princess Margaret and Tony Armstrong-Jones were married. The *Express* liked to tell it as it really was, from the inside.

The most dramatic evidence of Beaverbrook's hostility, particularly to the Mountbatten connection, occurred again in Green Park. A helicopter flew noisily overhead going slowly towards Buckingham Palace. The assumption in those days was that such a machine carried Prince Philip, who was probably at the controls. The Old Man appeared, just for a moment, to have taken leave of his senses. 'Bow down,' he shouted. 'Bow down. Bow down, Bob, before your Lord and Master!' I laughed, and neither of us said any more on the subject. Years later at Buckingham Palace Prince Philip said to me about Lord Beaverbrook: 'We tried several times to get him here. He would never come.'

Beaverbrook mostly travelled about London in his own taxi-cab, which was the same as any other except that it had no meter. One day after walking across Hampstead Heath we could not find the taxi at the appointed place (on other occasions he had his Rolls-Royce trail him through public parks, in true tycoon style). We paced up and down, and the Old Man resolved what seemed to be an insuperable crisis by suggesting that I hailed a cab. When we arrived at Arlington House he had no money and I had too little. 'That's Lord Beaverbrook,' I said to the dour taxi-driver mistakenly expecting him to be awestruck, before going up in the lift to borrow the fare from Mead, the butler. Arthur Brittenden, then chief correspondent of the *Sunday Express* in New York, wrote an amusing letter about my walks with the boss:

> You should know that you do not go unremembered in high places.
>
> After pounding through Central Park for two hours yesterday, Principal Reader announced the truth which had been bearing itself in on me for the previous 25 minutes: 'Mr. Brittenden, you have got me lost. I congratulate you on the speed and efficiency with which you have carried out the task. However, I shall now attempt to guide you to my motor car.'
>
> Twenty minutes later when the attempt had failed and we were sharing an isolated dell with a squirrel . . .
>
> 'Do you know Robert J. Edwards?'
>
> 'Indeed yes. I know him well.'
>
> 'I am not surprised. I should have expected you to say that Mr. Edwards and yourself know each other. For he is the only man worse than you are.'
>
> 'Worse than me at what, sir?'
>
> 'At getting me lost. Ah yes. Every time I go to London, Mr. Robert J. Edwards takes me for a walk. From Hampstead to Highgate.
>
> 'Every time Mr. Edwards gets me lost. Yes, every time. He has never failed once. Just think now. If I lost journalists like Mr. Edwards and yourself lose me, what would they say about me in Fleet Street?'

It was on Hampstead Heath that Beaverbrook gave me one of his sternest lectures. He had clearly felt for some time, or probably someone had suggested to him, that having a socialist as editor of the *Daily Express*, even a somewhat renegade one, had knocked the stuffing out of the leader column, except when he was in the country and dictating to George Malcolm Thomson. There was some truth in this. 'Do you really believe this stuff?' I recall once saying to another leader-writer, Jimmy McMillan. Actually, Jimmy did. He was a true believer. But most leader-writers perform much better when they get some inspiration from the editor or their proprietor. They choose to regard themselves morally like lawyers following a brief, acting for one side or the other, it does not matter which. They would not falsify facts unduly, but opinions are negotiable. Outstanding leader-writers like the late George Murray on the *Daily Mail*, who function best left alone, are rare. Someone had the sense to put him on page one, column one, each day when it was a full-size paper, and as with Joe Haines on the *Daily Mirror* showing the leader to the editor was merely an act of politeness, a formal acknowledgment that the editor has the last word even if that means the departure of the valued leader-writer, an unthinkable catastrophe.

There was no Murray or Haines on the *Daily Express*. George Malcolm Thomson's first love was his excellent book column in the *Evening Standard*; he has also written some fine historical books. But I suspected that he regarded Beaverbrook's policies with genial cynicism as befitted such an intelligent man. Without the Old Man on the other end of the telephone, the leader column was simply a question of filling the space in a style parodying his own. (George could do it superbly when he was moved: his column on the death of Beaverbrook was a masterpiece.) The late and jolly Michael Wolff, who became Ted Heath's highly respected head of propaganda at the Tory Central Office, was another member of the team. I would sit or stand reading their trite, short paragraphs at about 6.00 p.m. and short of changing the whole style and policies of the paper there was little I could do about it. Only nice Jimmy McMillan had fire in his belly. Alas, unlike Robert Pitman on the *Sunday Express*, he was no supreme stylist.

Beaverbrook gave me many scores of ideas for the Opinion column over the years. These were tape-recorded ('Am I on the machine?') and passed on to the understandably uninspired corps of leader-writers. But the only conversation he had with me about the merits of the column began on the Heath after we had gone down the steep little hill by Jack Straw's Castle. Beaverbrook descended the hill like one of those wooden dolls that walk unsteadily and too fast when a table is tilted, and I always felt particularly fond of him when he was vulnerable because of his age. I recall once going to the

Tate Gallery with him. 'When we get to the steps, Bob,' he said, 'I want you to put your arm in mine and hold on to me.'

A little stricken by the steep descent on to Hampstead Heath, Beaverbrook nevertheless got down immediately to what was on his mind in a conversation that he had clearly planned carefully. 'Blumenfeld,' he said, 'Blumenfeld was a very sensitive fellow.' R. D. Blumenfeld was editor of the *Daily Express* when Beaverbrook took over the ailing company in 1916. I waited patiently for him to enlarge on this apparently safe and interesting subject. 'He was so sensitive that he made things very difficult for me. If I criticised his paper, however kindly I did it, he would go into a sulk for weeks and become useless. If I did not criticise the paper, I had no influence on it.' Beaverbrook was describing a Catch 22 situation. Then he stopped, planted both feet on the ground in a familiar manner and looked directly and shrewdly at me.

'You're a sensitive fellow, too, Bob,' he said. 'Do you mind if I say something to you, and will you promise not to be sensitive?' I was utterly charmed. 'I promise,' I said. 'I promise absolutely.' The Old Man resumed walking. I followed dutifully. 'What I want to say to you, Bob,' his voice rising to a crescendo, 'is that I don't give a GODDAM what you say in the *Daily Express* as long as you say it with PASSION, say it with FEELING.' I had a vision of the bored leader-writers sitting around my office, apart from the eager but too simplistic Jimmy, looking forward to El Vino's or whichever club or restaurant they were to lunch in, and I knew exactly what Lord Beaverbrook meant. He was saying that I should say in the paper what he wanted me to say, but with the passion and feeling that was acutely lacking. There was no way in which I could be sensitive or hurt in view of his delicate approach to the subject, and after indicating that I would take his advice to heart I sought to change the subject by drawing his attention to the unusual sight, in those days, of a handsome young black man lying in the long grass with a white girl. He was riveted. His next words shocked me. 'Do you think, Bob,' he said, 'he puts his cock into her cunt?' He was, as I was to discover on other occasions, violently crude at times.

From the black man in the grass to the current news that Mr Jomo Kenyatta had been elected President of Kenya was not too big a leap. Beaverbrook stopped and planted his feet again. His face became contorted, his mouth cruel, his eyes those of a bigot. He ranted, that is the correct word, against black emancipation and to my horror described Kenyatta as a descendant of apes in trees. It was not simply because of Kenyatta's alleged former connection with Mau Mau. It was pure prejudice. Looking at him, probably quite coldly, my unspoken reaction was: 'I don't think I like this man. Why am I working for him?' Beaverbrook seemed to sense my feeling of revulsion. His face changed again dramatically. The mouth was no longer cruel but smiling hugely, as in Low's drawings of him. His eyes were bright once more. 'Well, Bob,' he said, 'how's that for passion, how's that for feeling?' Near the top of a hillock overlooking Kentish Town he made water. There were not many people around.

Beaverbrook's hostility to black Africa showed itself on another occasion, when he was a little tipsy. I had been summoned from the *Sunday Express* to Arlington House expecting to have the usual walk. 'I'm going down to the west country to inspect my farms,' he said. 'Would you care to come with me?' Never mind that I had neither razor nor change of suit for the following day, I thought it would be fun. We went to Paddington station in the Rolls-Royce where, to my surprise, we were met by two men in top hats, presumably the station master and his deputy. We were escorted to a compartment intended for six, the remaining member of our party being Raymond, his valet. There was much bowing and hand-shaking before the top hats departed, and as the train moved out of the station a lady at least as old as Lord Beaverbrook and possibly as rich tried to join us. 'You can't come in here,' said the devoted if sometimes amusingly insolent Raymond, and slid the door firmly shut again to keep her out. Beaverbrook was not perturbed by such bad manners, and he asked me to read him the first draft I had written of the Crossbencher column, which was in my pocket. He listened with his usual close attention while I read every word. 'That's no good, Bob, as you know,' he said. 'This is how you should do it.' He then dictated a few characteristic sentences, fell asleep, and I was able to complete the re-written version by the time he awoke at Newbury. It was then entirely to his satisfaction, trans-formed from the mediocre to the brilliant with a couple of trans-positions and a quaint phrase or two, a familiar exercise.

At Taunton we were met by his able chief farm manager, who later had the misfortune to go to prison for some breach of the agriculture laws. There were several cars waiting and the manager's Land Rover. I learned later that day that Beaverbrook owned five farms, each with its own manager. He would decide when he arrived at Taunton which one of the farms he would inspect, and so at all five farms a fire was burning in each dining-room and the table laid so that he could have lunch at any one of them, from a hamper

Raymond had brought with him. This seemed to me very hard on
the four managers' wives who were to be disappointed after all their
efforts, and even more traumatic for the one who was not. I looked
forward to accompanying Beaverbrook, as he stepped purposefully
into the Land Rover, but he said, 'I have duties to perform. You
must go to Cricket Malherbie and write that article on Africa.'
Since we had not, in fact, discussed an article on Africa I was in
some difficulties. It was a pleasant day and the small manor house
at his principal farm was as nice a place as anyone could wish to
have the simple lunch provided for an unexpected guest. There was
an atmosphere of relief that the dreaded though revered Lord had
chosen another farm to inspect and would not be arriving until later
to stay the night. Beaverbrook had a celebrated herd of Charollais
cattle, the first to be brought into Britain, and I was amused to
notice that there was not a trace of cow dung to be seen anywhere
in the conspicuously clean farm buildings and milking sheds. I
assumed that there was none to be seen in any of the other four
farms. There must have been a great deal of hosing from first light.
Eventually, and with great reluctance, I found a typewriter and
managed to compose a 1000-word leader-page article for the
Sunday Express on the now long forgotten crisis in Africa in 1957
that involved Egypt, the Sudan and Ethiopia. That night a very
jolly small dinner party had been assembled by Beaverbrook that
included Stanley Morison, the designer of Times Roman type who
was an anarchist and took the opposite view on almost every
subject. For some reason, Raymond was not there and Beaverbrook enjoyed the experience of serving the drink himself. This he
did with such gusto he became as near drunk as I ever saw him.
'The proceedings must end!' he said after several brandies and ban-
tering arguments with Stanley Morison. 'Bob and I have work to
do.' We went into another room that had a small suburban bookcase with a sliding glass door, half empty. 'Read your article,' said
the Old Man and his face showed surprise when I did. 'That's not
what we discussed,' he said. I explained we did not have a
discussion. 'Well,' he said, 'the subject is Abyssinia so get that atlas
out of the bookcase and let's see which countries are next to it.' It
was a 1914 atlas. 'Look at that, Bob,' cried Beaverbrook. 'Red
everywhere. Britain ruled the world!' He turned over the pages to
where there were pictures of primitive African tribesmen.
'Savages!' he shouted. 'We've given it all to them.' Happily, the
article Beaverbrook had in mind on the then current crisis gave no
indication of his views about the fitness of Africans to govern their

own countries. It was also one of the dullest on which my name has appeared. 'What do you think of it, John?' said the Old Man eagerly to John Junor who had it on his desk the following morning. 'Brilliant,' said JJ. Beaverbrook was delighted.

Beaverbrook's Empire ideas had a lot of appeal to me as a socialist. If the brotherhood of man was beyond reach, the brotherhood of the Commonwealth was a good second choice. Our links with Canada, Australia and New Zealand, who stood by us so magnificently in two world wars, should be treasured. I feared that the Common Market would undermine our Parliamentary rights and stretch these links to breaking point, with our lives being increasingly controlled by a fat cat bureaucracy across the Channel, utterly remote from our own people. The miracle of the Commonwealth was that it included so many black people, most of whom even then had self-rule. It was to me the nearest thing to a United Nations that really worked and the best force for good on this earth. Even when I was editor of the *Sunday Mirror*, a paper which under Cecil King's domination had doggedly advocated the Common Market, I voted against it in Harold Wilson's referendum, but by now not with any passion and uneasily aware that I was probably wrong. Beaverbrook's view of the Commonwealth, in reality, had little in common with mine. What he really believed in was a white Commonwealth and a black Empire under white domination. His attitude was typical of a Canadian provincial.

The *Observer*'s attitude was the exact opposite. It was having a prolonged love affair with 'the emergent' African nations and the distinguished expert on that continent, Colin Legum, could be depended on each Sunday to brief its readers at great length on every development. Where the *Daily Express* could see nothing right about the newly emancipated African countries the *Observer* could see nothing wrong. Although my support did not extend to reading these articles, my heart was with the *Observer*. I am a utopian, we should all try to love one another, sums up my beliefs. Beaverbrook was aware of this and one morning at Cherkley, with two or three other colleagues, the name of David Astor, then editor and owner of the *Observer*, came into the conversation. 'Would you like to meet him, Bob?' said Beaverbrook. I was astonished, because he was clearly implying that he could arrange a meeting, though the *Observer* had frequently attacked him and he had given every impression of hating Astor. How splendid, I thought, that though they were enemies in public they could meet in a civilised manner in private. I visualised a historic dinner party at Cherkley or Arlington House, laid on for my benefit, with guests who would never forget such a remarkable evening. 'Yes, I would,' I said modestly, indicating gratitude that he would go to such trouble. 'Well, put some boot polish on your face,' said Beaverbrook, 'and then he'll see you!'

A lot of one's time was spent talking to Lord Beaverbrook on the telephone. He never came to the office, and sometimes would call several times a day. 'What's the news?' he would say, without any preamble. The editor, possibly recovering from a good lunch, would try to think desperately of something that would especially interest him, glancing through the news schedule the news editor had given him at morning conference. 'What's going on?' was an alternative, or when he was in a poor mood, simply 'yarss?' (yes) said in his Brooklyn-like rasping accent. 'Get me Mr Edwards,' he would tell someone. One or other of the splendid secretaries who have looked after me down the years, phoned by one of his, would leap for the tape-recorder, switch it on and then tell me in as calm a voice as she could muster, 'Lord Beaverbrook on the telephone.' It was a tradition that when he came on during morning or evening conference, the room had to be cleared. The editor who said, 'Tell him I'm in conference' would be breaking the rules. I'm sure he called regularly at these times to assert his dominance. His appetite for information was insatiable, and the dullest item of political news could provoke a leader suggestion. 'You should say this in your newspaper,' he would advise, and would be astounded if you said, 'Well, actually, I don't agree.' But he always maintained the fiction that the editor was in command.

It was a relief to have an idea for a leader from him because this meant there was one less to think of for the editor or the bored leader-writers. The Old Man's thoughts were transcribed by the editor's secretary, handed to George Malcolm Thomson, and sent back to Beaverbrook on a teleprinter almost exactly as he had dictated them. Usually Beaverbrook's secretary would telephone to say the leader had been approved. Sometimes Beaverbrook would ring to say the idea had been misunderstood and another attempt on it would be made, but that seldom happened when George handled the leader. During Lord Beaverbrook's long absences abroad, except from his home at Cap d'Ail in the south of France, he seldom telephoned. That was a blessed relief, bestowed upon his editors by the difficulty in those days of making a trans-Atlantic call. I also sensed that he felt his editors and managers needed the break from his constant encouragement, as he called it, or harassment as others might put it. All was sweetness and light for a day or two before he went on his annual trips to Canada and Jamaica. He liked to leave in an atmosphere in which our devotion to him was the dominant emotion, rather than fear and annoyance at his constant nagging. 'Goodbye-ee,' he would say to me. 'Give my regards to your beautiful wife.' The moment he was safely aboard the Queen Mary or Queen Elizabeth, the editor knew he could go to Poppins (the pub next door to the Express) or El Vino's with his favourite cronies, like a true editor without fear of the telephone.

I learned from my predecessor Ted (later Sir Edward) Pickering that, even with Beaverbrook in the country, it was possible to have a reasonable social life early in the evening and yet answer the phone in sufficient time to keep the Old Man at bay. After the secretaries had gone, Pick would notify the night news desk that he was going to have a 'discussion', his pleasing euphemism for a drink, with Keith Howard, the news editor, or another colleague. The telephone exchange knew the drill precisely. Lord Beaverbrook seldom put through a call personally. If he did, it was almost invariably a disaster ending in wrong numbers and frustration. So if there was no answer from Pick's office, the exchange would say to the person instructed by Lord Beaverbrook to get him on the line, 'He's not in his office at the moment. We'll find him and ring back immediately.' Lord Beaverbrook's secretary would then know that he, or later I, was in the pub and that it was all stations go to get us back to the office. Every Fleet Street newspaper's telephone exchange had the numbers of the local public houses. It was a simple matter for the helpful exchange (and there was no finer body of men than those at the Express), to find out the editor's whereabouts from the night news desk and give him the red alert personally on the pub phone. Pick had the knack of disappearing from the group he was with as quickly as the Cheshire cat's smile. A few minutes later he would be phoning Cherkley, Arlington House, or less frequently Cap d'Ail. Just as Lord Beaverbrook would be about to shout, and sometimes did, 'Where's Pickering?' (or later Edwards) the editor was on the phone as calmly as if he had just returned from sorting out a problem in the composing room. He would then return to the pub and because, unlike me, Pick is a very private man, no one would indicate that they knew he had been absent and moving at something approaching the speed of light.

El Vino's was a problem. It was just that much too far. Calls were therefore switched through direct to the phone behind the bar.

Successive editors somehow gave the impression they were hard at work in their office despite the sounds of revelry and cries of 'Cheers, old man' in the background. On one occasion Charles Wintour was asked where he was because of the unusual sound effects. It was the day the convict Alfie Hinds, later proved innocent, was found on the run in Calais by the *Daily Mail*. 'El Vino,' said the brave Charles. 'You won't find Alfie Hinds in there,' said Beaverbrook triumphantly.

It was during my second term as editor of the *Daily Express* that a tiny and totally dedicated office manager called Mr Dunkum recommended that I should have two tape-recorders to monitor calls from the Lord (as managers invariably called him: we, as somewhat superior mortals, never did). This was after an incident involving Leonard Mosley, one of the *Express's* highly talented writers. Some book had been written about the Battle of Britain, with a shrewdly generous reference to Lord Beaverbrook's role as Minister of Aircraft Production. No sensible editor would have that book reviewed without taking advice. So I put through a call to Arlington House. 'Oh, dear,' said the Old Man, showing off to someone. 'Oh, dear, oh, dear. You a young lion and you have to bother an Old Man.' I knew he was delighted. 'Who are you going to get to do it, Bob?' 'I suggest Leonard Mosley.' Mosley was a film critic, a very good one, and occasional book reviewer and general writer. He seldom met Lord Beaverbrook, but I knew that because of his talents and helpful attitude he was a sure-fire winner for the Old Man's approval. 'Put him on the telephone, Bob.'

The smart-suited, urbane and wholly delightful Mosley came, in his relaxed manner, to my office and I explained the situation. The Old Man had, it turned out, already seen the book and wanted to talk about it. I left Mosley sitting in the editor's chair, with the out-of-date, Empire-dominated map of the world inherited from Arthur Christiansen and Ted Pickering behind him, the tape-recorder carefully switched on. I thought his slight humiliation at being told what to write should be done in private, and I wandered to the features department to see what inspiration, if any, they had had that day. When I returned to my office my secretary, Pam Spooner, Mr Dunkum and sundry others were standing in deep concern, as if witnesses of a traffic accident, round the tape-recorder, which was making a noise like an excitable Egyptian with a high-pitched voice seeking to sell his wares in a Cairo street market. 'It's gone wrong,' said Pam. 'We can't hear a word he's saying.' I showed the cool appropriate to an editor of a great national paper. 'Can't you slow it down?' I suggested. 'We've tried that,' said the faithful Dunkum. 'It has the same effect as a gramophone that needs winding up. Incomprehensible.'

Leonard Mosley had gone to lunch, probably to The Ivy, and I said I would speak to him when he returned for the transcription. He sauntered in later. 'The tape-recorder has bust,' I explained. 'Presumably you can remember what he said and took some notes?' 'Unfortunately,' said Leonard, 'I can't and I didn't. But surely there's no problem?' 'Why not?' 'Well, shouldn't I just phone the Old Man and get him to repeat it?' The idea intrigued me. 'Go ahead, Leonard,' I said and waited for the fun.

'Mosley here, Lord Beaverbrook,' said Leonard. 'I'm sorry to tell you Mr Edwards's tape-recorder is out of order.' Beaverbrook's reply was instant. 'So am I,' he shouted, and put the phone on the hook. Later Beaverbrook complained bitterly to me. 'Look,' I said, 'I'll take responsibility for the paper. But I'm damned if I'll take the blame for a faulty tape-recorder.' 'Aw, forget it, Bob,' he said, instantly contrite. Somehow the article worked out all right, and from that moment onwards two large tape-recorders worked impeccably every time he came on the telephone.

Once I had the misfortune to have a temporary secretary in my office when Lord Beaverbrook himself came directly on the telephone. I had drilled it into her that when I agreed to speak to someone she should always get them personally on the phone before putting them through, or at least 'go through together' as they say in top secretaries' circles. The following dialogue between Beaverbrook and my 'temp' took place: 'Editor's office.' 'Mr Edwards, please.' 'Who wants him?' 'Lord Beaverbrook' (I have no doubt menacingly). 'Have you got Lord Beaverbrook already on the phone?' she said, still not realising it was him. He sent a hurt note to Tom Blackburn, the joint chairman. 'I was asked the question have you got Lord Beaverbrook on the telephone by a female secretary. I wish you to look into this and have a talk with Mr Edwards about it. It won't do for the editor of the *Daily Express* to take the attitude to the public that he must ask have you got the person calling him on the telephone before undertaking to speak.'

I read into this that Beaverbrook was deeply offended that his commanding voice was not instantly recognised and that he could be mistaken for a male secretary or valet. It always upset him not to be recognised. On a morning walk in Mayfair, when he was feeling particularly warm towards me, we looked into a small shop window full of teddy bears and toy cats and dogs. They were meant as

sugar-daddies' presents for escorts at local night clubs like Churchill's. Beaverbrook said, 'Would you like two for your children?' He
went in and picked two that were outrageously expensive. 'You
know who I am?' said Beaverbrook when it came to sending him the
bill. 'No, I don't, I'm afraid,' said the girl shop assistant, politely.
When told 'I'm Lord Beaverbrook,' she had the sense to agree to
posting an account, but Beaverbrook's first act on returning to his
flat was to shout a message to Mr Blackburn into the dictaphone
saying that under no circumstances was an account to be opened
with the shop. The bill was to be paid and they must be told 'no more
transactions'. A kind act had been spoiled by childish behaviour. My
two oldest children treasured the presents for years.

9
LA CAPPONCINA

I always enjoyed visiting Lord Beaverbrook. I particularly enjoyed going to the south of France to stay with him at his home, La Capponcina, overlooking the sea a mile or two from Monte Carlo. Work was a pretence. The plane would fly to Nice. The chauffeur would pick you up in the Rolls-Royce. This was the life.

'The Lord is in the garden,' they would say, and you would go out unescorted to find him, being careful not to walk on the blue grass, which even caused him to shout at much-loved journalists like Ian Aitken. 'Aw, hello, Bob, good flight? Come and sit down beside me. Now, Miss Rosenberg, tell Mr Blackburn, say to him ...' and he would continue working. Drinks were difficult to get hold of except at meal times. Sometimes he realised his journalist guests might have withdrawal symptoms and a whisky would be offered. I could have taken some with me but felt this misdemeanour might be reported. At lunch and dinner he occasionally served still champagne, which I have disliked to this day, but mostly there was champagne of varying quality, depending on the mood he was in and how much he wanted to impress his guests. I have known him to serve different champagne to different people at the same table. Chicken, as in England, was served with monotonous regularity, but there was asparagus, very good soufflés, cheese from his west country farms. Nobody could reasonably complain. He did not appear at breakfast, which was simple and French. You were left to gauge the right time to have it and when he expected your company, and you walked in to his small study and said 'good morning' as if you were simply a house guest instead of a paid employee. 'Good morning,' he would reply with great emphasis and warmth, and then you sat patiently, a bit like a faithful labrador, awaiting the morning walk. Since there was nowhere much to go in that affluent corner of France, with almost every centimetre owned by millionaires, it was usually along a precarious cliff path, and I wondered what people would surmise if in my company he fell off it on to the rocks below.

When the weather was hot, there was a good chance of a picnic on what he called his 'yatt'. In fact, it was a beautifully varnished, large, motor launch. Every day in fine weather everyone would look anxiously out to sea in the hope that it was totally calm, which would mean hours of relaxation for the personal staff who remained behind and pleasure for those who went with 'the Lord' and his guests. We picnicked one scorching day just inside the harbour at Villefranche. There was no wind and no tide. Each piece of food, including the melons, was removed from the hampers by Raymond the valet, individually wrapped in tissue paper. There were several of us on board, and Beaverbrook had a simple method of disposing of litter. He dropped it in the sea. We all followed his bad example. It included several emptied bottles of still and real champagne. When the meal was over Beaverbrook looked at the remarkable amount of debris floating round our boat, murmured 'Good God!' in affected shock and took a squint at me to see if this was something I would remember. I thought the scene on this splendid day would have graced a French film about the decadent bourgeoisie.

Even the most skilled courtiers can cause offence. Something I had said had displeased Beaverbrook. Possibly at dinner the previous night I had persisted in an opinion different to his own. The punishment for my wickedness is that I was sentenced to write an article instead of going on the yacht. Mead the butler placed a bottle of 'plonk' and piece of cold chicken beside me as we watched the boat sail away along the coast. 'It don't seem right, do it?' said nice old Mead. 'Them with all of that and us with nothing.'

My most dangerous moment involved Josephine Rosenberg, the Old Man's extremely attractive secretary. Lord Thomson, the newspaper magnate, had been to dinner and, as always, Beaverbrook's treatment of him verged on rudeness, to the extent that the meal was over by 9.15 p.m. and Beaverbrook indicated that the proceedings had concluded by saying to me, 'Now, Mr Edwards, will you please escort Miss Rosenberg to her lodgings up the hill.' Jo regularly joined the Old Man for dinner and I was delighted to accompany her. She had managed to smuggle a bottle of liqueur from the house into her rooms above the garage, and after three or four days at La Capponcina I was beginning to feel stir crazy and in need of female company. We stayed together for some time, and although I have nothing exciting to confess in the fashion of contemporary autobiographies, she did wish me good night in a pleasing dressing gown. I was surprised to find Beaverbrook's house in total darkness. There was no doubt I had been locked out. Mead eventually turned on the lights and answered the bell. 'I'm sorry, sir,' he said, looking sadly at me as if I was done for, 'the Lord told me to tell you he had gone to bed and that I was to put out the lights and lock the door.' 'Oh dear,' I said, and went to bed thinking of Miss Rosenberg. The following morning I made sure I breakfasted early. I met the Old Man in the long corridor, overlooking the fish pond outside, as he went to his study. His right eyelid flickered alarmingly and he got to the point at once. In his curious Brooklyn-style voice, he said, 'You're distoibing my household.' Angry, I replied, 'There's a very simple solution to that problem.' I was forgiven. 'Forget it,' he said. I told this story to John Junor. 'Oh, my God,' he said, in his splendid Scottish accent, 'don't tell me you put your finger in that little pie.'

Another little drama at La Capponcina concerned Peter Forster, the *Daily Express* book critic I had appointed. While it may be true, as journalists who cannot write frequently say, that 'no one is bigger than the paper', some contributors are virtually irreplaceable. Nobody could replace Nathaniel Gubbins, the marvellously witty *Sunday Express* columnist during and before the war. Beaverbrook is reputed not to have understood his fictional humour that included a thoroughly believable, self-centred couple of ladies in a safe hotel during the blitz and an equally believable but lovable chimney sweep commenting with native shrewdness on current events. Possibly because of this flaw in Beaverbrook's abilities, Gubbins moved to the inferior *Sunday Dispatch* and lost his inspiration in a sea of trash and mediocrity. Several have tried to copy John Junor's column in the *Sunday Express*; all have impaled themselves because, except by *Private Eye*'s satirists, it is inimitable. Equally the *Daily Express* was totally stuck when James Agate could no longer write his famous book column. Under Ted Pickering's editorship George Millar was given a whirl at his friend Max Aitken's suggestion. He finally succumbed to a barrage from Lord Beaverbrook far more accurate than the Germans had to face at the Battle of the Somme, in part, I suspected, because of his friendship with Max. Then, as Pick's deputy, I was told by the Old Man to nominate a substitute. Foxed, I asked my wife, Laura, and it was she who suggested Forster, then writing an inspired TV column in the *Spectator*. 'Go ahead,' approved Beaverbrook, and I was a little daunted when a delighted but awesomely solemn Forster, safely under contract, told me he thought one of his principal duties was to appeal to publishers. I did not like to tell him at the start of his new career that this was not the idea at all. The only people he had to appeal to were the readers, as Agate did abundantly in an eccentric column mostly about himself, and of course the Principal Reader.

All went well for many months as far as the last requirement was concerned. Beaverbrook had decided, like a true publisher, that he personally had discovered Forster, who wrote conscientiously and well with great appeal to publishers and literary people. Then the tide turned dramatically. A book was published, I think about Somerset Maugham, and, since the subject interested Beaverbrook, Forster was summoned to discuss it with him. 'Take a pencil,' I probably said. 'Do your best for the old boy.' Later, when a copy of Forster's article had been submitted, Beaverbrook rang me in a pained voice, 'Bob, he did not listen to a word I said.' I thought the best way to protect Peter Forster was to send Bob Pitman to do the article instead. He could be depended upon to deliver, and he did so brilliantly, full of unacknowledged reminiscences from the Old Man.

From this moment there was a steady drip of criticism over many months, during which I became editor, of Forster's thoroughly worthy contributions, until the run up to Christmas when a desperate features department, reeling from one drunken party to the next, filled the bottom half of the leader page with an essay by Forster on Scrooge. Bereft, as they were, of inspiration they had probably asked him to do it. The day it appeared my wife and I had arrived on a brief visit to La Capponcina ending on Christmas Eve. Beaverbrook's opinion of the article rapidly became clear.

Laura and I sat opposite each other in his small study, she on a yellow armchair and I on a matching settee. Beaverbrook was standing at his lectern, wearing a straw hat and admiring himself in a full length mirror. ('You shouldn't have that mirror there,' I heard Lady Beaverbrook say on another occasion. 'It makes you look vain.') The Old Man got down to business. 'Do you mind, Bob, if I attack you in front of your wife?' The answer I gave was no. 'Well then, Bob, what the hell is the *Daily Express* doing publishing an article on Scrooge, for God's sake?' Secretly I agreed with him, but loyalty demanded that I defended the article, which I did as best I could.

'Huh!' said Beaverbrook, and pressed the bell on his lectern once. This produced Mead, the kindly and traditional butler. His employer handed him an envelope which clearly contained his Christmas box. 'Merry Christmas, Mead,' said Beaverbrook, and without pausing added, 'Tell me, is there anybody at all left in England who wants to read about Scrooge?' Mead gave me an affectionate and concerned glance, placed the envelope carefully in his pocket and replied with apparent lack of guile, 'Oh, yes, sir, everyone in England is interested in Scrooge. They put the play on the radio every Christmas.' He left, almost walking backwards, and Beaverbrook pressed the bell again, this time twice. Raymond the valet pranced into the room. He, too, was handed an envelope clearly containing money, asked the same question and, with a similar glance at me, gave the same answer.

Beaverbrook sat next to me on the settee, picked up the *Daily Express*, and read the offending article carefully all through. Then he threw the paper on the carpet so that it lay spread open at his feet. 'Do you know why I've done that?' he shouted, his rage at least half-genuine. 'No, sir,' I smiled. He explained, 'So that I can pick it up and throw it down again!' It was time to surrender. 'That's OK,' I said, 'Forster goes.' Sorry, Peter. A quarter of a century later, when I told this story to Michael Foot, he told me Beaverbrook could not stand Charles Dickens.

Life at La Capponcina could become excruciatingly dull. Beaverbrook's dinner guests were often rich, snobbish and boring. One night they were discussing the appointment of Frank Cousins, a dreaded left-winger, as general secretary of the Transport and General Workers' Union. Patrick Hennessy, boss of Fords in Britain, gave his conventional view and Beaverbrook decided to enliven the place. He turned to me, a seemingly harmless, diffident young man in a dinner-jacket. 'You're a communist,' he shouted. 'What do you say to that?' The effect was electric. They all knew Beaverbrook was capable of employing a communist. Stupidly, I took offence. 'I'm not a communist,' I said, 'but I'll become one if I work for you long enough.' The next morning I made amends by joining Beaverbrook for his morning dip off the rocks into the sea, which I did not enjoy. He smiled serenely.

He and Lady Beaverbrook took Laura and myself to dinner with Arpad and Madame Plesch. The only reason he could have enjoyed their company was because of their enormous wealth. 'He's a Hungarian Jew,' he said to me on the way there in the Rolls-Royce. 'Made all his money selling sugar to the Nazis in the war.' The drawing-room was littered with small tables and priceless ornaments. I picked up a small gold lighter that needed a new flint. For this unpardonable negligence, a German flunkey in a footman's uniform received a severe reprimand from Madame Plesch in his native tongue. Beaverbrook picked up a ball he had found and threw it the length of the room, dangerously pursued by the Pleschs's four small dogs. Dinner was the kind served with burning twigs at considerable risk to the four white-gloved footmen. Conversation flagged. Eventually coffee was served that tasted like the dregs from a car sump. I looked to see how Beaverbrook was coping with it. He caught my eye. 'What wonderful coffee,' he exclaimed to Madame Plesch. He took out a small pad he always carried. 'Tell me, where did you get it?' Our hostess was thrilled. 'We always say what wonderful coffee we have in your house,' she said. 'I will tell you where we get ours if you tell us where you get yours.' It was a deal. Madame Plesch named a company in Istanbul and said she would forward the address. 'And now,' she said, like one of those women in a Marx Brothers film, 'where do you get yours?' 'Lyons Corner House,' said the Old Man triumphantly.

The six of us went to the Russian Circus in Nice. When the Cossacks rode into the ring, Laura and I stood up and cheered wildly. We had had enough of rich people for one day.

One cloudy, miserable day in the south of France he was as bored as the rest of us. He had despatched missiles to his editors and managers, and made copious alterations to documents put in front of him by Josephine Rosenberg and a young ex-graduate and journalist, Ivan Yates, who was his current assistant with high hopes of a job on one of his papers after a period of servility. Ivan, unusually for a Beaverbrook choice, was not physically blessed, though not an unpleasant person. He was tall, stooping, thin and wore unflattering horn-rimmed glasses. Earlier the Old Man had dictated to Tom Blackburn, the joint chairman, yet another complaint about the filtration system in the swimming-pool which faced us in the garden. The truth was that he only liked to swim in the sea, which he did off uncomfortable rocks, but it pleased him to complain about the blackguard contractors whose incompetence he said had caused the pool to become a slimy haven for algae, water spiders and other bugs. I suspected that the system worked perfectly well, but he had not allowed the gardeners to switch it on for the required periods. Under his straw hat he eyed his young assistant menacingly. 'Ivan,' he said, 'you have toiled hard in the vineyard. You have earned a reward. Take a swim.'

Ivan did not feel able to decline. He went miserably to his bedroom and emerged wearing large bathing trunks and looking like the 'before' part of one of the 'You too can have a body like mine' advertisements. Watched by his employer, he flopped into the pool. Beaverbrook turned to his secretary. 'Miss Rosenberg, you should join Ivan in the water,' he ordered. Jo was well looked after for pleasing her boss. She came through the french windows in a sensationally skimpy bikini and I was as interested as Beaverbrook as she dived off the top board. 'I think Miss Rosenberg's the better swimmer, don't you, Bob?' he said, well pleased with the show. And then he tried his luck for the third time. 'Why don't you go in?' he said. I declined. Editors have their rights.

Beaverbrook, I suppose, could not be blamed entirely for having some fun at the expense of his more grovelling employees. Several times I witnessed him ring off when someone was in mid-sentence, ruining that person's day. I felt a badge for courage was deserved by one of his older secretaries who reproved him for doing it yet again. 'He was still talking,' she said, quite sternly. Beaverbrook raised his eyebrows in affected surprise. The secretary some years later told me she was terrified of him.

He showed his sadistic trait one day after he had dictated a particularly violent memo to Ted Pickering on his dictaphone. It gave him pleasure to rebuke editors in front of their deputies, as I was then. Beaverbrook did not regard Pick as any more of a toady than the rest of us, possibly less so. 'He's an old soldier,' he said to me, with variations, on several occasions, outrageously since Pickering was my supposed boss. 'Every time the *Daily Mail* gets a story it's because they have, by good fortune, a reporter who lives next door. Or the telephone lines to our office were down. Or our wonderful fellow was ill, poor chap.' Pick would only admit that the *Daily Express* had erred as a very last resort; and even then he would explain that the culprit's error was inexplicable in view of his utter devotion and years of outstanding service. His loyalty to his staff made him a very popular editor, and he was highly successful, but less so with Beaverbrook. 'That will make him stutter,' he said savagely, when he had dictated the memo.

Beaverbrook may have thought I would be pleased, since my ambition was obvious. In fact, I was shocked, but unlike the brave secretary did not say so. Every now and then, when I too was defending the paper, he would say, 'You're becoming an old soldier like Pickering.' He preferred sackcloth and ashes, the penitent's stool. And his desire for me to be editor against Max Aitken's and others' loyal support for Pick bubbled over on an evil morning at Arlington House. 'Why don't you move into his chair?' he said, apparently in deadly earnest. 'Sit behind his desk and take over!' I could think of nothing to say, but imagined that five years earlier he had probably said the same thing to Pick about his editor, Arthur Christiansen.

Often I wondered if he was simply acting and hugely enjoying the performance. He would rage over the phone, his face contorted, like no other I have seen, replace the receiver and immediately resume the most sunny and kindly of expressions. He very seldom shouted at me, possibly because I was 'too sensitive', but he had his moments all the same. At Cherkley a remarkable lift, built for one, had been installed to transport him to his bedroom. When he stepped into it in the vast hall it looked like any other small lift, but all traces of it disappeared as he ascended. He had the habit of asking me a question which required a long answer just before he slammed the gate. I would follow his Elijah-like progress by walking up the great winding staircase, addressing him in a loud voice across the considerable chasm. Perhaps he was simply easily bored, but I did not think so. He pulled the same trick with a chair-lift, also built for one, that took him from the cliff walk to the villa La Capponcina at a gradient of at least 1 in 3. His faithful subjects were expected to stumble up the narrow path beside it, continuing the conversation. I rapidly learned to make an excuse and leave him when this absurd moment arrived. He liked me to read newspapers to him as we zig-zagged up the French Alps on picnics and other excursions. It made me feel as queasy as travelling in a car when I was a child. 'More, more,' he would say, 'what else is interesting today?'

He told me with great satisfaction how Tom Driberg, later the Labour MP but then an incomparable William Hickey, pleaded with him to persuade the other press barons to suppress reports of proceedings against him for homosexual offences. 'I was in the bath when I saw him,' said the Old Man, joyously recalling this sadistic touch. 'It was buggery, you know. I noticed that he had developed quite a large belly. "You're not so beautiful as you were, Tom", I thought, as he pleaded with me to kill the story.' Which Beaverbrook did. Sometimes he saw people while sitting on the lavatory. I presumed he selected those timid souls most likely to be embarrassed, and I was told he would occasionally see journalists in his bedroom, walking around naked for maximum effect.

Several times he gleefully recalled how Lord Francis-Williams, the eminent socialist and press critic, had, as a young journalist on the *Daily Express*, driven four dray horses and a cart loaded with newsprint through the picket lines in the 1926 General Strike. I have seen a paragraph printed at the time acknowledging this Wild West performance. He also told me that Brian Chapman, another well-known socialist, had written the notorious SOCIALIST GESTAPO headline in the 1945 election, when Churchill and Beaverbrook cooked up the ludicrous scare that Professor Laski as chairman of the Labour National Executive would take over as dictator if Labour won. It seemed to me that he and Mammon had something in common, and he appeared to be saying: 'Don't let it worry you if you write something you don't believe. Join the Club.' I was deeply moved at the funeral in a Putney church of Percy Elland, the thoroughly nice editor of the *Evening Standard* who died of a heart attack at the age of fifty-eight. But the only comment I heard Beaverbrook make was to Ted Pickering inside the church directly after the service. 'I saw you opening and shutting your mouth,' he said, genially. 'But you did not know the words!'

There was another side altogether to Beaverbrook's character. Time and again he wrote to sick or bereaved colleagues, as the Beaverbrook papers in the House of Lords library bear witness. I had only to suggest he should send a letter to someone of whose misfortune he was unaware and he would dictate one immediately, in his unique and stylish manner. These brought great comfort and I thought highly of him for his concern. But he enjoyed his little flirtations with Beelzebub. He liked to describe journalism as 'the black art', and one day he saw me looking at a framed photo on one of his desks of a fearsome, patriarchal, bearded figure of great age. 'That was my father,' he said. 'He was a Presbyterian Minister. In his latter years he often asked me for cash,' by which Beaverbrook meant that his father liked the stuff, 'and by the time he died I think he no longer believed.' There was an unmistakable note of triumph in his voice. There was also a clear implication that Beaverbrook did not believe either, despite his much publicised financial support for the Presbyterian Church. Was much of it play-acting? I think so. Beaverbrook did not need a Saatchi and Saatchi to create an image for himself. He was the most astonishing character I have met and even in his wicked moments he was vastly interesting.

IO

CUTTING ROSES

In the first half of the 1960s, the *Daily Express* sold more copies than ever before. There was a record over several months in 1960 of about 4,300,000. That was when Edward Pickering was editor and I was his deputy. Three years later under my editorship we achieved the highest figure for August in the paper's history, 4,382,000 copies, and we broke other monthly records. Roger Wood, who was slotted between my two periods in the hot seat, did not disgrace himself either, before being forcibly moved on to Cudlipp's ill-fated *Sun*, then Australia, and eventually the stunning job of editing Rupert Murdoch's *New York Post*, of which he later became editor-in-chief. Something else must be added, which I discovered only recently in my diligent research for this book; the paper was unquestioningly better than in the latter years of the great Arthur Christiansen's editorship. That cannot be said of the *Daily Express* after Lord Beaverbrook's death and (I like to feel) my final departure a year later.

Pick was the first editor during this period of advance and, since editors get the blame when things go wrong, he also deserves the credit. Beaverbrook, however, had other ideas. In October 1961, a curious item appeared on page one, column one, the spot traditionally reserved for the paper's blurbs, under the headline IS THERE A HAPPY GREMLIN IN THE EXPRESS? It went on:

> One of the most baffling mysteries in newspaper production is that the Daily Express continues to go on from success to success no matter what happens to its staff in any department.
>
> Indeed, it may be said that nobody moulds the Daily Express; the paper moulds its staff.
>
> Over the years many production executives of the Daily Express have left for other papers and have tried to put upon them the stamp of the Daily Express. They have always failed.
>
> Their replacements at the Express have always succeeded. There must be some happy gremlin at work, some good fairy who guides

newcomers and makes them do whatever they have to do in the
manner in which only the Express wants it done.

The secret must lie with Lord Beaverbrook . . .

This item was from an article in the *Newsagents' Journal*. It
delighted Lord Beaverbrook who, like another of my bosses later
on, Robert Maxwell, was not one for false modesty. That was
something he preferred from his editors. I had recently taken over
from Ted Pickering and felt suitably humbled. If the editor of the
Daily Express today held half the sales figures of that period he
would probably be granted a Rolls-Royce Corniche, a company
yacht, and the right to stub out his cigar upon the chairman's desk.
All papers were doing well but only the *Daily Mirror* sold more. It
did not then have the competition of the *Sun*, Hugh Cudlipp's
disastrous gift to Murdoch to save 2000 jobs and prevent industrial
trouble at the *Mirror*. Research figures in those glittering days at the
Daily Express show its remarkable dominance. One third of the
readers came from the top social group, known as AB, higher in
percentage and numbers than the *Daily Telegraph*, its nearest rival
in this market. Thirty-nine per cent came from the next social group
C1, high-grade white- and blue-collar workers, beating the *Daily
Mirror* by 12 per cent and the *Express*'s traditional rival the *Daily
Mail* by 13 per cent. The rest came from what is known, for want of a
better term, as the working class (C2 and D1) where the *Mirror* was
far in the lead. Thus the *Daily Express* was a truly classless paper. It
was unique and no one but Lord Beaverbrook deserves the credit for
that. In Scotland, our least class-conscious country, it was a total
triumph, far outselling the others. Recently I talked to Terence
Lancaster, former foreign editor of the *Express* who became the
highly respected political editor of the *Daily Mirror*. 'We called it
the world's greatest newspaper,' I said. 'Well, it was,' he replied
instantly. Something like 40 per cent of its readers supported Labour
and slightly more the Tories in a properly conducted poll. Beaverbrook preached high wages and full employment, and when the
paper showed typically middle class hostility to a generous pay deal
for miners he sent an angry note to Max Aitken saying that the paper
was not 'anti-labour'. He added the shrewd footnote, in case his
rebuke was misinterpreted, 'I don't mean we are not anti-Labour
with a capital L.' Beaverbrook applied his pro-labour policies in all
four of his newspaper centres. During all the time I worked for him I
do not recall a single crisis with the workforce, whereas on the
Mirror Group in pre-Maxwell days the management seemed to

devote almost all their energies to avoiding stoppages and few to promoting papers in their care. The malpractices that caused the closing down of *The Times* and *Sunday Times* in 1978/9 for nearly a year before Murdoch took over from Lord Thomson's defeated son; the dramatic switch to Wapping by Murdoch himself; the threat by Maxwell on the *Mirror* and later his admirer David Stevens on the *Express* to close down their papers unless a third of the workforce left; all began in the days of the great press barons. The explanation is simple. Their profits were enormous, in Beaverbrook's case despite his expenditure on gathering news. Weaker rivals could not afford the high wages and the rackets, and went under. Beaverbrook sent me a note complaining that I had wasted an expensive envelope when replying to him. Much energy was devoted by secretaries in finding suitable old envelopes for this purpose. But the most diligent study of the Beaverbrook papers in the House of Lords would fail to yield a single memo to Tom Blackburn complaining about the cost of all the fiddles in the warehouse, the machine room and process department, and truly astonishing piecework payments to compositors which by the early 1980s were up to £50,000 a year in some offices. Max Aitken, chairman of the board of Beaverbrook Newspapers, wrote in his annual report published on 5 December 1959: 'I am happy to say our relations with labour have never been better.' You could say that again.

The strength of the *Daily Express* above all else was its news and picture coverage. Beaverbrook could not tolerate being beaten on a story anywhere. One afternoon a photo came from Camera Press, the Aspreys of picture agencies, whose boss Tom Blau skilfully exploited the pressure on the paper that it had to win every time, which showed Jackie Kennedy falling off her horse over a hedge. The picture was good in its own right. It had the additional merit that Beaverbrook hated the Kennedys. Blau said the price was £2000. He never came down with us. I knew that if we said no he would let the *Daily Mail* have it for £600, the picture's real worth at that time, and I consulted Tom Blackburn. With infinite sadness he agreed the price. Next day Beaverbrook sent for me. 'What did you pay for it?' he snarled, standing behind the usual pile of documents. 'Pay for what, sir?' 'You're an old soldier like Pickering – the picture of Jackie, o' course!' These things remain imprinted in the memory. When I told him, there was a pause, then a gentle 'Good God.' He picked up the dictaphone. 'Mr Blackburn, you've all gone mad at the *Express*. Mad, mad, mad.' 'Well, sir,' I said, 'we both thought we would rather face your wrath over paying so much than tell you we let it go to the *Daily Mail*.' The message to Blackburn was cancelled after I had gone.

One evening Ted Pickering and I were on the backbench when the picture editor brought us dramatic exclusive photographs of four maids leaping to their deaths from a burning hotel in Rome. In each case their nighties had lifted, revealing their naked bodies. It would not have happened in 'The Front Page', but neither of us had the stomach to ask the picture retoucher to paint in panties or extend the nighties. Without any discussion we turned the picture down. Sure enough, it appeared suitably altered in the *Daily Mail* with the hypocritical claim that it was being published as a warning against fire. Beaverbrook asked why the *Mail* had the pictures and we did not. I explained and that was that.

Pick and I worked well together. Harold Keeble, the associate editor who was never allowed to be in charge of the paper, having had a brief disastrous period at the *Sunday Express* before John Junor took over, was our resident genius. He looked like James Cagney, walked with an attractive limp, and was utterly malevolent. Nobody except the first editors of *Picture Post* and *Paris-Match* has ever handled pictures better. He read *Life* and *Time* magazine from cover to cover but seldom ever glanced at the articles he displayed with such panache in the *Daily Express*. He would snap his fingers and say to Clive Irving, Denis Hackett or whatever other talent was at hand, 'What's it all about, what's it about?' As he sketched out the page, he would not even choose the type for the headline but somehow the end result was, as sports editors are fond of saying, magic. With pictures for Photonews he had what he called a policy of rejection. The ever-patient and gentle picture editor, Gerry Cook, would bring in one set of pictures after another until the right one was found. They would end up strewn over the floor and, even though no one ever saw Keeble do this, pushed under the carpet. With a friend or two he drank probably half a crate of Pouilly Fumé a day, mostly at the Caprice, and he was so devious that praise from him induced a feeling of uneasiness. He drove around the West End in an expensive convertible with every known extra and insisted that his driver wore a chauffeur's hat. He was a star, and had the unnerving habit of disappearing at moments of decision.

For some reason, he was missing all day and Pick was off duty when I published one of the many pictures I have never forgotten. It was of the funeral of Countess Mountbatten which took place at sea. There were a lot of false rumours in Fleet Street about her death in Malaysia, and the form of burial added spice to them. Everybody looked careworn and bored at morning conference, as they often do when the deputy is in charge, and I decided as usual to jerk them into life. 'Do you mean to say,' I asked, 'that we've been invited to photograph her coffin in mid-air?' The answer, in a sense, was yes. The national press was to have a photographer on a minesweeper facing the frigate on which the funeral service was to take place. I enthused about the dramatic qualities of such a picture, which should appear tastefully on the page following the one carrying the photograph of the Mountbatten family mourners standing on deck around the draped coffin. I enquired anxiously whether we had a good features sub-editor on duty to write the caption. We had. His headlines were THE END, WITH FULL NAVAL HONOURS. THE LAST VOYAGE TO SEA OF THE SAILOR'S WIFE. His caption, set all full out as we say in the trade, read:

'... we therefore commit her body to the deep.' With these words, spoken by the Archbishop of Canterbury, and the wail of the bosuns' calls, Lady Mountbatten's coffin slides from under its covering Union Jack and plunges into the Channel. The moment of silence following the gentle splash is broken by the ringing note of Royal Marine buglers sounding the funereal Last Post, followed by the stirring Reveille which signifies an immortal awakening. On the quarter deck of the frigate Wakeful Earl Mountbatten makes his last farewell a minute later. He takes his wreath, touches it momentarily to his lips and drops it overboard on to the dull sea.

Beneath this, in case anyone thought we were intruding by publishing the picture, I put an acknowledgment 'Official Rota Picture by Keystone' in bold type. When the rivals came in later that night, I was shaken to notice that although they had all had it not one of them had used the picture. Doing my best not to look worried, I said to Eric Raybould, 'Are they all crazy?' to which he gave the daunting reply, 'May I see you in your room?' Sucking his irritating Manikin, with a matchstick stuck in the mouth end, he said, 'You did not ask me, Bob. I hate it.' And then, because he was loyal, he added, 'I hate pictures of coffins anyway.' This was no comfort, so I consulted the trusted and splendid night news editor, John Knight, a gentleman, Lord's Taverner and altogether a marvellous person. 'I wish', he said, looking at me gravely as if he feared I also was about to be tipped into the sea, 'I didn't have to say this. I fear it is a mistake.' With that he wished me a polite good night.

I was alone, as people in charge of newspapers often are in these situations, when Harold Keeble suddenly appeared, clutching the first edition of the *Daily Express* which had clearly been delivered to him at the Caprice or another five-star restaurant. 'Bob,' he cried. 'I had to come in. I had to congratulate you. That's a great picture. You know the one I mean. It's a total breakthrough. It takes journalism into a whole new dimension.' Then came the *coup de grâce*. 'It's the best since I published the picture all over page one of the three Queens in mourning. Next day there were two thousand letters of protest. Two thousand! I almost lost my job.' He was gone and I was now lonelier than ever. Then inspiration struck. I called in Ben Vos, the deputy night news editor. In those days we did not have television screens in the news room. 'Find out whether the BBC and ITN showed the coffin in mid-air,' I said. And, of course, they did. It was then that I realised that TV had altered everything. Not a single person protested to the paper.

Some while earlier there was a terrible train crash in a tunnel at Lewisham. Harold Keeble hurried to the backbench with a chilling, evocative picture that showed an unidentifiable man hanging grotesquely upside down from the wreckage, which was shrouded in fog. I was against the picture because of the pain it would cause relatives of the many victims, but did not press my objections because I felt that sometimes I was too cautious. Until then newspapers never published pictures of bodies in domestic disasters like this, though foreign plane crashes abroad were regarded as fair game. Keeble headlined the picture THE VICTIM. No reader complained on this occasion either because they had seen far worse on TV.

While Pickering was editor, Keeble wrote a long, handwritten letter to Lord Beaverbrook listing all the faults of the features department. It was a typically disloyal act because, of course, the department's performance was ultimately the editor's responsibility, and up to a point the deputy editor's too, but he had a case. The leader page was often an act of desperation and the women's features were weak. The paper's great strength was in its home and foreign news, pictures and sport, apart from having two of the world's greatest cartoonists, Carl Giles and Osbert Lancaster, the two best racing correspondents, Clive Graham and Peter O'Sullevan, and the incomparable layout that reflected Beaverbrook's policy of a classless, buoyant paper that wanted everyone to have two cars and plenty of money. Junor would have demanded Keeble's instant dismissal, and so would I, but no doubt Pickering responded with his usual tolerance. Beaverbrook could not wait to show me the letter. I said it was one of the most startling confessions I had read, since Harold Keeble himself as associate editor had been put in charge of the features department and could make any changes he wished, subject to the editor's approval. Thus Keeble effectively demolished himself. He was involved in an appalling car crash, with his correctly attired chauffeur at the wheel, permanently forsook Pouilly Fumé for Coca-Cola, and after a brief stay at the *Daily Mirror*, where he designed a classic layout for Cassandra (Bill Connor) and trained the Mirror Group's present editor-in-chief Mike Molloy in typography, moved to the *Daily Mail* to its great benefit.

Despite his incurable treacherousness, his was one of the greatest talents I have known. We spent many hours going through pictures together. One awful evening it was well past the deadline for Photonews and we had nothing worth printing. Keeble remembered a story mentioned at morning conference of a closed-down railway line in Norfolk that local people thought should be turned into a road along the same track. 'Have we got a picture of it?' said Harold, and sure enough we had from one of our 60 photographers. The picture showed two railway tracks with nothing on them in a nondescript rural setting, but with Harold's flair for presentation we got away with it. The space taken was the equivalent of a whole page in a tabloid newspaper. He could spot a memorable quality in an apparently ordinary picture. Twenty-seven years later I can recall precisely a half-page Photonews of the portly Dr Richard Beeching, the newly appointed boss of British Rail, mowing his lawn with an outsize Atco, his mock-Tudor home in the background. The usual, unimaginative, news page layout man would have given it three columns and no more and it would have been instantly forgotten. Across the news room in Ted Pickering's time Harold had erected a vast banner in startling colours: IMPACT! GET IT IN YOUR FIRST PARAGRAPH! GET IT IN YOUR PICTURES! ABOVE ALL GET IT IN YOUR HEADLINES! I had it removed. A good newspaper does not scream at the readers on every page. The 'slow-burning' first paragraph is often better than a sledge-hammer. Fleet Street still talks of the gently written, witty *Daily Express* page one centre columns of that period, that were masterpieces of sub-editing.

How incredible that the paper of the Swinging Sixties was dominated by a man in his eighties who conspired to put Lloyd George into No. 10 over forty years earlier. I met the Beatles in a photo session at the *Daily Express* after they had been discovered by the *Evening Standard*. Nearly a quarter of a century later I said to Paul

McCartney, 'Do you remember, we met once in the dark room of the *Daily Express*?' 'How could I ever forget?' he replied in a deliberately camp voice. Unlike the pop papers today, there was no trash in the *Express* despite the recurring problem of the leader page. Again past the deadline, I found the features editor – I think he was the able Clive Irving who became an authority on journalism – in a state of utter dejection. He was sprawled in an ancient armchair, which had a broken spring sticking through its cover, in the features room overlooking Fleet Street. 'It's happened,' he said. 'There is nothing. Nothing whatsoever.' He pointed in the direction of the feature writers' room. 'They're useless. Hopeless. Nothing.' I asked about a woman writer Keeble projected, as we put it, in neon lights. 'Her!' spat Clive. 'Can never write a last sentence. Today she hasn't even written a first.' In a leader page crisis I always thought of our legion of foreign correspondents. 'What about René McColl?' 'He's written an utterly boring article from Brazil. Who the hell cares about Brazil? I have put it on a flong page.' Flong pages were to help production in periods of big papers. They were not for the following day but the one after, and were usually dropped in the later editions. We never spiked René. 'He is incapable of writing a bad article,' I said. 'Take him off the flong and put him on the leader page.' Thus, unknown to the readers, were the agonies of producing the brightest paper in journalism. Whatever they thought of René's revelations from South America, the Principal Reader would not complain.

Other important pages presented no such problems. If the present editor of the *Daily Express* devoted two pages almost every day to the arts both his staff and his rivals would think he had suicidal tendencies. Yet that is what the *Express* did in the 1960s as a matter of routine. Its full-size page then, with advertisements, was the equivalent of a 'double-spread' with advertisements in today's tabloid. Beaverbrook drummed home the message: we must be a good paper for the West End. Thus it was nothing unusual to have Clive Barnes reviewing an opera, Noel Goodwin a concert, John Rydon an art exhibition, somebody else ballet, Bernard Levin the theatre and Nancy Spain on TV, all on page 4. I have discovered that it was the Happy Gremlin himself who put them all on one page. Previously they were strewn through the paper for production reasons. 'Your readers like to know where things are,' said Beaverbrook to me in a note from his dictaphone. 'In a well-ordered paper, there are familiar places they can be sure of finding.' The objections of the production people were magically overcome. Doubtless the next complaint from the Old Man was that the paper was not getting away on time. He may have made things a little harder in the composing room, but he had created probably the best paper on the arts in the history of popular journalism.

Some of the other things the *Express* did in the Swinging Sixties would have astounded today's cost-constrained editors. When Hemingway died in 1961, I sent one of our New York reporters Andrew Fyall to Sun Valley, Idaho, to cover the funeral. The report was not in the Hemingway league, but it was good enough:

> In a sun-kissed valley cradled in the lap of the foothills of the Sawtooth Mountains of Idaho they laid Ernest Hemingway to rest today. There were no stars, no personalities at the graveside. No boxers or bull-fighters, no one from the corps of celebrities who surrounded him during a lifetime of success.

But the *Express* was there. And a photographer. Ours was the only British paper to cover this event, which even today is of interest.

I shall not forget, and nor will the photographer who was on the assignment, the burning of the *Laconia* at Christmas in 1963. Gerry Cook, then the picture editor, was the first person I called in after hearing the news that the liner packed with British holidaymakers was on fire off the Portuguese coast. 'No problem,' he said. 'With your permission I am hiring a Viscount. We are sharing the cost with *Time* magazine. With luck we will be there in three or four hours.' Such were the eccentricities of Beaverbrook's management, the editor was supposed to check with Tom Blackburn or Max Aitken if he wanted to spend more than £100 on buying a picture. But at a cost of £2000 he could charter a four-engined Viscount to cover a (literally) hot story like this without reference to the management and there would be no comeback so long as the picture was eventually used. If it was not, the editor had to justify his expenditure. Gerry Cook, the best picture editor I have known, had one bad habit that may have appealed to my predecessor. He kept bad news from the editor. Four hours later I sent for him again. 'Any news of our aeroplane?' I asked. 'No one's heard a word,' he said. The awful possibility was that it might have ditched in the sea. Gerry and I looked at each other. Neither of us could face the possibility of being scooped by the *Daily Mail* with a picture across six columns on page one of the *Laconia* smoking from stem to stern and passengers leaping into the sea. 'We will have to send another plane,' said Gerry. The best picture turned out to be one taken by an American air force pilot stationed in Portugal. It cost us nothing. The Viscount that had lost contact had landed safely in a rare snowstorm in Lisbon and we used one of the pictures taken by our photographer to avoid an inquest. Fortunately we had been unable to locate a second plane to hire. The photographer had to spend Christmas in Lisbon away from his family. He came up to me in a pub the other day. 'You sent me a nice telegram,' he said.

With such determination, and fear of the consequences if we failed, we always seemed to get the best pictures. How the others must have envied PICASSO'S WEDDING BREAKFAST. EXPRESS PHOTO-NEWS GETS THE ONLY PICTURE. And the words were good, too: 'The telephone rang in Pablo Picasso's villa, La California, high on a hill above Cannes. "Be a good boy and answer that, will you?" yelled the painter to his 30-year-old son Paul. Paul did, returning with his face wrinkled in astonishment. "Papa," he called, "they say you are married!"'

Harold Macmillan's 'wind of change' speech is now recognised as probably the most statesmanlike of any British Prime Minister since the war. The *Express* published it as the page one lead under the heading CHALLENGE ON AFRICA. MACMILLAN ISSUES IT FEARLESSLY. The key phrase, 'The wind of change is blowing through the continent', was the second headline on page two, but I am relieved to say it was there. Two thousand words of the speech were reported by René McColl. Today it would probably be accorded a third of the space and take second place to a hyped-up story about Joan Collins or EastEnders. Major murder reports read in the 1960s like something by Dashiell Hammett. They were mostly written by someone known only in Fleet Street called Peter Hedley. I got him the biggest rise ever given to a *Daily Express* sub-editor after he had said he was hard-pressed to pay his children's school fees. My ploy was to name six of Beaverbrook's favourite journalists to Tom Blackburn and say that I would rather lose any of them than the unknown Hedley. Headlines did indeed have the impact demanded by Keeble. When Archbishop Makarios, formerly a prisoner of the British, paid his first official visit the picture was headlined GUEST OF H.M. GOVERN-MENT AGAIN! The caption recalled that previously he was our guest on the Seychelles 'without the option'.

On a Sunday when I was deputising for Pickering the only news at morning conference was that Mr Krushchev was sailing through the English Channel on his visit to the United States. There was an atmosphere of extreme lethargy and the pubs did not open until twelve. 'Well,' I said, 'have we sent him a message? He loves grabbing the headlines. Ask him if he wants to say anything to the British people.' To my great surprise, because my real purpose was to wake up the conference, he sent a long reply by Morse code thirty hours later, in time for Tuesday's paper. As if ship to shore telephones had not been invented, it was picked up by an astonished radio operator at Land's End. The Russian liner was only just within range, and the following day we interviewed the radio operator to drive home the chagrin of our rivals. On 14 December 1960, the *Daily Express* noted on page one that it had staff reporters covering stories for that issue in Suva, Dortmund, Paraguay, Beirut, New Delhi, Lagos, Nairobi, Aden, Cyprus and Sebring as well as staff men in permanent or temporary bureaux in Moscow, Paris, Bonn, New York, Washington and Havana. Harold Keeble had the idea in another issue of publishing a Photonews picture, taken by a freelance, of all 60 *Express* photographers. I was with Beaverbrook when he saw the page. 'Good God,' he said, as if we were all crazy. His joy was obvious.

William Rees-Mogg, then chief leader-writer of the *Financial Times*, gave the Cambridge Union his views on the press, as I was to do many years later. He said of the press lords: 'They seem to be a pretty innocent body of men these days. There's still Lord Beaverbrook. Long may he survive. A remarkable example of what press lords used to be like. But they don't come that way nowadays.' This was before Rupert Murdoch was allowed into Fleet Street by the owners of the *News of the World* in order to keep Robert Maxwell out. Rees-Mogg said of the *Express*: 'It revolutionised newspaper layout throughout the world. It is still most remarkably laid out. And pleasant and interesting to read.' And he praised its news service: 'I myself have to try and report occasions to which a team of *Daily Express* journalists have been sent.' Naturally, with this reference to Lord Beaverbrook, we published a report of Rees-Mogg's speech on page one. As long as he was given the credit, it would have been a dereliction of duty to have done otherwise. I probably thought at the time that Rees-Mogg was fishing for a job with us. He would have been a much better editor of the *Express* than many who later had the job.

On the *Evening Standard* and *Sunday Express*, it was possible to have a reasonable private life. For Pick and I, for at least five days a week, all our waking hours were devoted to the *Daily Express*. My eldest daughter, Helen, says she recalls me at that period as someone she occasionally saw cutting roses at our country vicarage. I had a flat, paid for by the company, in Clifford's Inn and, despite all rumours to the contrary, invariably spent the night alone in it. My day would begin at about 8.00 a.m. when with some care, since I was naked, I would open the flat door to retrieve the 'roll-up' newspapers that had been delivered by the circulation department. 'You must be very fond of reading them,' a stranger said to me on a train from Manchester as I went through a pile of national newspapers. 'Not necessarily,' I said. 'I get paid for this.' At the flat I would slit open the wrapper round the papers and strew them like a pack of cards on the floor so that I could see all the front pages at a glance. This was a precaution in case, as frequently happened, Beaverbrook would call me up. Sometimes he did this when I was asleep. I would know it would be him and what followed was like a speeded-up film sequence until I had spread out the papers and was ready to answer the phone. 'Anything in the other papers?' he would growl. I had already read the first editions at the office and after a swift glance at the front pages was able to give the impression that I was already well into my working day. An invitation to go for a walk or come to lunch usually followed. I breakfasted at a Lyons tea shop. Assuming the day's routine had not been disturbed by Beaverbrook, it was back to the flat for further intensive reading of the papers and I was in my office some time before 11.0 a.m.

Oddly, morning conference at the *Express* was not at a fixed time. The editor would tell his secretary. She would beat the jungle drums. Fifteen or more highly paid people would crowd into his office and, very frequently, no sooner had they arrived than Beaverbrook was on the telephone. Pick would indicate this with no more than a raised eyebrow and they would troop out again into the corridor. This sometimes happened two or three times at morning conference. It indicated very clearly who was in charge. Sometimes the call would be for me. My secretary would hand me a note, an unnecessary formality since no one else was allowed to interrupt conference. I would raise my eyebrow to the editor and go into my office next door. Ted Pickering must have found this irritating and embarrassing when it occurred several times during a conference. When I became editor I asked Beaverbrook to deal only with me about the conduct of the paper. Invariably the best performer at conference was Keith Howard, a superb news editor until the strain of the toughest job in the office became too much. His reading of the home news schedule had the comic quality of Hancock in his famous Half Hour. Some of his best stories never materialised into actual copy for the paper, but of all the entertainers I have known at newspaper conferences he was the greatest. 'All you seem to do in there is laugh,' said my secretary, Pamela Spooner, approvingly. The best newspaper offices are like that.

For some who attended it, the end of morning conference was the signal for the first drinks of the day. Although I am told Sir Alistair Burnet broke the rule some years later when, curiously, he moved from editing *The Economist* brilliantly to editing the *Daily Express* considerably less well, prohibition applied in the Express building, except in Bill Needham's office. He was the formidable, large and apparently upper-crust advertising director and was expected to drink with clients in the interests of revenue, a task he performed diligently. Burnet liked a Scotch or two while lesser colleagues with a similar need made for El Vino or Poppins, the pub next door to the *Express* where the news editor held court. The leader conference immediately followed morning conference. I was expected to attend as Beaverbrook's man. It was a dismal affair: four or five intelligent men trying to think of several subjects in pursuit of a policy that interested none of them, except the earnest Jimmy McMillan. The atmosphere when we discussed leaders on the *Sunday Express* was entirely different. John Junor seemed to dominate everything and we were scarcely conscious of Beaverbrook's influence. It was there, of course, but well hidden.

Every day was banquet day for many journalists in Fleet Street. In my years on the Express and Mirror groups I ate enough oysters and lobsters at Wheeler's in Old Compton Street to fill a skip with their shells, and never once saw a cockroach. I was introduced to Wheeler's by Nancy Spain, the lesbian journalist, who was much more fun than the homosexual Godfrey Winn, and died as sensationally as she had lived in a light aeroplane crash on her way to Goodwood. Wheeler's was one of the few good restaurants open on bank holidays. On those days it was almost entirely filled with journalists from the same and rival newspapers. There was a carnival atmosphere. Office drivers smiled cynically when they were told to be back at 2.45 p.m. They could safely go to their favourite canteen at what I assumed for some time was a cabbies' haunt in the Mall, visit the bookie's shop, return at 3.30 p.m. and still have to wait half an hour. 'The Mall', as drivers called it, turned out to be cockney pronunciation for the *Mail*. Associated Newspapers, owners of the *Daily Mail*, were reputed to have the best canteen and for a change of scene the *Daily Telegraph*'s was also highly rated. Anybody who had the nerve could eat at newspaper canteens except, of course, at Fortress Wapping, where Rupert Murdoch achieved a degree of management control without parallel.

I complained gently at the Savoy restaurant, with its pleasing views across trees to the Thames, about the invariable delay in getting the bill. 'You don't need to worry about that,' said the head waiter, 'just leave without signing.' This I did for years, enhancing my reputation with people who are impressed by such things. My liking for the Savoy remains undimmed. It is a pleasure to be greeted like an old friend by the man in charge of the loo, and I have noticed how quite grand if rather dim characters, who are probably non-executive directors of forty companies, enjoy the social cachet of being known by the person who hands them a towel, or apparently known as one attendant confided to me recently. The double is to hand an overcoat to the cloakroom attendant and not receive a ticket in return. This means you are recognised. I stayed at the Savoy on Friday and Saturday nights for years when I edited Sunday newspapers. Without any prompting from me, or a single word drawing my attention to its generosity, the hotel put me in ever larger suites for the price of a single room with bath on these evenings when business tended to be slack. Eventually the man in tails, solemnly carrying my small case, would escort me to quarters with a drawing-room, French clocks, and an enormous marble bathroom fit for an Arab oil sheik. They are good at PR at the Savoy. Before my second wife, Brigid, and I were married we went for dinner elsewhere and I persuaded her to stay the night with me at the hotel. For some reason she decided I was as false and faithless as the next man and to emphasise her view left the hotel in the early hours with my trousers. Such was my confidence in the Savoy, I felt this would present no problem. In the morning I would simply call up one of the men in tails, tell him of my need and he would produce a pair of trousers from somewhere as if it was an everyday occurrence. Regrettably, from the point of view of this story, the hotel was not put to the test. An hour or so later there was a gentle knock on the door. My partner had returned with my trousers and I was forgiven.

After what many would regard as the meal of a lifetime it was work in earnest at the *Express* with temperamental writers to calm down, endless copy to read, pages to plan, pictures to choose, people to interview and the great moving belt called a newspaper to be brought under some semblance of control, plus almost inevitably calls from Beaverbrook. At 9.30 p.m., or considerably earlier when the paper was big, it was desperation time if the last few paragraphs of the page one 'splash' and the final sports headlines were not on their way to the printer. Pick would have approved the page one make up and after a visit or two to Poppins gone for his supper. I would go down to the composing room, where Raybould, the number three and previously night editor, would be putting on a great show of activity in his shirt-sleeves. There would be arguments with Basil Denny and Willie Crumley, two 'prodnoses' in days when grammatical errors and compliance with the paper's style book still mattered in Fleet Street. The night lawyer would clash with at least one sub-editor. A careful ruling had to be given. It was usually arrived at by mutual agreement because sensible editors do not override the lawyer. Then I would go home for dinner, during the period when I lived in London, or when my home was in the country to another restaurant, usually the now defunct Versailles in Frith Street. This was packed at lunchtime, mostly with Tin Pan Alley expense account people like Johnny Johnson who composed famous jingles for TV commercials, and almost empty at night. Often the lonely figure of Billy Cotton, the bandleader, was at one end and I was by the window at the other with a telephone on the table to keep in touch with the office. He regularly ate 'bangers and mash', as in the song sung by Alan Breeze, whom he loathed. We became close friends.

I was back at the office in time to sneer at the rivals when they came in through the usual questionable channels, or to jerk the backbench, night news or foreign desks into action when the *Daily Mail* or *Daily Telegraph*, in particular, both of whose first editions were carefully monitored for Lord Beaverbrook, had a good exclusive or a story that our chief sub-editor or the copy-taker had annoyingly put on the spike, causing Pick and me a lot of trouble the next day when the Old Man complained. Suddenly the editor would materialise behind us. 'Oh, very good,' he would say, almost always. He was the most reassuring editor I have known, which I sometimes found irritating. Like Beaverbrook I was aware that the higher you are, the further you have to fall. Like Beaverbrook also, I was convinced that I should be editor. This is the view usually held by deputy editors, and was later the view of at least one of mine. Not many of them are like Beaverbrook's favourite politician, Bonar Law, who is mainly remembered for his loyalty to chiefs others wished him to replace. I once saw Pick design page one himself when a not very good sub-editor was handling the page. He did it with great professional ease and skill. It was a revelation to me that I was in severe danger of misjudging the man.

If there was a big story running at night the routine was entirely different. There was only time for a quick dash to the pub for sandwiches and a drink while waiting for copy and the latest pictures from the dark room. Excitement was high and, though we had been on duty for twice as long as most of the staff, Pick and I generally found it impossible simply to go home to bed when the plans for the main London edition had been completed shortly after midnight. 'Shall we go and have one at the Press Club?' were the fatal words. Raybould and Peter Johnson, the night editor, joined us after the edition had gone to press, plus sundry sub-editors and noted imbibers on the day staff who had been drinking in the local pub until well after the legal closing time. I do not recall ever seeing an editor of a rival paper in the Press Club at that hour. This was possibly because they did not have a proprietor like Lord Beaverbrook who expected them to be on duty at all hours, or possibly because the editors of the other papers had their own drinks cupboards. The same two or three depressing people were there almost every morning, including a sub-editor with a severe alcohol problem who a few hours later would by some miraculous process of recovery cobble together a front page for the first edition on his evening paper. Apparently asleep, he would sit alone on a tall stool for hours, his head between his hands, as ever more garrulously we rejoiced in the follies of our rivals and exchanged Fleet Street gossip. Early one morning our talk was interrupted when the sub-editor fell from his stool, crashing to the floor, we assumed in a stupor. To our surprise he stood up, a little unsteadily, and said, 'I am sorry. I must have dropped off.'

Our long suffering drivers would wait for us outside the Press Club in St Bride's Place if they did not like a drink, and inside if they did. The hours they worked were nearly as long as ours. Their tedium was relieved by their own company and the large sums they earned in overtime. These were pre-breathalyser days. Drivers who had similar thirsts to ours would stand in the passage to the Press Club bar where we would keep them well supplied with pints of bitter. There are legends about all editors. Driving me home to Hemel Hempstead well after dawn one morning, a driver called George told me about Ted Pickering. George had, for a fast driver, an interesting astigmatism. He also drank prodigious quantities of bitter. The conversation began when I confided to him, as we sped round a succession of roundabouts that led to the Watford by-pass, my belief that I was drunk. George fixed me with his good eye.

'Never, sir,' he said. 'Never.'

'Oh, yes, I am,' I replied. 'There are two certain signs. One is that it will soon be six o'clock. The second is that I know that when I get home I will cut you some roses.'

'Never seen you drunk,' George insisted. 'Like Mr Pickering. Never seen him drunk neither. I remember once . . . he had had such a busy day, in a manner of speaking as you will understand. At dinner time (he meant lunch) I took him to the Boulestin and he had someone important with him and they talked a long time, till nearly half-past three. In the evening he spent a long time talking with Mr Howard in Poppins, about something important I have no doubt, and then later than he had said, he went to a restaurant and when we got back to the office he said, "I won't be long George," and sure enough he was down before long and said he was just going across to the Press Club for a few minutes because he had to talk to someone. Well, after the usual time I went across and he was having this important discussion and I had several pints of bitter as you will understand. It was a horrible, foggy night and as I was driving him home to Haslemere he fell asleep, being very tired, and he fell across me a couple of times. Well, I was bursting, if you will forgive the expression, and the fog was terrible, but I knew a lay-by on top of the Hog's Back. So I stopped there, leaving the engine running so I wouldn't wake up Mr Pickering, and when I came back to the car he was gone. "Mr Pickering!" I shouted, just to make sure he was all right. Then I heard his voice through the fog. "Good night, George," he cried from quite a distance. "Come back, Mr Pickering," I shouted. "You ain't home yet."'

Newspaper life is great fun. I made tea for George, as usual, and cut him some roses.

II
'STUDY MY ANSWERS
PLEASE.'

Mr Edwards.—

Study my
answer please.

O happy is the
man who hears
instructions
voice

As I charted my way through the perilous waters of Beaverbrook Newspapers the Great Barrier Reef, as far as I was concerned, was Beaverbrook's son and chairman of the board Max Aitken, DFC. He and I could not hit it off, though I got on well with his co-chairman Tom Blackburn. When I finally departed in 1965 a year after his father's death, we both felt that we were well rid of each other. Max was a conventional Tory and he viewed my employment as a former editor of *Tribune* with the same hostility shown to the *Socialist Worker* editor, Paul Foot, when he was appointed to write a column in the *Daily Mirror* many years later. I thought it was wrong that someone lacking in either business or editorial flair should be in charge of such a great company simply because he was his father's son. The loser was bound to be me, but there were far deeper reasons than these superficial ones for our mutual hostility.

Some years after I left the company and was editing the *Sunday Mirror* Hugh Cudlipp invited me to spend the day with him and his wife Jodi on his yacht on the Hamble. 'I had a call on the ship-to-shore phone from an old friend of yours,' he said when I arrived. He explained that Max had telephoned from his home at Cowes asking him and Jodi to lunch. Because he had said I was coming down I had been invited too. With Willie Soutar, the *Daily Mirror*'s art editor, in charge of navigation we sailed across the Solent to Max's impressive private mooring. He was surrounded by his usual large male friends like Captain Johnny Coote in blazers, and one or two pretty girls. His male servant known as the bos'n distributed drinks and sausages at a fast pace. Eventually Max turned to me and said loudly so that everyone could hear, 'The trouble between us, Bob, was my father. From now on you call me Max and we are friends for life.' He kissed me on both cheeks and then he added an even more surprising P.S., 'Why don't you come back and work for me? What would you like, the *Sunday Express*?' Even without the P.S., I would have liked him for his remarkable gesture. The *Sunday Express* offer seemed an unlikely one. John Junor might have objected. I assumed he was being difficult at the time. The last occasion I met Max was at the dinner Lord Matthews gave John on his twenty-fifth year as editor. Max had had two bad strokes and was sitting in a wheelchair at a table by the door. JJ had put me, one of the few editors to be invited, in a place of honour. After dinner Max's secretary and good friend Anne Westover came across and asked me to say hello to him. 'He won't be able to say a word,' she said, 'but he would love you to do that.' So the two unequally matched sparring partners met again. 'Hello, Max,' I said. 'Hello, Bob,' he replied, to the stunned surprise of everyone at his table.

It was something of a tragedy for me that we made it up too late. It was also a tragedy for Ted Pickering that while he was much liked by Max he did not get on as well with Beaverbrook as I did. Arthur Christiansen rapidly succeeded Beverley Baxter as editor of the *Daily Express* in 1933 when the circulation for the last six months of the year was 1,884,666. By 1950, with Beaverbrook's hand firmly over his on the tiller, he had taken it to 4,220,592, without a single tit or bum picture or any kind of salacity. The paper had reached the remarkable figure of 4 million in 1949 and remained above it for the rest of his editorship. It was selling 4,111,000 copies a day when Ted Pickering took over in 1957 and after a slightly unnerving fall in 1958 rose to a record 4,313,063 in the first half of 1961. This was, to Fleet Street's astonishment, the moment Beaverbrook chose to enforce his will and put me in charge of the paper. As a concession to Max, I was given the curious title of acting editor, as was my successor Roger Wood, in his case as a concession to Lord Beaver-brook. He was Max's choice. Roger said, 'There is no such animal. I am the editor in law and in fact.' Pick was put in charge of the *Farming Express* and other curious projects and was soon rescued by Hugh Cudlipp to pursue his distinguished career first as editorial director then chairman of the Mirror Group. He later became executive vice-chairman of Times Newspapers Ltd and one of Rupert Murdoch's most trusted colleagues. When Sir Alex Jarratt, chairman of Reed International which then owned the Mirror Group, was asking editors who should succeed Pick on his retirement, I said I hoped he would be suitably honoured. 'Yes, I must do something about that,' said Alex, as much an Estab-lishment figure as Bob Maxwell is not. I felt I owed Pick that suggestion at least. Whether it had anything to do with his sub-sequent knighthood I have no idea.

In my first six months in charge of the *Daily Express* in 1961 the sales reached an even higher record figure of 4,328,524, despite a price increase from 2½d. to 3d. But these were dangerous days indeed, both for me and some members of the staff. Beaverbrook had perfected a system of monitoring the *Daily Express* first editions against the rivals'. It was one paper against all the rest, a huge disadvantage, and he became convinced that we were missing too many stories and heads should roll. 'Are you in favour of a reign of terror?' he shouted over the telephone. 'Answer!' I should have realised that this was par for the course for the editor of the *Daily Express*. I began to appreciate what Pick must have been through, though he never complained to me, and why Christiansen so wryly echoed my word 'fun' about being editor of the *Express*. Beaver-brook's way with the chief of his flagship was to harass and harass. It began in 1917 with his first letter of criticism to R. D. Blumenfeld, as recorded in A. J. P. Taylor's masterly work *Beaverbrook*:

My dear Blum,

I have had time this morning to make a critical examination of the Daily Express and I'm sure you won't mind my giving you the results of it.

The Smaller Advts are either being eliminated or are not coming in in a satisfactory way. This requires treatment. The Theatre Advts don't pay well enough to be put on the Leader page and should go on the back page.

It is not good business to attack Lord Rothermere even by implication. We are in the middle of complex paper deals with him, and he has always been generous in these matters.

On the front page there are frequently important news items from the night before. Surely there ought to be enough completely fresh matter for that page.

I notice this morning that we missed the Boom Towers claim. There ought to be a man put on to read the other papers and check anyone responsible for missing these things on The Express.

The By-the-Way column is worse than that of The Daily News or The Star.

As to the Editorials they are a strange mixture of good and bad. I attribute this to their being written by one hand and then altered by other. I sometimes notice a lack of consistency between the various parts. There is also on Wednesday a flat contradiction between the leader and the Parliamentary Correspondent: the former advising L-G to follow Borden and go for an election while the Correspondent pours cold water on the whole idea.

An arrangement cannot be a good one, if it produces these contradictions. I am entirely in favour of short leaders written in a simple and direct style, but it seems to me that the Editor ought to have someone competent to write these on his own without any help from the Editor, and if he has not such a man he ought to find him. Wilson, Dach, & Farthing are all men of first class capacity, and I believe that if they are given real responsibility they will deliver the goods.

But I gathered from a telephone conversation I had with Wilson the other night that when you are in retreat at Dunmow everything has to be telephoned through to you. My own view is that working at the pressure you do, you ought to have 2 or 3 nights off, but on those occasions the man on the spot ought to be in charge. If we haven't got men we can trust to do this – which I believe we have – we must get new ones. Please don't trouble to answer this letter which merely consists of suggestions I hope you may find useful.

At least, as Alan Taylor says later in his book, Blumenfeld had the guts to tell his tormentor to go to hell. Or, as Beaverbrook put it to me, he was 'sensitive' and therefore a difficult man to criticise. But although he was unquestionably the greatest editor in the paper's history Christiansen took everything that was thrown at him, and also took care to have no political opinions of his own. In his autobiography *Headlines All My Life*, he tells the unintentionally revealing story of how he was shocked when he saw that Chamberlain had described Czechoslovakia as a 'far away country about which we know little.' He imagined that Beaverbrook would be shocked too, and rang to tell him. 'Well, it is, isn't it?' was Beaverbrook's predictable response. Christiansen ends this story by saying he realised Beaverbrook was right and 'got on with my proper job of editing the paper.' In fact his job as a proper newspaper editor should have been to attack Chamberlain's infamous remark. He showed his political naivety in believing Beaverbrook would be shocked, and his true role by meekly giving in. He set the pace for future editors. They were there to be bullied and I was no exception.

Here are some examples of memos from Beaverbrook, exactly as I received them, misspellings and obscurities included:

Here, Mr. Edwards, is a cutting which I wish to bring to your attention. It is the quotation from the D. Mail, it is in quotation marks therefore it must have been in the hand-out that was given by the Common Market people in Brussels. I want to know once more why you didn't have it. I have had your explanation that the DX story is a better one that the D. Mail, but my patience is somewhat exhausted by that statement. Now I am asking that we should seriously discuss the effects of the DX and not find excuses for, and not find any more excuses for the deficiences of our paper which are serious.

Mr. Edwards, you have failed to let me know about Peter Chambers, Peter Chambers did not appear in the paper again on Saturday, but no message from you about it, and yet I am doing my best to sustain an interest in the boy and in you.

I wish to make it clear to you Mr. Edwards, that the DX no longer engages in supression.

I have notified Mr. Blackburn to that effect. I now tell you and everybody else who can possibly be responsible for supression in the future, attempts at supression, for there won't be any real supression.

Mr. Edwards, what about our second man in the City. We would look after him and bring him along, nothing, nothing, nothing, ever heard about it since. When do you let me know.

Mr. Edwards – Mr. Colin Clark spoke to members of the Farmers Club in London on the 10th Jan. He made some extraordinary statements about the changes that would take place in farming in the event that the Common Market came into force ... that farmers should be compensated.

Why didn't you have this in your paper?

Mr. Edwards. Did you have the story on the 11th of the nuclear-disarmament candidate against Desmond Donnelly. If not, why? And didn't the DExp have the Keep Britain Great story on Tuesday, in Tuesday's issue, or Monday's issue rather. If not, why not.

The statement that Mr. Spaak warns Britain, "New Members must accept not only economic dispositions of the European Community, they must also subscribe to its political ideal." Will you tell me why you did not have that statement in your story.

Answer, Mr. Edwards, at once, by letter.

I am not very good at picking out stories, but as I read it seems to me that the story in the D. Mail, B.B.C. on page 3, B.B.C. runs into trouble, is not in the DX. Answer please.

On page 5, extracts from the paper called Which about car testing, car testers, I can't see that story in the DX. Possibly I am short sighted. Answer, Mr. Edwards.

See the story about the Co-operative society selling Danish butter. Did the express print it, if not, why not. Directed to Mr. Edwards.

Is Sir Roy Harrod against the Common Market, Mr. Edwards, if so why isn't he on you list of possible contributors to your newspaper. Answer.

Mr. Edwards I was talking with Somerset Maugham who was discussing newspapers with extraordinary vigour and also much perception. He said all articles in the DX are too long. He said each feature should be not more than one column in length. You might let me know what you have got to say to that.

So many of these missives arrived in the office, my personal assistant Peter Drake spent much of his day getting answers to them. Eventually, with Max Aitken's over-eager consent, I decided to turn the tables on Beaverbrook by checking on the first editions of our rivals versus all the rest as he did against us. As I expected, the *Daily Express* came out of this much fairer comparison best of all. I sent a vast pile of cuttings to Cherkley to uphold this triumphant finding. They were returned next day with a handwritten note from Beaverbrook: 'Not interested in other papers. Only the *Daily Express*.' On another occasion, I wrote: 'With respect, I find that it is not a good policy to inquire into all the stories we have not carried. I try to pick those I think are important. Otherwise, too much of the day is spent on inquests and not enough on the next day's news. Also, I find that inquests on stories that are relatively trivial undermine the value of inquests in general.' Beaverbrook did not believe that anything that interested him was the least bit trivial. He would not have liked the note, but I found that by answering back once in a while the flow of memos was notably reduced.

Some of his memos were pure pique. He was jealous of anyone

other than himself getting credit for the success of the *Express*. Sefton Delmer, who had for years been the paper's distinguished chief European correspondent, was the subject of a 'This Is Your Life' programme. It was a tremendous plug not only for him and his famous scoops but for the paper as well, but I shrewdly cleared it with Max Aitken before giving a good show to our report of the programme. Sure enough, Beaverbrook complained: 'I may have asked you before Mr Edwards – if not I will ask you again, why did you print the Sefton Delmer story at such length in William Hickey?' I replied: 'Sefton Delmer's appearance on "This Is Your Life" was extremely successful. It obviously made a big impression on the public and it was one of the best programmes in the entire series. It seemed to me a good piece of propaganda for the *Daily Express* to publish a generous extract from this programme about a man who had produced so many *Daily Express* scoops. I consulted about this, and my view was shared.' Sefton Delmer, like Morley Richards the former news editor, was one of the people legend has it I sacked at that period. In fact I declined in both cases, on the grounds that they had served the paper too well for such a fate and they were sacked by Max Aitken and Tom Blackburn. However, many of Beaverbrook's complaints were thoroughly justified if dispiriting, and his suggestions often reflected great journalistic flair. Here is the note, referred to elsewhere, in which among other things he argued the case for putting all the critics on one page:

> The Daily Express needs a constant brake on its display, especially on inside pages. In the Daily Express the type which used to be reserved for one page now dominates several news pages in the paper.

> I have been reading your New York column. I did not read in the Daily Express that when Joan Sutherland hit that high E-flat in New York there was a roar from the audience which went on for five minutes. Nor did I read that after order had been restored and she had finished the scene, there was another roar that lasted for twelve minutes. Is this not the news whether you are interested in music or not? As it so happens, Joan Sutherland is Australian, not USA.

> Arising out of this, I feel that the Daily Express is losing its importance as the West End Show business paper – due not so much to the fact that the Critics are not of high quality, but to the fact that first nights and other show business news is scattered indiscriminately all over the paper. The Daily Mail has copied the Express by devoting page Three every day to Show Business. Maybe Hickey is in its right place on page Three, but could not a regular place be found in the Daily Express to which interested readers could turn automatically.

I have always been a strong believer that the public is habitual and needs the same news in the same place day after day. The great trick is surely to make the news look different by good headline writing and ingenious display.

The Daily Mail has a distinct drag on the Daily Express in relation to financial news. I suggested to Max some time ago that financial news should be transferred to a righthand page at the back of the paper so that it would not be at the mercy of the amount of vital sports coverage each day. This problem has existed for years. Needham opposes the transfer of financial news to a page on which general advertising has to be sold. Could not prestige advertising for motorcars be sold against financial news attractively presented?

Two other examples of the constructive approach:

Mr. Edwards. It would have been better in the leader column if you had said Mr. and Mrs. Bygraves and not Max and Blossom Bygraves. You must maintain dignity of your leader column. Don't feel hurt if I give you too many criticisms – if you think I give you too many criticisms.

I hate to see the picture of the new Mr. Sagan on page 9 of the Daily Express. My view of that all is to hell with Mr. Sagan. We have no interest in her at all here.

When Wall Street goes up in a big way, put a note on the front page. When Wall Street goes down in a big way, put a note on the front page.

Sometimes his letters were kindly in tone. This one contained in the third paragraph sound advice that should have applied to Delmer and Richards, and which I never forgot:

From Lord Beaverbrook

September 21, 1961

Dear Bob,

Very many thanks for your letter.

It is well to be firm, but at the same time to give leadership, thus instilling confidence to your staff.

Our journalists should not assume that their positions are secure irrespective of their manner of performing their services. But those who do well should be quite certain that their employment is permanent, and their places in the organization are fixed and even engraved in marble.

I am glad that you got Kretzmer. His article on Lord Russell was excellent.

Let me know when you attain happiness with your women's features.

I do not know quite how to go about the Keith Howard position. If you would write me some particular event where he shows judgment and energy, then I could send him a letter.

Don't fail to keep me informed. Do not leave me in ignorance.

Tell me your troubles as well as your triumphs.

And sometimes I won hands down, as in this exchange of notes:

Beaverbrook to Editor:

Mr. Edwards, it took five or ten minutes to get through to you today. I am wondering why there should be such a long delay. It seems to me that your telephone should be, you should be easy to get through, I think it is essential that you should have telecommunications available all the time. Just let me know about it please. You must be subject to many calls during the day, so I suppose you tell the telephone operator where to find you.

Editor to Beaverbrook:

I am sorry you had difficulty in getting through to me immediately. I have always found it a good policy to spend some time each day in the various departments stirring things up, and giving advice and judgment. It often works better than getting the executives to come and see me.

Usually my secretary can find me in a moment, but there is bound to be a slight delay sometimes if I am not to stay in my own office all the time. It should certainly never take 5 minutes. On this occasion my secretary failed to find me as quickly as usual. I will make a point in future of telling her exactly where I am.

Whenever I am out of the office, the telephone exchange always know where to find me.

Beaverbrook to Editor:

Dear Bob,

Do not change your habits on my account.

The more time you spend with your various departments, the better I will like it.

It is only by personal touch with your group that you can build up a well staffed office.

Yours sincerely,

Looking at them all again today, I wonder how I managed to put up with the tone of most of the memos in my first period as editor of the *Express*. It was a baptism of fire not helped by Max's jealousy over the special position I had held with his father. He also stoked the furnace, as this note from Lord Beaverbrook demonstrates:

> Mr. Edwards, I have seen a note from you really intended for Max Aitken addressed to me about the Mavrolian divorce case which evidently you did not carry in the first edition, and you give the reason you didn't carry it because it had been run in the evening papers. But, Mr. Edwards, the evening papers do not circulate to our first edition public. Our first edition paper is in many respects an evening paper, should be covering the evening paper news. I hope you will take that into account and see that in future that you carry divorce cases in the first edition even if you leave them out in later editions, even if you throw them out in the London edition.

> Max Aitken points out there is no possible justification for putting it in the last edition if you fail to put it in the first and he says you were really edited in this case by the Daily Mail, will you answer that point.

It was a no win situation with the *Daily Mail*. There was trouble if they had a story and we did not, and trouble when we picked it up from them because that was being 'edited by the *Mail*', a favourite expression. Ironically, many of the stories we did pick up we would not have bothered about but for the constant inquests. If anyone was edited by the *Mail*, Beaverbrook was, never mind that compared to our 4,300,000 sales the *Mail*'s were only 2,600,000, with 600,000 of that from the recently absorbed *News Chronicle*. He needed a stick to beat over the editor's head, as he had been accustomed to with Christiansen, and what better for that purpose than the traditional rival? In fact, it was a good paper at the time as now, well edited by William Hardcastle who became the famous 'World at One' pre-senter on BBC radio. He only lasted three years. In response to Beaverbrook's cries for a reign of terror against complacency, I sacked two or three people. They became a legion in Fleet Street mythology.

A quarter of a century later one of them saw my name in the visitors' book at the Red Lion, Steeple Aston. 'Please can I have my job back?' he wrote beside it. At a farewell party for Arthur Christiansen, Beaverbrook said, 'Hands up those who were sacked by Chris?' A surprising number were raised. The policy I adopted was that if someone was young and did not fit in he should, after all efforts with him had failed, make way for someone who did. Several of Fleet Street's best journalists today were taken on by me. One

Express feature writer specialised in writing about problem people. He was a problem himself, and frequently got away with nothing either in the paper or on paper for weeks on end. In desperation I summoned Clive Irving, the features editor. 'Look, Clive,' I said, 'I know you will think it cruel and ruthless but if he doesn't produce something soon I am going to sack him. It's up to you.' Clive, like his predecessors, failed to such a degree that I suspected our offending colleague had other interests. I called him in. He sat in 'the disloyal deputy's chair', stared earnestly at me and said, 'Bob, I know exactly what you are going to say, and you would be right to say it. But I beg you not to. I implore you.' I gave way. He survived several editors after me until at last there was one who did not succumb to his charms.

The pressures grew even stronger. It was understandable that some of the old gang resented my attempts to tighten up the paper after Pickering's successful but easy-going régime. It was understandable if Max passed on his doubts and fears whenever he had the right opening. I should have seen what was happening when Beaverbrook began to play my deputy Roger Wood off against me as he had tried to play me off against Pick, and to some degree Max. This is well illustrated in a memo he sent me about the leader page he loathed of 23 December 1961, which contained not only the article Peter Forster wrote on Scrooge, that I have mentioned earlier, but two other articles by Peter Chambers and Shirley Lowe, both talented writers:

Mr Edwards, you say in a memo to me dated 28th that in the Manchester office there are too many old hands. I am asking you and I am asking Mr. Wood here, what are you going to do about that.

Mr. Edwards, I am talking here with Mr. Wood, and I am complaining very seriously to him, very seriously indeed about the leader page of Saturday, December 23rd. I hope you will hear the serious notes in my voice because it is a matter of some importance to me that the leader page should now be put right. I have gone on long enough urging the action, now action must be taken. If it is not taken I will have to intervene.

A bad article by Peter Chambers should not be printed. The article on December 23rd is a bad article.

But my principal complaint is against an article by Shirley Lowe. I am not satisfied to be told that Shirley Lowe is now departed. That doesn't make any difference to me. What makes a difference to me is that the control of the paper is such that a bad article can find a place in what ought to be a good page. I hope now you will recognise the seriousness of my complaint. I hope you recognise that I am determined that this page should be put right. And if that page is not put right, I tell you I will have to intervene.

That I have told Mr. Wood also.

Mr. Edwards, I forgot to ask you, did you read the Shirley Lowe story before it went in the paper.

It is deeply wounding and full of menace for an editor when his deputy is asked to visit the proprietor and be told the paper's failings. I should have replied: 'You try and produce a good issue on December 23rd when half the staff is blind drunk.' Instead I did my best to protect the features editor, whom I carefully did not name:

I agree with your criticism of Shirley Lowe's article in the issue of December 23. I disagree with your opinion of Peter Chambers' article, which I thought was good.

As I have explained, I rejected an article by Nancy Banks-Smith and this was the only suitable alternative the features department could offer me on the eve of Christmas. I told them it would need a lot of work to get it ready and then I left, before the edition, not having seen the finished article, in order to be able to leave early next morning to visit you at Nice.

I would never have approved such an article if I had seen it in its finished form.

The features editor is full of chagrin that we should have published such a bad article at the end of a week in which he did quite exceptionally well.

He is seeking to improve the leader page along the lines of our discussion.

Early in February, I was paying my first visit to the office of the *Scottish Daily Express* in Glasgow. A marvellous lunch had been laid on for me to meet the staff. We arrived back rather late in the afternoon and very happy. 'There's a call from your secretary,' I was told. When I called her back, she said: 'Mr Aitken says would you please be in his office at ten o'clock tomorrow morning.' 'Whatever for?' I exclaimed. And then it dawned on me. 'Good heavens, sweetheart,' I said. 'They are going to sack me.' 'Surely not,' replied

Dorothy Shaw, the highly professional secretary I had inherited from Ted Pickering.

Max was with Tom Blackburn when I arrived on time. Obviously Tom was there as a witness. Max told me they had decided to appoint another editor. 'Who?' I asked. 'Roger,' said Max. He said I would be welcome to stay on as deputy editor of the *Evening Standard*. I said I preferred to go. At this, to my surprise, tears came into his eyes. 'I'm the one who should be weeping,' I said. 'I can see why you asked me in at ten in the morning. So that you could wipe the blood off the walls and have me out of the office before my friends come in.' I left to go home to my wife and returned to pick up my documents from the front hall. With them was a letter from the new editor Roger Wood. It said simply:

> Dear Bob,
>
> > What did you do? I need to know.
>
> > > Yours ever,
>
> > > > Roger

The departure of the editor of the *Daily Express* was news in those days. Mine led the news bulletins and caused much comment. Almost all the journalists of importance on the paper wrote to me expressing their regrets. This astounded Beaverbrook when I mentioned it to him later. 'I was told a lot of them were against you,' he said. 'Please show them to me.' This I did. One in the eye for Max, I thought. Just why I was fired I did not understand. They always say that editors are the last to know. Possibly Beaverbrook's faith in me had been skilfully undermined. Possibly he thought that after a period on the *Evening Standard* as number two I would be more compliant, although I felt he had no justified complaints on that score.

A few weeks after I had cleared out of the office as fast as a Director General of the BBC, he rang me at home. I was sitting in the rose garden, the telephone beside me on a long extension. 'How are you?' he said. 'Roger tells me you're going to do nothing for a year. That's bad for you, bad for you.' I put my hand over the mouthpiece and said grinning to Laura, 'The bastard's ticking me off and I'm not even working for him.' On an inspiration I wrote to him that night saying that when I left the *Express* there was a vacancy for the editorship of the *Evening Citizen* in Glasgow, and volunteered for the job, 'if no one else has been appointed', I was careful to add.

Next day I was having lunch with Woodrow Wyatt, a foul-weather friend, at the Caprice. To my astonishment, Lord Beaverbrook's butler, Mead, came to the table before Woodrow had arrived. 'The Lord sends you his compliments,' said Mead, 'and would be glad if you would join him either before or after your lunch.' Beaverbrook had discovered where I was from my wife. With commendable cool, and with due respect to Woodrow, I said I would see him afterwards. The Caprice is on the ground floor of Arlington House where Lord Beaverbrook lived. The lunch went on a long time. We met Beaverbrook in the entrance hall as we left. He turned round, took me back with him to his flat and to Fleet Street's surprise I became editor of the Scottish evening paper. 'You've heard a lot of things about me,' I told the assembled tough but fearful staff. 'Believe only the nice things. We will have a great time.' We did, I believe. It was my third editorship. Just over a year later the familiar voice was on the phone. 'Why didn't you tell me what would happen if you were no longer editor of the *Express*?' he said. 'You must come back. Don't tell a soul.'

12

LEAGUE
OF FRIENDS

The job of a Fleet Street newspaper editor must be a far riskier occupation even than that of a football manager, a comparison which is often made. So many of us have been fired, we really ought to form an association. Sir Edward Pickering, who was pushed aside by Beaverbrook to make way for me, should be president. He is the grandest of us all and goes on for ever. As an executive vice-chairman of *The Times* at the age of seventy-five and chairman and governing member of many other bodies he could easily take the presidency of such a convivial if a trifle unmanageable group in his stride. Pick could be depended upon to preside or be present at the more important social and Establishment occasions in Fleet Street, before it was destroyed by the madness of the union chapels and the brilliance of Murdoch's move to Fortress Wapping. When Tony Miles, our genial pre-Maxwell, pre-Thornton chairman and I were about to attend such gatherings we invariably (as we refreshed ourselves liberally beforehand, possibly in the company of two or three other like minds) speculated on whether he would be present. He invariably was, even to the extent of emerging as some kind of church grandee in a gown at memorial services for beloved (or otherwise regarded) colleagues.

Harold Evans would be a leading member. He was the cleverest, though not the wisest, of us all. He transformed the *Sunday Times* from a sedate, respected journal of the upper classes into possibly the most vigorous, brilliant newspaper in the world. Such is the paranoia from which most editors understandably suffer, he believed (so I suspect) that Murdoch promoted him to the editorship of *The Times* as a plot to get rid of him. I do not share that belief. Even such a skilled wheeler-dealer as Murdoch does not give the most treasured gift (still) in British journalism to someone for such a fiendish purpose. Harold Evans proved that a genius in journalism does not necessarily have the powers of delegation and leadership to run a national daily. Why his fellow cockney Lord Matthews ('the builder') should have appointed Derek Jameson as editor of the *Daily Express* is more of a mystery. I suspect, heaven preserve me, that he is a better radio and TV presenter and newspaper columnist than he is an editor, which in reality is quite a hard, slogging job out of the limelight if it is done properly. He surprised everybody by not making much of his previous newspaper editorship of the *News of the World*, from which he got the chop, but possibly the N.O.W. (as Fleet Street called it) requires an even more gentlemanly editor than the *Daily Express* to complete the comedy. The celebrated, egotistical Stafford Somerfield was the prototype. A big shot among those who practise country pursuits, he currently writes a column in the *Dog World*. As one would expect of someone who for ten years edited Britain's principal publish and be damned newspaper, it has a lot of bite. 'Staff' ('a' as in WAAF) gave the strong impression as an editor that he did not give a toss for anyone except his bibacious proprietor Sir William ('Pissy Billy') Carr.

That, I suspect, is the proper attitude for an editor to take, a virtue that eluded me. I felt sorry for John Profumo and at the height of the scandal when he had been forced to resign declined to publish a picture of him in the William Hickey column dressed as a Roman General at a fancy dress party. Valerie Profumo personally appealed to me not to use it. She said it had been taken long before at a private party and was a present from her to him. Peter Baker, my disloyal deputy, sneaked to Beaverbrook that I had let the side down, but I heard no more from the Old Man after I explained that apart from moral considerations and responding decently to the heroine of the hour there was a question of copyright. I felt sorry for Jeremy Thorpe and handed him the lethal correspondence with Norman Scott, discovered by three building workers, also on convenient legal grounds. And I was wrong, very wrong, about that.

When Staff could not get along with Murdoch, he ended a memorable TV news interview by turning away from the camera and saying, 'Did someone mention a drink?' Derek Jameson did his best job as editor-in-chief of the *Daily Star*, a paper he and the eccentric editor (my former chief sub-editor on the *Sunday Mirror*) Peter Grimsditch created at the very bottom end of the market. All would qualify to join the association I have suggested, along with many others and half a dozen or so ex-editors of the *Daily Express*, none of whom have my distinction of having been editor twice. My fellow CBE John Thompson and William ('Bill') now Lord Deedes may not seem to be eligible since they left the editorship of the *Sunday* and *Daily Telegraph* respectively by 'mutual consent' after the Canadian financier Conrad Black moved in his millions to take over the papers, but those who think they are in the know would not quibble. Was John Junor finally eased out of the editorship of the *Sunday Express* by another financier turned press baron David Stevens? Unthinkable.

When I returned to edit the *Daily Express* again, all went very well for a few weeks. On one day Beaverbrook sent me examples of replies to his notes to demonstrate the dreadful decline of the paper (which I must say was not obvious to me) during my exile in Glasgow, the Gorky of Fleet Street:

From Lord Beaverbrook   7th March 1963
To Robert Edwards

I send you these two notes. They are for your information and then destroy them. Don't return them to me.

From Lord Beaverbrook   7th March 1963
To Robert Edwards

If you will read my numerous complaints (attached) and the futile answers I was given, you will see what is wrong with the Daily Express – and it is a good bit.

Apart from the treacherous but otherwise not unpleasing Peter Baker, I had no enemies on the paper. All those who so kindly wrote expressing shock, amazement and support when I was fired a year earlier must have been glad they did so, and such was my warmth towards them I returned in the role of Mr Chips rather than the hard man and sacker of the innocent I was reputed to be. It was correctly rumoured that my pay-off had been £10,000 and when a further rumour suggested that I might return and oust my successor Roger Wood, some office wit said, 'Bob Edwards has been seen in York with ten thousand men.' Such was Fleet Street, this not bad joke immediately circulated in every hostelry. Beaverbrook's relationship with me at first was mellow, but as all previous editors had found – Blumenfeld, Baxter, Christiansen and Pickering – it was not to last. On the day Beaverbrook had sent me the notes demonstrating the infamies of the previous regime, Godfrey Winn had complained to him that I had turned down one of his articles. Beaverbrook asked me to send it to him and later said he could find nothing wrong with it. His judgment was muddied by the homosexual writer's blazingly insincere, breathless flattery. ('You are the great Teacher, I am the humble pupil at your feet'. I have yet to encounter a proprietor who does not wilt before such onslaughts.) The article described the ordeal Winn had suffered being on a convalescent holiday in Barbados, the ordeal being there at all when he would have preferred to be among *Daily Express* readers in Britain despite an Arctic spell:

> How glad I am to be back in England. Yes, and the spring so far away, and my pipes frozen like yours. And no hot water for a bath. And my writing room, after the tropical heat I have been savouring, like an icy morgue. But how glad. How very glad.

He described what anyone else would regard as the lyrical joys of his holiday, which naturally included being shown round 'the superbly colourful gardens' at Government House by the Governor's wife, and at tedious length recalled a conversation with a lady with a naval crown in the brooch of her dress, at a party on a moonlit patio, about the joys of English rain. 'My heart missed a beat. It wasn't the strain of the heat, it was the stabbing, joyful realisation that this time tomorrow, I would be . . . home. My sense of excitement mounted the moment I got on board the BOAC Boeing.' To the experienced eye, this meant that BOAC had picked up the tab for the trip. I wrote briefly to Beaverbrook to explain why I had rejected the article:

> I think this is a bad article by Godfrey Winn. I do not see how any Editor could defend printing if he was asked. The idea that Godfrey Winn was secretly suffering while living in splendour in a sunny clime would produce ribaldry among too many of our readers.

Like Hannen Swaffer, Godfrey Winn always succeeded in writing about himself, no matter how cataclysmic or magnificent the event he was supposed to be reporting. In 1961, 34 English schoolboys and two masters were killed on a flight to Stavanger. Winn was given the task of visiting one of the families, and succeeded in using this as a cue to describe how his life was 'saved' in the war by a Coastal Command pilot who fought off an attack by three Messerschmitt 109s on the Hudson in which Winn was flying for a single trip as a reporter. Anyone not impressed by Winn's gushing prose would have recognised instantly that his purpose was to demonstrate not the pilot's bravery but his own in going on such a mission. The intelligent reader would also have guessed in the same instant that the pilot's primary concern was to save his own life. This article remained etched in my mind as an example of tasteless cant typical of a small group of undeclared gays much sought after, strictly professionally, by the proprietors of national papers and the editors of women's magazines for three decades.

The news desk, from the news editor to the lowliest reporter, loathed it when Godfrey Winn was sent on a big story. On one occasion John Christopher, an excellent *Daily Express* staff man stationed in South Wales, had worked almost round the clock for 72 hours covering a mining disaster. Eventually the story was beginning to pall, so I agreed to solve the usual leader page problem by sending Godfrey Winn to write one of his cloying colour pieces. He asked me if he could be met at Swansea railway station by a reporter, which displeased the news desk greatly. As always, however, they agreed, and Christopher was given the task. Unfortunately, Godfrey caught the wrong train, an earlier one, and when the reporter finally arrived in time for the correct train raged at him in a flood of camp fury, not failing to mention his years of service for Lord Beaverbrook and their warm friendship. 'And Winn was totally in the wrong?' I said to Keith Howard, the news editor. 'Totally,' said Keith. 'Well,' I said, 'Christopher should have told him to fuck himself.' 'That's the whole point,' said Howard, 'he did. He dismembered him on Swansea railway station. He did such a good job, he felt you should be told because Godfrey Winn is bound to complain if not to you, to the Old Man.' Howard passed on Christopher's apologies for any trouble he might have caused me. My warmth for our man in South Wales from this incident onwards was enormous. A glow went through me recently when I read that he had retired.

Godfrey Winn spent 24 hours, escorted by Christopher, covering the aftermath of the tragedy. Instead of complaining, he sent me a letter of praise and appreciation for the reporter's help. 'Just shows,' said Keith Howard when I handed it to him over my desk, 'if you stand up to him, he caves in. Obviously he wants Christopher to keep quiet about what he said.' I had another explanation. 'Perhaps he's fallen in love with Christopher.' The thought of Christopher resisting Winn's advances was as good an excuse as any for a quick trip to Poppins for the first drink of the day. Godfrey Winn's article on the Stavanger air disaster ended: 'I had gone to try to comfort them and instead the whole family had given me a new standard of courage to live by.' A writer sent on such a distinctly yellow assignment who claims his motive is 'to try to comfort' the grieving family transforms the ruthless reporter played by Kirk Douglas in 'Ace in

the Hole' into a paragon of virtue. Shortly after explaining to
Beaverbrook why I had rejected Winn's article, he said to me as we
walked down a steep hill·in Monte Carlo, 'If you don't think so much
of his articles, why do you run them?' 'To please you,' I said. He
stopped, faced me, and planted his feet firmly. 'You don't have to
run them,' he said. And that was the end of Godfrey Winn's career
with the *Daily Express*. I did not mind his homosexuality. It was the
sickening insincerity that accompanied it which offended me. I
doubted if he picked anyone up. He seemed to me as neutered as a
doctored cat.

The slow crescendo to the usual barrage of endless attacks on the
paper began in earnest on 8th April 1963. Beaverbrook's note is
gentle enough in tone but he was sufficiently concerned about my
feelings to take the unusual step of telling George Millar to have it
shown to him before dispatch. After reading it through he made only
one minor alteration in his own hand. The note is convincing evidence of his skills as a newspaper boss and his knowledge of the
craft. Much of his fire is directed at one of Britain's most respected
show business writers, David Lewin. Possibly the strength of his
criticism was influenced by Lewin's known friendship with Bernard
(now Lord) Delfont. The note is worth reprinting in full, exactly as
Beaverbrook sent it to me, as an example of the 84-year-old press
baron at work, his mind undiminished by age and his love for his
number one paper undiminished:

Mr. Edwards, I don't want to send you a lot of criticisms of your
paper. I would like to send you a great deal of praise, the paper has
improved tremendously as I have been telling Mr. Max Aitken and
Mr. Blackburn. Besides I am giving kindly advice now. I have been rid
of the worry of the DX that was so very much on my mind. But I am
shocked at the purchase of the memoirs of Christine for £2,000.

Were you in on the racket. If so just let me know your part and your
reason for it will you.

Then again, your leaders are wanting drive and point. Who is running
them now, is it George Malcolm Thomson, or just where are you
getting the inspiration.

In Saturday's paper I make no objection to the White House and the
Kremlin leader. But one leader was enough. That would have had
some punch if I had had my way. The Salisbury leader is very good
too. No objection, but it has got no punch to it. Scrap all the laws!!
Are you going to scrap the early closing laws for instance, I hope not.

Note the difference, Mr. Edwards, between your story of King Farouk and the D.Mail story which is on page 2 of Saturdays paper.

Mr. Edwards, I am reading the article by David Lewin. Is this the first announcement in his story of Charles Forte taking up theatres, is this the first time we have been told it. If so, it is good news. If it is not the first time it has been told but is simply raking over an old story, then it shouldn't have any place in your Saturday page, should it?

What is the idea of telling us that Delfont is a clever fellow, and that Forte has a new item on his balance sheet, namely I assume his investment in Bernard Delfont's Company. What is the idea there? I don't entirely follow it.

"There is no limit to the money E.M.I. is prepared to invest in this country." Is this country in the U.S.A. or Great Britain. If E.M.I. is news, this purchase of theatres is news then that is first-rate, but if it is old hat, if it appeared in the D.Mail last week, then I am not so enthusiastic, are you?

Now then we are told that the television West and Wales has bought into a producing company here in London, and this producing company is very successful, it has produced Oliver and other plays. If this is news, good, good, good. If old hat, what then.

I am told that R.C.A. Victor has bought in one place, and Associated Rediffusion in another. Is that news, sure? Hot news.

Where did I first hear that story about Columbia, the Columbia Co. in America buying My Fair Lady. Where did I first hear that. Dear, dear, has Mr. Lewin been reading back numbers?

Now, is the story about the success of the long playing record of My Fair Lady something new? Something that has just come out this Saturday for the first time in the DX.

Is it the first time Lockwood has spoken in these terms about musical comedies and plays. If so good news, ought to be at the top of the column.

In my reply I tried to defend myself for introducing the *Daily Express* to cheque book journalism by buying up Christine Keeler. I was not the least bit critical of either Miss Keeler or Mandy Rice-Davies; nor had I admired Labour's ruthless pursuit of Mr Profumo, and I was delighted when Lord Denning ruled, as I had believed, that there was no security risk. But buying up Christine Keeler against Beaverbrook's hostility to 'that racket' was such an act of bravado, though done with the best of motives – to sell the paper – that I decided to concede his other criticisms:

To: Lord Beaverbrook   From: Robert Edwards

April 9th, 1963

Thank you for these comments.

1) In the case of Christine Keeler it seemed to me essential that we should get the story of where she had been, and also – which to me appeared even more important – the first picture of her since all the tremendous fuss about her disappearance. She was a missing person of the most sensational kind, and I would have hated seeing her story anywhere else than in the Daily Express. I was extremely careful in handling the story to take out anything in the nature of hints and innuendoes against anybody else, although I thought her reference to the Russian Naval Attache was permissible. I don't think anybody in Westminster or elsewhere regarded the story that day as a smear on anybody or even yellow journalism. It seemed to me a first class piece of news gathering that readers would expect the Express to have about a girl who had been discussed in parliament and society. I know there was great gloom elsewhere that we had the story.

I tried hard not to be inhibited against good news judgement because of past difficulties about Miss Keeler, and that was why I went for the story.

2) The Daily Mail story of King Farouk's engagement was indeed much better than our own. I did not spot this, and am now having an enquiry about why our staff man failed to file as good an account.

3) Your criticism of David Lewin's article is devastating, and absolutely correct. I thought that many of the facts were new, but after an enquiry I find that none of them were. All he had done was to put into one piece what was really common knowledge in the theatre. I will watch this kind of point in future.

R.J.E.

I was aware that a lot of people were giving their opinions of the *Daily Express* to Lord Beaverbrook, and that to disagree with him was not therefore so heinous. Also I felt that he was expressing himself too strongly because he feared that he was losing his grip on the paper through his great age. Like other editors working for a powerful boss, I adopted the posture of the Cabinet Secretary in 'Yes, Prime Minister' and expressed agreement while clearly indicating the opposite. Thus someone must have said during a gap in the conversation at lunch or dinner that the *Daily Mirror*, which I did not once see Lord Beaverbrook reading, was strong on animal pictures. Too many, or even any but the most outstanding, would soon have had Lord Beaverbrook reaching for his dictaphone, so that when he sent me a note complaining about the lack of them I sent him a reply that would not have disgraced Sir Humphrey Appleby himself:

I have had a word with the Picture Editor and other executives about stepping up the supply of animal pictures. I have stressed, however, this is not to be overdone. Too many animal pictures, in my opinion, have the effect of cheapening the paper.

Here is another note a few days later in the Sir Humphrey manner with the same insolent undertones:

I was most distressed that we did not use the picture of the black man chasing the white man, which appeared in Wednesday's Daily Mirror. This was the first thing I raised with the Picture Editor when I came in on Wednesday morning.

It was an Agency picture which arrived at 6.00 a.m. on Tuesday morning. It was used in the early editions of the evening newspapers, and then dropped. It was discarded by our back bench on the grounds that it had been running in the early evening papers, but if I had seen it I would certainly have said that it should have been used – even though all the other morning newspapers apart from the Mirror rejected it on similar grounds.

Often I had my back to the wall.

From: Lord Beaverbrook   29th May, 1963
To: Mr. Robert Edwards

Mr. Edwards, see how the Daily Telegraph publishes news that is days old like Rockefeller's popularity down after marriage. Days old so far as the Americans are concerned but published over here for the first time.

Mr. Edwards, I want you to notice that paper, it is packed full of news, whereas the DX is packed full of features.

To: Lord Beaverbrook   29th May, 1963
From: Robert Edwards

I will watch the Telegraph carefully.

Like you, I am all against having too many features in the Express. More people will read a news page than can ever be persuaded to read any than the most brilliant feature page. I think, however, that features give a paper its tone and character, and that my problem is to create a happy balance.

I have spoken to Mr. Baker and Mr. Raybould warning them, as I have before, that I don't want the paper over-featured.

From: Lord Beaverbrook   30th May, 1963
To: Mr. Robert Edwards

What are you going to do about it? Curtail some of your features or not?

How right he was. A few years later I studied readership research figures on the *People*. These showed that probably twice as many people read news stories as run-of-the-mill features, the exception being the stars, which more than 80 per cent of women could be depended upon to read. The *Daily Express* did not have readership surveys. The Principal Reader was the one who mattered. He acted for all the rest. For all his criticisms, or possibly partly because of them, the *Daily Express* was a remarkably good newspaper at this period. The nearest parallel I can think of today would be a popular version of the *Independent* or, for that matter, *The Times*. In those days the quality papers were dull. The *Daily Express* was disappointed if it did not cover the big stories better than anyone. Contrary to myth, it far outshone the *Daily Mirror* on pictures though not (I felt) on political sagacity. Not one of Beaverbrook's stream of notes to me criticised the *Express*'s coverage of really major events. It was niggling stuff, so I too readily convinced myself, fed by his little team who had the easy task of pointing out what we had missed. Six months after my triumphant return, for all the warmth and hospitality Beaverbrook poured upon me as his man for the top job, I blew my top.

It was 10.00 a.m. He had phoned me at my flat at 8 o'clock and, as usual, I had stood with nothing on with the papers strewn in front of me. Somehow I could never bring myself to talk to him sitting up in bed. When I greeted him in Arlington House, he was standing by his small desk with a pile of papers which I recall as being about six inches high in front of him. His right eyelid flickered menacingly as it did when he simulated anger. There was trouble ahead, and I was in a genuine bad temper myself. It was hard work editing the *Daily Express*, and while I was a temperamental and over-sensitive person to deal with I had a whole staff some of whom were infinitely worse. I was also a keen Labour supporter. It was a long way to the Winter of Discontent in 1979, Brent Council and the other manifestations that shook to the foundations my love for the Party. I had convinced myself that it was better that I should edit the paper than a Tory, and respected Beaverbrook for appointing me. But if I found things too wearing, I would leave and back Wilson, whom I liked and admired – that could be a good thing and would cause a nice stir.

Beaverbrook began from the top of an obviously carefully compiled pile with some criticism or other of the *Express*. As he reached for the second paper in the pile, I said, 'If everything there is an attack on the *Daily Express* you will achieve nothing except to knock the stuffing out of me and the staff.' He stopped, and his reaction was immediate. He looked at the clock and I am sure I read his mind correctly. He thought, 'I've got to get rid of this fellow. But what am I going to do between now and my next appointment at 10.30?' He liked to keep himself occupied.

He said, 'Then there is no purpose in continuing this conversation.' For the first time he showed me not merely to the door of the flat but to the lift. He pressed the button and as we waited I wondered if he would say to me, as he had when he and Christiansen parted at the same spot, 'I am sorry to see you going down.' Instead he gravely shook me by the hand and said goodbye. Unfortunately the pub opposite the Caprice downstairs was not yet open. I was not fired, nor threatened. Beaverbrook and I simply did not speak and I had the unique experience under him of editing his principal newspaper for several months without exchanging a single word or memo. The whole staff must have known but nobody ever mentioned the curious silence from Cherkley and Arlington House. George Malcolm Thomson was far too polite and wise to comment on the Old Man's new habit of invariably telephoning leaders direct to him. I now feel that I treated Beaverbrook very badly. He was indeed an old man and I was so deeply fond of him that I dream about him affectionately to this day, as indeed I do about Maxwell, which I find difficult to explain.

I should have written to Beaverbrook, but I was enjoying my freedom too much. I am a much better editor when I am left alone. That is true of all proper editors, which I think I can reasonably believe I was. John Junor ran an even better (I am speaking professionally) jingoistic, xenophobic paper after Beaverbrook's death

than he did before and knew exactly the right note to sound for
Sunday Express readers. I had scarcely any guidance in my six years
as editor of the *People* and thirteen as *Sunday Mirror* editor, and the
political tone of both papers was markedly different to the *Daily
Mirror*'s. Today, under Maxwell's influence, it is the same on all
three papers, to the ludicrous extent that one Sunday the *People* and
the *Sunday Mirror* not only said the same thing but ran exactly the
same leader. I would not have tolerated that, and I am sure that
neither editor was happy about it. It was another example of Maxwell's curious interpretation of his promise not to interfere with the
papers editorially.

While Beaverbrook was having his troubles with me, his relationship with Junor was scarcely better. He had been trying to persuade
his most difficult editor to soften his leader page and pursue more
moderate policies, and no doubt there were other quarrels between
the two. John brought the matter to a head by resigning on the
grounds that while Beaverbrook had the absolute right as proprietor
to decide his papers' policies, as editor he would on grounds of
conscience be unable to support Harold Macmillan when he called a
general election. Beaverbrook insisted that John worked his notice
and suggested he wrote articles during that period. John refused and
said he must either continue to edit the paper until the notice expired
or be paid off. Beaverbrook conceded. One day, before I too fell out
with him, he asked me to lunch at Arlington House alone with him
and Lady Beaverbrook. I knew he had something very special on his
mind when, at the end of his meal, he sent for one of his special
cigars. Both he and Lady Beaverbrook leaned forward eagerly as he
asked, 'Tell me, Bob, who should be editor of the *Sunday Express*?'

I decided to play act a little and feign reluctance on the grounds
that no doubt he had asked Max Aitken and if my answer was
different to his it would not improve our relationship. 'Oh, come on,
Bob,' he said, knowing he would win. 'There is only one answer,' I
replied. 'John Junor. No one is a better editor of the *Sunday
Express*.' I felt I had done in whoever Beaverbrook had been
tempted to play with as a new editor. (The choice, in fact, was Derek
Marks.) A few months later, after Macmillan had totally justified
Junor's contempt for him at the time, he announced that he was to
have a prostate gland operation. Beaverbrook, exulting, rang Junor.
'We are saved,' he cried. 'He's bound to go and you can stay.' To
this day I wonder how great a role I had played in this rappro-
chement. But he was still not talking to me, his other favoured son.

Then, on 22 November 1963, came what I thought was a chance to heal our relationship. Everybody remembers what they were doing when Kennedy was shot. I was standing in front of my desk in the office of the editor of the *Daily Express* when the foreign editor, Terence Lancaster, rushed in with the news. I knew my duty, rather like Christiansen in the film 'The Day the Earth Caught Fire' in which he played himself. 'Get me the Old Man,' I shouted to my secretary Pam Sprinzel. She discovered he was at Arlington House with Max Aitken. Raymond, the amusingly insolent valet, was on the line. 'Lord Beaverbrook, please,' I said. He knew that I was in the doghouse and his voice showed it. Instead of the usual 'certainly' he said, 'I'll go and find out.' A moment later he announced triumphantly, 'The Lord's busy and can't talk to you.' 'Well, then,' I said, 'in that case can I have Mr Aitken.' There was no question mark at the end, and Raymond's joy was boundless when he came back to tell me, 'Mr Aitken's with the Lord and can't speak to you.' I then uttered a line I was proud of. 'Tell him Kennedy's been shot and see if he will speak to me.' He did, but Beaverbrook did not. Eventually a well-rehearsed Tom Blackburn, the joint chairman, called me up, several weeks after our stunningly good coverage of Kennedy's death, much of it written by David English, now editor of the *Daily Mail*, whom I appointed foreign editor in 1965.

Tom spoke to me in a tone of great resolution and leadership. 'I have been talking to the Old Man,' he said, as he unfolded his unlikely tale. 'I told him it's absolutely ridiculous that he is not speaking to the editor of his most important newspaper. I told him it can't go on, it's got to end.' Both of us stopped to marvel at the thought of Tom speaking to Beaverbrook in these terms. I waited for the punch line. 'There is only one solution,' he said to me. 'You will have to write a letter of apology. Show it to me first.' 'I will write to him,' I said, knowing who had written his script. 'But I won't show you the letter.' I did not want Tom to be in trouble over what I wrote, nor to try to persuade me to alter it. My letter simply said I was sorry that he was not talking to me, I stressed my undying affection for and loyalty to him, but did not know what to apologise for since I did not feel I had done anything wrong. I sent the letter round by hand. That evening there was a familiar voice on the phone. He said gruffly just three words, 'Not good enough,' and rang off. The following morning he rang as though there had been no rift between us and asked if I would like to go walking. Never again did he send me a note complaining about stories missed by the *Daily Express*. I had succeeded where all previous editors had failed. His little research team was diverted to other tasks, and I am sure he was much happier not to be reminded each morning that all was not totally perfect, as it could not be, even with his hugely successful paper riding as high as it had ever done in the days of the great Arthur Christiansen.

The first time I knew there was something wrong with Beaverbrook was in the summer of that year. His ancient Rolls-Royce was waiting outside the front door at Cherkley. As usual, he had not told me where he was going or whether I was going with him. There was the famous occasion, probably true, when he had some particularly obsequious, eager journalist accompany him on a cross-country trip and shortly before arriving at his destination dropped the young man at a lonely bus stop, where only good fortune would produce a bus within an hour. Mead, the wholly wonderful butler, arrived with Beaverbrook's black Homburg and overcoat. The Old Man, his hat at the usual rakish angle, turned to me. 'You can come in the car,' he said. 'I am going to see Churchill' (pronounced 'Choichill'). We climbed into the Rolls-Royce, rich in mahogany, rugs and thick carpet and the size of a small drawing-room. 'I am lucky,' he said, as we drove through the mile-long avenue of trees to his front gate near Leatherhead (if it was not actually a mile, that is what it seemed). 'Churchill is dying from the head downwards. I am dying from the feet upwards.' He opened the glass partition between ourselves and the driver. 'We will drop Mr Edwards at a railway station some-where,' he said. An hour later the editor of the *Daily Express* stood on the platform of a branch line in Kent, a lonely figure.

An older person than I would have known Beaverbrook was saying he had cancer. Max Aitken, several years after his father's death, had someone telephone me to ask if Beaverbrook had told me he had the disease. I decided he had, and that poor Max was jealous because I was so favoured, hoping I would deny the story some mutual friend had passed on to him. This particular visit to Churchill occurred at about the time of Beaverbrook's 84th birth-day. There was an incident I recall vividly that showed his increasing fragility. The usual vast quantity of presents had been sent by employees, friends and family from all over the world. As usual he enjoyed opening the parcels himself, the more difficult the task the better. (Among the presents there were still more paper knives. He had enough already to fill a display unit at Harrods.) One par-ticularly enterprising present, which would ensure someone's con-tinuing employment for several months, was a rare collection of seeds culled from botanists in many countries. They were in little individual packets with their names written by hand in Latin. The chap had gone to a lot of trouble. Beaverbrook was immensely excited. For the first time I saw the small electric vehicle on which he was transported inside the grounds of Cherkley when he was too tired to walk. He and Lady Beaverbrook, whom he adored and who was a great gift to him in his final years, got on board and moved slowly along the path to the far side of the great lawn. Beaverbrook held the seeds. I followed dutifully. To my surprise he advanced on to the lawn, his arm held by his wife, and distributed the seeds over it like some biblical figure. Even with my limited knowledge, it was obvious that not a single one would grow and if it did it would immediately be shorn by the lawn-mower. And did I imagine it, or were the birds watching expectantly from the trees? Suddenly, as he hurled the seeds about, Beaverbrook fell. He had somehow tripped, and as he half lay on his back on the ground he shouted at Lady Beaverbrook, 'Damn you!' He did not mean it. He was just a very old person, and he was afraid. I loved him a lot.

That year he did not go abroad for Christmas. Along with every other journalist on his staff whom he knew personally, I sent the usual card carefully chosen by my wife Laura, with the usual carefully constructed message. At the last moment we were invited to dinner, I think on Christmas Eve. Panic. We would need a present. 'Flowers,' said Laura, 'for them both.' We stopped at a shop on Clapham Common, on the way to Cherkley, and bought enough to grace a Mafia gangster's funeral in Prohibition. Beaverbrook was in the hall when we arrived and I handed him the flowers. 'Give them to Lady Beaverbrook,' he said to Mead. There were flowers everywhere, in enormous vases. Suddenly ours were reduced to the size of a child's posy. It was a very small party. Beaverbrook gave Laura a cheque for £100 when I was out of the room, pouring his charm upon her. Lady Beaverbrook later gave her an expensive leather make-up bag and handed me a gold-plated lighter in an Asprey's box. The lighter did not work.

Passing Asprey's one day, I went in to complain. A man in tails examined it gravely and politely asked who had given it to me. 'Lady Beaverbrook,' I said, 'but you must not tell her.' 'Certainly not, sir,' he replied. 'If I may speak to you in confidence, she did not buy it from us, but she is a valued customer and we will be happy to renovate it for you.' Like Laura and me, she was caught off guard by Beaverbrook's sudden whim to have us to dinner. I remember his saying in wonderment to me shortly after they were married in June that year, 'Do you realise, Bob, she has more money than I have? I am the poor man in this house.' Cracks were being filled in the walls. The whole house was being renovated. The attractively shabby dining-room, scene of much repartee, sycophancy and gossip, was being changed into something quite grand, with gold leaf on the mouldings. For weeks guests ate in a humble second dining-room, and if they worked for him had to share the unspeakable diet Lady Beaverbrook had discovered in the battle to prolong his life.

Almost until the end his interest in his newspapers was undimmed. He was more benign, partly because of a remarkable letter Max Aitken wrote by hand which called for praise as well as criticism, and which pointed out that the *Daily Express* had the editor of his choice and all his papers were doing better than ever. Here is a typical note dictated two months before he died:

From Lord Beaverbrook   14 April 1964
To   Mr. Robert Edwards

(1) Please get rid of the term 'another self-made man' in the Christopher Rowlands article. It is a cliche.

Also, the last line needs sub-editing, to remove the term 'a quart into a pint pot'.

(2) There is a lot of old stuff in the TV column.

I return both columns.

Another such note would not have pleased today's distinguished editor of the *Daily Mail* if I had shown it to him. 'Mr. Edwards,' the Old Man dictated with almost the old acerbity, 'too much space is given to David English's telegram from Hollywood about somebody named Samantha Eggar, it's a silly little story', to which I gave an old soldier or 'Yes, Prime Minister' reply which said we were wrong, of course, but for the right reasons: 'I certainly agree with the criticism given to the space on the story from Hollywood today. We were conscious that the paper was rather heavy, and it was allowed to run with greater prominence than we would usually give, in order to bring some light relief to the pages.' Lies, lies. We obviously thought the article was jolly good and of great interest to our readers. For the record (a phrase banned by Beaverbrook) I produce, after diligent research, my favourite old soldier note to him, written in 1961 about some story or other some creep had pointed out to him that we had missed:

I was extremely disturbed that the Mirror had the story about Earl Poulett and the row with the Rector of Crewkerne. There was an immediate investigation next morning.

It appears that the Mirror alone were telephoned by a Parishioner. Our correspondent at Crewkerne, who in fact, normally goes to church every Sunday, was ill, and did not hear about it. He got out of his sick bed and turned in a first class follow-up next day – but that, of course, is no consolation.

In general we are most satisfied with our Crewkerne reporter.

Much discussion went on between Beaverbrook and myself about strengthening the staff of women writers following Jill Butterfield's marriage and departure. I took on Deirdre MacSharry, then the unknown fashion editor of the *Evening News*, mainly because I liked her smile. She became a huge success, edited *Cosmopolitan* for years and is revered. I also discovered Ann Leslie, and such was my confidence in her ability I gave her a weekly column on the leader page at the age of twenty-two. It reads well today and she went on to become one of Fleet Street's most respected writers, but at the time it was thought to be a mistake. Beaverbrook clearly was not sure because for once only he passed on Lady Beaverbrook's criticisms instead of his own. My reply was rather haughty:

> Thank you for letting me see Lady Beaverbrook's comments on Ann Leslie's column. I think these criticisms are extremely sound, and I must bear the burden of them, because I passed the column which comes under my personal direction like all the other columns.

I have prided myself on spotting some of Fleet Street's most talented people, but sometimes I got it wrong. 'I have also seen Miss Jean Rook, fashion editor of the Newnes magazine *Flair*,' I wrote to Beaverbrook, 'but I thought her a bit too stolid.' I thus rejected the only genuine star in the post-Beaverbrook *Express* who was claimed, without too much hyperbole, to be the first lady of Fleet Street. Various notes exchanged between Beaverbrook and myself show that I resisted pressure from him to appoint Clive Barnes as TV critic to compete with the celebrated Peter Black on the *Daily Mail*. He became probably the most famous theatre critic in the world on the *New York Times*. 'I would like to have a talk with you about doing the television column you have suggested on a strictly trial basis, not for publication in the first instance,' I wrote to Beaverbrook, stalling. He replied encouragingly: 'Go ahead with Clive Barnes. Satisfy yourself by experience that he is worth it.' Later I wrote: 'Clive Barnes's second attempt at a TV column is again a failure.' I nominated Martin Jackson on the grounds that people would prefer to read news about current programmes and personalities than criticism. 'It might be that under close tuition his writing style will improve dramatically,' I added, which cannot have convinced Beaverbrook that he was wrong. As it was, we were both right. Jackson became a leading television journalist and editor of *TV Times*. But Beaverbrook was more right than I was. I console myself that Clive Barnes always gives me the credit for introducing him to the *Express* as ballet critic and stand-in for Noel Goodwin on music and Leonard Mosley on films. He was paid £6 per concert and up to £30 for a film column.

We had another discussion about the merits of Henry Fairlie, possibly the most respected political commentator of the time, whom I had introduced to the *Daily Express*. Henry was a friend of George Gale, Peregrine Worsthorne, now editor of the *Sunday Telegraph*, and Paul Johnson, who had written a Paris column for me in *Tribune* under the pseudonym Paul Henriques. We had some pleasant parties together at George's house in Staines. The notorious Staines Set we might have been called if *Private Eye* had been invented. Henry is now a sage in Washington. In the 1960s he fulfilled the J. L. Garvin role by writing articles of great portentousness in the *Spectator*, the immensely heavy Sundays and elsewhere where readers took a proper interest in affairs. Since he was also a fine writer, he would have settled down nicely in the *Daily Express* but for one grave disability in Beaverbrook's eyes. 'Mr Edwards,' he said into his Soundscriber, 'I see that you published five articles in the past month from Henry Fairlie. How far is he right in these articles, these five articles? Let me know please. One article was entitled Queen Insists, of course he was wrong there.' My reply got to the heart of the matter, at least at that time. Listing his mistakes in the five articles, which included predictions that Macmillan would stay on a day or two before he resigned; that he would be succeeded by Mr R. A. Butler, who was ignominiously poleaxed (with Macmillan's help) by Lord Home; and that Wilson had united the Labour Party but crushed its spirit (subsequently disproved when Wilson ended the Tories' thirteen-year rule), I stated the obvious: 'There is no doubt that Henry Fairlie has an aptitude for coming to the wrong conclusion about politics ... Yet despite his failure to interpret events correctly, which I suppose is true of most political correspondents, he has a most extraordinary influence ... I have never had much faith in his judgment, but I do have a profound respect for his reputation.' As a sop to Beaverbrook, I added: 'It seems to me that he is a good person to have in the *Daily Express* for the time being. But I am totally opposed to putting him under contract.' All of this, in a Jeeves-like manner, was meant to indicate that I thought Fairlie was jolly good. He did not last. Contrary to his reputation in socialist circles, Beaverbrook was a stickler for getting it right, although he allowed himself greater latitude.

Beaverbrook's concern for accuracy and his paper's reputation showed itself over a dramatic page one 'splash' five weeks before his death. 2 BRITISH SOLDIERS BEHEADED screamed the headline. Stephen Harper, a veteran *Express* foreign correspondent, reported that two soldiers whom he named had been ambushed by Yemeni tribesmen and suffered this unfortunate fate. No other paper had the story. Beaverbrook did not believe it. Nor did the Foreign Office, and the State Department in Washington issued a denial from its consul-general in Taiz, where the incident was supposed to have occurred. In fact, Harper had got the story from Major-General John Cubbon, General Commanding Middle East Land Forces in Aden after the two soldiers had disappeared. Eleven days later their bodies were found, decapitated. I decided to await Beaverbrook's evening call. 'By the way,' I said, after relating the rest of the day's news, 'they've found those two soldiers. They were beheaded.' 'By God,' said Beaverbrook in a reply that only a newspaperman will understand, 'that's good news.' Then he corrected himself, 'I mean it's terrible.'

On his 85th birthday, at my instigation, he gave an interview to George Gale, the least ingratiating writer on his staff, who wrote brilliantly if a little patronisingly: 'And almost against one's better judgment one has again realised that one likes the Old Man. With the worst will in the world it is impossible not to warm to him, to feel towards him a kind of surprised affection.' That may not be the level of praise that Bob Maxwell will regard as sufficient in the *Daily Mirror* on his 85th birthday, but the reluctant admirer Gale got some good quotes from the Old Man. 'Of all things', he told George, 'I'd like the people to say the *Daily Express* is better than it used to be. I mean that when I die I'd like it to be believed that it was better than when I lived.' That I severely doubted, but he made a comment I felt he meant about the imminent conversion of the Labour *Daily Herald* into the *Sun*: 'A great pity, that paper going out. They should put Hugh Cudlipp in charge of that paper instead of the *Sun*. He'd make a much greater success. He's dissipating one and a half million faithful readers.' Another passage from the George Gale interview is worth quoting in full for all my friends who were perplexed by the *Daily Express* expressing views that were clearly the opposite of mine:

> I remarked that a leading article in the previous day's Express bore I thought his characteristic imprint.
> 'Which one was that?'
> 'The one about beef and foreigners.'
> 'Ah, yes, I think it was mine. We have a system, you know. I speak at this end and there is a machine at the other end and it comes out with a leading article.'

The greatest occasion I have attended in my life was the famous birthday party in 1964 given by Lord Thomson in honour of Lord Beaverbrook. His speech was the best I have ever heard, a masterpiece of wit, brevity and style, written unaided by a desperately sick, utterly brave old man of eighty-five on the very edge of death. The occasion was enriched still further for me because I knew that Beaverbrook regarded his fellow countryman Thomson as being strictly in the second division as a newspaper baron, and Garfield Weston, the biscuit tycoon who had contributed an enormous cake, as a crashing bore. ('I have to leave you for half an hour,' Beaverbrook once said to me at Cherkley. 'Garfield Weston has come for tea. He is one of life's burdens.') Beaverbrook's speech ended with his astonishing farewell: 'It is time for me to become an apprentice once more. I am not certain in which direction, but somewhere, sometime, soon . . . ' and that was the last but one time I saw this marvellous man. The final occasion was after some unperceptive manager had revealed the total sum spent by the *Daily Express* on editorial expenses in the previous financial year. Beaverbrook was probably quite proud of the impressive figure, accounted for by innumerable lunches and much first-class foreign travel, but he affected shock. After battering Tom Blackburn, the joint chairman, he summoned me to Cherkley. The sun was shining as usual as I was shown into the garden. He was sitting on a wicker-work seat outside the library with his feet on another. From chest to ankles he was covered in an old-fashioned car rug. He smiled at me genially. 'By God, Bob,' he said, after telling me the dreadful sum that had been spent, 'I'm going to sort out this racket if it's the last thing I do before I die. Will you support a reign of terror?' I said that most naturally I would, of course. He explained that Mr Blackburn had decided to send a stern note to every member of the editorial staff. 'Anything to say about that?' he asked, eyeing me shrewdly from beneath his straw hat. 'Well, sir,' I replied, 'perhaps you might not wish to have such a note sent to key members of your staff like René McColl, Trevor Evans, Percy Hoskins, Ian Aitken, George Malcolm Thomson . . . ' and I named all his favourites. Lord Beaverbrook picked up the Soundscriber for his last message in my presence. 'Mr Blackburn,' he shouted into the machine, 'Mr Blackburn, Mr Blackburn. Check every name on your list with Mr Edwards before sending out that letter.' That was the end of the great purge on expenses. The letter was never sent.

From that moment there was silence from Cherkley. We all sensed that Beaverbrook was ill but did not like to face the unthinkable. One morning Tom Blackburn said to me, 'I hope you are ready if the worst happens.' Three days later on 10 June 1964 we led the paper:

At 4.15 pm – two weeks

after his 85th birthday

BEAVERBROOK DIES

It was a pretty good paper. George Malcolm Thomson had written an obituary years earlier that Ted Pickering had passed on to me. He wrote an inspired editorial that ended: 'To others it is left to admire and wonder at Beaverbrook. We loved the man.' Max Aitken said: 'Certainly in my lifetime there will be only one Lord Beaverbrook,' a statement I suspected George coined. I had the idea of printing Beaverbrook's birthday speech for the first time in full. It read magnificently. Max Aitken was delighted with the paper and rather superfluously, I thought, confirmed my appointment. The following morning Lady Beaverbrook phoned to ask if I would come to Cherkley to view her husband's body. 'You were one of the people he really liked,' she said. George Malcolm Thomson and Tom Blackburn were also asked, and Beaverbrook's favourite *Daily Express* photographer, the young, fiendishly skilled Harry Benson. Beaverbrook was lying in the big drawing-room where I had drunk many of his unspeakable cocktails. We were in the small drawing-room next door. I took the photographer to one side. 'I know you, Harry,' I said. 'Don't take any pictures, just this once.' Beaverbrook's face looked calm and smaller than it had seemed in life.

Lunch was late, instead of punctual as with him, and while Mead served the soup I noticed as I looked behind me out of the window that the remnants of Garfield Weston's enormous cake were lying on the lawn like a miniature fortress. Several crows and other birds were feeding on it. 'Good Lord,' I said involuntarily to George, 'have you seen the cake on the lawn?' 'Yes, I have,' he replied solemnly. 'It's to feed the birds,' said Lady Beaverbrook. I felt that the Old Man in the next room would have appreciated the scene. As we left the table at the end of the meal, Lady Beaverbrook said to the butler, 'Take the cake off the lawn, Mead. Mr Garfield Weston is coming down this afternoon.' Our cars passed in the drive and we waved at him far too enthusiastically. He must have wondered why. Back at the office when he and I were alone I said to Harry Benson, 'Did you take some pictures of the Old Man?' He confessed he had. 'Hand over the roll,' I said. I still have it somewhere.

13
AFTER
BEAVERBROOK

Beaverbrook once said to me, 'You have to know how to handle the people above you, as well as those below.' I did not know at the time what prompted this remark, nor does it seem particularly profound, but somehow it has stuck with me. Certainly I did not know how to handle his son Max Aitken, and scarcely tried. Even as brave and independent a person as John Junor has always showed a sensible and apparently genuine respect for whoever was in financial command of his newspaper following Beaverbrook's death. Max's hostility to me was not simply because of my socialist views but because of my scarcely disguised hostility to him. I was defending myself against what I thought was a Max-inspired criticism over the phone, and Beaverbrook shouted at me, 'If you are trying to divide Max and me, you will never succeed!' Hair-raising stuff, I thought. I also felt that if Max was there with him, as I suspected, it would probably do me more good than harm, which perhaps was what the Old Man intended. Even after Beaverbrook died, I made little effort to win over Max despite the nicest of letters from him: 'I thought your treatment of the paper over the last sad week has been very fine. Right in the tradition of the *Daily Express*.' I decided he could not possibly fit into his father's shoes and I should preserve morale and do my best to fill the vacuum by showing that I was in total command. 'Keep the bastards out,' I liked to say. 'Pour molten lead over them.' This reference to the management included Max Aitken and was not calculated to endear me to him. 'The editor I have appointed, Robert Edwards, is 38,' he wrote in a page one message on the twenty thousandth issue of the *Daily Express*. 'He is the youngest editor of any national newspaper. And he is an old man compared with most of his staff!' Friendly words. I really should have taken my mentor's good advice.

My first clash with him came after we turned several of the middle pages into a weekly Saturday magazine. It was called, hideously, 'Leisurescope' and was designed to provide light reading on Saturdays to compete with similar pages everyone in Fleet Street knew were to appear in Cudlipp's *Sun*. The *Daily Mail* did the same, so great were the fears about this new publication and the man behind it. I was against the idea and resisted changing the highly successful formula of the *Express*, which recognised that even on a Saturday a newspaper was far more likely to be read than one on cycling or even fishing, the premier participant sport. Although he was an immensely gallant Battle of Britain pilot and an intrepid sailor, Max's nerve as a newspaper boss was not as strong and he insisted, as Beaverbrook would have contemptuously described it, on letting the as yet unborn *Sun* edit the *Daily Express*. I agreed to allow Jocelyn Stevens, the renowned editor of *Queen*, to edit the pages provided I had the last word, on the grounds as Max put it, 'You and I know nothing about magazines. We are newspapermen.' Jocelyn brought in Denis Hackett, later to transform *You* magazine for the *Mail on Sunday* and edit *Today*. I could not have thought of a better team, but the idea flopped because it was wrong for the *Daily Express*. One Friday someone said, 'You had better look at this week's magazine.' From one end to the other, it was a clever spoof edition of the *Express*, complete with phoney Osbert Lancaster cartoon. I knew that it would baffle millions of *Express* readers and probably bring a frightful visitation from the Old Man himself. I blazed a trail to Max. 'You have probably only had time to glance at it,' I said. 'Take my word for it. We can't print it.' 'You're the editor,' was all he said. Downstairs I called in Raybould. 'An interesting exercise for you, Ray,' I said. 'You have got eight extra news pages to fill in tomorrow's paper.' That evening Jocelyn was on the phone. 'I always knew you were against me,' he said. We made it up later.

Some interesting in-fighting developed with Peter Baker, the paper's number two and a prototype disloyal deputy. He convinced himself, a common and understandable failing among deputies, that he would make a better editor and took the usual step of putting this notion to Max after earnest discussions with cronies, who may not have shared his convictions to the same degree. Max rewarded his disloyalty with a thousand a year increase and gave a similar rise to Raybould to keep him happy. All this was done without my know-ledge, but I was well enough attuned to suspect a plot. 'What's going on, Ray?' I asked. 'All I know is that I've had a thousand a year increase and so has Peter,' he replied after I pressed him further, 'and I've said you're a jolly good editor.' That told me everything. At the next meeting with Max, which included Peter Baker, Ray-bould and two other assistants, I went through what I imagined were

Peter's complaints to Max. These included criticisms of Deirdre McSharry and of Robin Esser, whom I had recently put in charge of features and now edits the *Sunday Express*. I said that if either had deficiencies, which I did not concede, we had better appoint someone to guide them as Harold Keeble would have done, because I simply did not have the time. The implication was obvious. If there was anyone at fault, it was my deputy. The scene would have been good enough for inclusion in Wilfred Greatorex's series 'The Power Game', then compulsive TV viewing. Raybould gruffly supported everything I said. Afterwards Max held me back. 'I am giving you a rise of a thousand,' he said. 'Peter Baker is a shit. You can fire him if you like.' I had to have the last word. 'I won't sack him,' I said, 'but next time he complains to you about me, please ask if he has had the courtesy to tell me first.' The effect on Peter of my obviously successful counter-attack was astounding. He took to gambling and drinking all night, came to work drunk, and within a few days quit without any prompting from me. I was shocked many years afterwards when I heard that he had died of a heart attack on a yacht in Long Island. Despite everything, I liked him, probably because of his striking good looks. Raybould became my deputy. He looked more the traditional journalist and toiler by night.

In October 1964 I had the unusual experience as a known socialist of editing the *Daily Express* during a general election. Max thought that was bad and regarded me as a Trojan horse. Some of my more earnest friends thought it was awful, too, and felt I had sold out. Had I not been a Labour candidate as recently as the election before last, and one who was regarded in those days as left-wing? A couple of years later 'What the Papers Say' did a programme about me which ended with a rendering of the Vicar of Bray. My recollection is that it was by Bernard Levin, but he denies this. At any rate it was very well done. I felt that my critics misunderstood the *Daily Express*. Today it is a conventional Tory paper but it was not then. It bitterly opposed the Common Market, as I did along with most Bevanites. It was committed to full employment and high wages. It supported the unions and if Beaverbrook had lived as long as Noah would probably (wrongly) have opposed Mr Tebbit's laws that so effectively restored the democratic rights of individual members, on the grounds that this was an interference with the freedom of the unions to run their own affairs. Just as he campaigned month after month against Ted Heath's admirable abolition of resale price maintenance because, in his view, this endangered small shopkeepers and publicans and favoured the great shopping chains. A public opinion poll in the

Observer shortly after the election showed that 45.7 per cent of *Daily Express* readers who expressed a view claimed Tory allegiance, 40.1 per cent Labour allegiance, and 10 per cent Liberal. What was surprising to people who did not understand the *Express* were the number of Labour supporters, greater than the entire circulation of the paper today. The *Daily Mirror*'s figures surprised no one: 64.5 per cent Labour, 22.1 per cent Tory. The *Daily Express* disgraced itself in the 1945 election, but that was because of Beaverbrook's devotion to Churchill.

Reading through the *Daily Express* election coverage in 1959, the last with Beaverbrook in command, it remained lukewarm towards the Tories throughout the campaign, and came out in tepid support on polling day. There was no comparison between this and the *Daily Mail*'s traditional frenetic excesses, which accurately reflected its readership profile. JOBS FOR ALL was the election theme of the *Express* and it advised its readers to weigh up which of the parties would serve this cause best. I was on duty as deputy editor one evening when Gaitskell replied to an attack on him by Macmillan, reported on page one of that day's *Daily Express*. 'On the front page there was a wonderful photograph of him,' said Gaitskell. 'And I am sure they will do the same in my reply to him tonight and give us another good photograph and a front page story.' That is a politicians' ploy familiar to reporters, but I duly obliged and wrote the headline A NICE PICTURE (ALL PART OF THE EXPRESS SERVICE) FOR HUGH. There was no squawk from either the editor, Ted Pickering, or Beaverbrook.

At the start of the 1964 election, I arranged a page one pronouncement, probably written by George Malcolm Thomson. 'The *Daily Express* is an independent, classless newspaper. It holds strong views about national policy and expresses them with vehemence and consistency. What is its first duty towards the public in the General Election? First, to give each of the parties in the contest a fair show in the news.' And it repeated, as Beaverbrook would have decreed: 'The conception of full employment is inextricably bound up with the philosophy of the paper.' Ian Aitken, to my great regret, resigned as political correspondent rather than face what he thought might be the horrors of working for the *Express* during an election in that role. I tried to dissuade him and promised that nothing he wrote would be distorted, our coverage would be a model of propriety, but he said with simple honesty, 'My family don't like me working for the *Express*.' The dog, I felt, had a bad name it did not deserve, but I understood. His father George was a distinguished servant of the

Amalgamated Engineering Union, and he had married into the radical Mackie clan in Scotland who kept fastidious Nye Bevan supplied with salmon. He went to his natural home on the *Guardian* and emerged as an outstanding, notably fair, political commentator. What had kept him at the *Express* so long, I felt, was his liking for Beaverbrook. They had the warmest relationship and he had none of the flak inflicted on editors. I replaced him with Terence Lancaster, one of Fleet Street's great wits, foreign affairs expert and devotee and friend of Harold Wilson. He later became the *Daily Mirror*'s leading political writer, much admired by Hugh Cudlipp. Joe Haines, who now gives the *Mirror* its political clout, was brought to the paper by him.

The man who turned out to be the *Express* star of the 1964 election was George Gale, cantankerous, gravel-voiced and incorruptible, an arch-Tory with a liking shared by many for Fleet Street hostelries. His clothes looked as if they had been rejected by the Salvation Army. With rare intuition, and to enliven a bored editorial conference one morning, I suggested sending him on a train with R. A. Butler, who occasionally delighted the nation with statements of calculated ambiguity. 'He's dying to say something indiscreet,' I said to the sea of faces around me. 'Let's give him the chance. No photographer. Just him and George together when he goes off to speak somewhere.' The result that same day was an interview that became the sensation of the election. I wrote the headlines:

ON TOUR YESTERDAY, THE MAN ON THE EDGE OF THINGS

George Gale talks to the 'Marvellous, devious man,' R. A. Butler, who says:

THE RESULT? '20 SEATS EITHER WAY'

It is not customary for Government ministers to predict in an election campaign that they might lose. In Butler's case this was particularly piquant because he had been the obvious choice as leader. 'The bags under his eyes sag less with weariness than with the accumulated weight of political experience,' wrote George. 'Matured indiscretions, like ripened fruit from apple trees, fell from his lips.' How was the election going? 'Very close. We're running neck and neck. I'll be surprised if there's much in it, say 20 seats either way. But things might start slipping away in the last few days.' Slipping away? 'Yes, they won't slip towards us.' He disputed a statement by his leader on foreign policy. 'After all, I would know. I am,' he said, sitting beside his Foreign Office box, 'the Foreign Secretary.' He spoke of a recent outburst by Quintin Hogg (now Lord Hailsham) who made the not unreasonable point that only if there were no adulterers on the Labour front bench could they complain about Profumo: 'A great pity. It brings up the past. It reminds people of the last year of the Macmillan government.' George rounded off the interview with this gem: 'I mentioned that Sir Alec, whenever he makes a big speech with a platform of Tory notables behind him, goes out of his way to sing the praises of "young, dynamic" Mr Edward Heath. "Oh, does he? I think that's very interesting. I think Alec's a bit bored by him – not as a Minister, of course." '

Some commentators were surprised that I put this classic interview on page nine. The reason I did so was because I feared that if I made it the main story on page one, which it deserved, it might have finished off Butler, a man I admired. 'Is George sure Butler knew this was on the record?' I asked Raybould. 'Absolutely,' he said. Gale repeated the assurance to me when he got back to the office. At a party given by Lady Pamela Berry a day or two after I left the *Express* for a second time, Butler ambled across to me and said to my surprise, 'If there is any help I can give you, let me know.' 'Well,' I said after thanking him, 'I can now ask if you thought you were talking to George Gale off the record.' Butler smiled enigmatically. 'I never complain about journalists,' he replied. He did not seem the least bit unhappy about it all. The *Daily Express* came out half-heartedly in favour of the Tories on polling day, too late to have any influence, and afterwards Oliver Poole complained to Max Aitken that they would have won if he had not had a socialist as editor.

Max did his best to get on with me. I could not convince myself that he was up to his job. The end was inevitable, because I was not making any effort to avert it. One morning he threw a piece of paper across his desk towards me. 'What's your answer to this?' he said aggressively. I threw the paper back to him. 'Pass it to me in a civil manner and I'll answer your question,' I replied. He looked at me and said, 'Just as I thought we were getting on together.' It was high noon and that is how editors in Fleet Street bit the dust. I have no idea what was on the piece of paper. A week later Max asked if I would like to have Derek Marks, then deputy editor of the *Evening Standard* under Charles Wintour, as a political commentator and assistant editor. I was delighted and played hell because he was given a dingy office. Derek did not seem the least perturbed, and I should have guessed why. It was Sir Trevor Evans, the paper's great

industrial correspondent, who told me. He gripped my arm on the
way back from a banquet and said conspiratorially in my ear, a habit
shared by crime reporters, 'I hear you're on your way again, old boy.
I'm very sorry.' It was decent of him and I kept it to myself.

The scene was as before, Max in his chair and Tom Blackburn
beside him as the other, in his case reluctant, executioner. As Max
began, I interrupted, 'We don't need Tom here. Let's do it properly
this time.' Tom left. I told Max I would consult Lord Goodman, my
friend through many troubles, and persuaded him to let me tell the
staff myself at the following morning's conference. He seemed
surprised when I asked who was going to be editor. Derek Marks,
unsportingly I thought, declined to attend the conference. Keith
Howard, the news editor, produced his usual half-fictitious
schedule. There was much laughter, and right at the end with
suitable bombshell effect I announced my departure. Several of the
staff took me to El Vino's, and on to a late lunch at the Caprice.
Fleet Street loved a sensation and liked its editors best of all when
they had been fired. John Junor invited me on his yacht that
weekend. We sailed past Max's house on the waterfront at Cowes.

14
SUNDAY EDITOR

It was John Junor who first rang me one morning in 1966. 'Have you heard the sad news?' he said. 'Sam Campbell is dead.' There was a brief pause. 'You must apply for the job immediately.' The next call was from someone on Keith Howard's news desk at the *Daily Express*. 'Keith has asked me to tell you that Sam Campbell has died. He says that you in particular should be told.' I felt it was a bit much to seek Sam's job on the *People* even before his funeral, and besides there was no need to ask. They would tell me if I was wanted. I was more or less the only person in Britain out of work in those days of full employment. Words like redundancy had not been heard of. I rang the Labour Exchange at Maidenhead to see if I was entitled to the dole. A man with a northern accent was sympathetic at first. 'Would I be right in assuming that you are in this situation through no impropriety on your part?' he asked. 'Correct,' I said. 'Would you have had a month's pay?' he continued. 'More than that,' I replied. 'Three months?' I told him it was eighteen months. His voice noticeably hardened, but he was still polite. 'Apply again at the end of that period,' he said.

For £40 a time, far more than on the dole, I regularly did the BBC's weekly review, then on the Home Service, of the daily newspapers. The fact that I wanted one of them to employ me as an editor somewhat cramped my style. It was a gentler version of Granada's 'What the Papers Say'. I would intone: 'And what did the *Daily Sketch* say?' Kenneth Kendall would read the extract. He did the popular papers. 'And now let's hear from *The Times*,' I would continue. John Snagge did the heavies. 'The *Daily Mail*, on the other hand ...' In case anyone is interested, the *Mail* was in Kendall's court. The programme was put on tape shortly before it went on the air. If we fluffed a line, we had to start again at the beginning of the sentence. One of the original Asian immigrants, a rather irritable man, would cut out the mistakes and stick the tape together again, usually about five times as far as I was concerned. One Friday,

Kendall, Snagge and I each scored one. I was delighted, since their invariable score had been nought. 'A warm glow possesses me,' I told Snagge as we sipped coffee. 'Sometimes,' said the great man, 'one sees something that isn't there. It has to do with the design of typewriter lettering.' He went into a long story about a famous announcer who, reading every news bulletin on both the Home and Light programmes, would have a large Scotch at the pub near the BBC after each broadcast. The midnight bulletin ended with the latest cricket scores. 'Larwood ill,' said the announcer. 'I'm sorry, I'll read that again. Larwood one hundred and eleven.'

Despite Sam's demise, I went on a cruise to the Canaries on the ill-fated *Laconia*'s sister ship. I had been inspired by a previous cruise on which I became friends with a stunning and intriguing girl who, unfortunately, was an undeviating lesbian. My wife stayed at home and I hoped for better luck. Instead I became friends with the ship's doctor, who had dirty finger nails, and the ship's sister who might have appealed to the stunning girl if she favoured the Sister George type. This voyage became a Fleet Street legend, thanks to skilful stage management by Hugh Cudlipp. The myth was that it was a banana boat and Cudlipp scoured the oceans to find me. Now at last the truth can be told, as we often wrote in desperation. I went ashore to a hotel in Tenerife with my two friends and we stayed by the pool. In the changing-room afterwards I showed the doctor a little growth on my inner thigh. He volunteered to cut it off and send it for analysis, but I thought that was risky. The three of us went to the bar where a man who looked and played the piano like Hoagy Carmichael entertained. We got very drunk. I staggered from side to side down the corridor to my cabin wishing there was at least one attractive girl on board. I poured a large whisky, lit a cigarette and went to bed with a Raymond Chandler book I had read ten times.

In the morning the light was still on. I had placed the whisky glass, undrunk, safely on the floor. The cigarette had bored a small hole in the bunk. I vaguely remembered opening and reading a telegram. Did I dream it? The telegram was there. 'PLEASE RETURN LONDON URGENTEST. REGARDS, PICKERING', it said. I looked out of the port-hole. We were docked in Las Palmas. Cudlipp had found out where I was by phoning my wife. He planted stories in the *Evening Standard* and *Guardian* diaries about the great search. Fleet Street hummed with speculation and wild stories. It was a first-class P.R. job. One paper described me as indestructible. UK Press Gazette reported: 'His name was the only one seriously mentioned among the vast Fleet Street gathering that stood around the grounds of Aldershot crematorium after Monday's last farewell to his predecessor.' In a hatchet job, the *Financial Times* gossip writer described me as 'tall, slim and elegant', possessing 'some wit and an undeniable talent: but he is not memorably tactful.' Someone I had fired, perhaps. The *Mirror* diary, at Cudlipp's instigation, described me as 'an ebullient and controversial figure ... He stepped off a cargo boat at Las Palmas last night to find an urgent cable awaiting his attention.'

On the Boeing 707 from Las Palmas, travelling first-class again, I could not eat the caviar and lobster or drink the champagne. I realised that having been sacked so publicly, twice, had taken its toll. I asked my doctor in Maidenhead for pills so that I could cope next day with my interview with Cudlipp. In the end, I did not take one. What the hell. I got the job. The *Sunday Times* wrote: 'Mr Edwards has twice been editor of the *Daily Express* but his new appointment will probably be his most challenging of all.' Cudlipp was full of charm and style. He planted more stories all over the place to give me the best possible start. Newspapermen like to be edited by a legend.

I enjoyed editing the *People*. I was left alone. No editor can ask for more. Despite Sam Campbell's cavalier attitude to truth when I was a *People* reporter fifteen years earlier, the paper had a skilled investigative team led by a remarkable figure, Laurie Manifold, who would have made an inspired and incorruptible police chief. This sort of journalism was frowned upon by Beaverbrook. 'Never put the police on anyone,' he would say, which would remind me of his early buccaneering days as a financier, although no evidence against him has ever been sustained. I thought it was great crusading stuff. Even Sir Denis Hamilton, editor-in-chief of the *Sunday Times*, paid tribute to the skills of *People* reporters. Just before he died, Sam had been exposing famous drugs firms for making outrageous profits on health service prescriptions. The despairing manager told me it had cost the *People* over £300,000 in lost advertising revenue.

The changes I made to the paper were subtle. Terence Lancaster came from the *Daily Express*, where he was unhappy with the new team, to write what many people thought was the best political column. Sam's Dr Goodenough was an old gentleman who looked, from an artist's imaginary impression, like Alfred Hitchcock in profile. I had him redrawn to resemble the sort of modern doctor familiar to our younger readers. His age was reduced by at least thirty years, his nose straightened and we put him in a white coat. None of the hypochondriacs who gave the column such a high readership seemed to notice. We revealed to a shocked nation the

new suburban practice of wife-swapping, which we ran and ran to
prove to the staff that their new editor knew on which side his paper's
bread was buttered. More respectably, we exposed what we predictably called the Great L Scandal. Anybody could run a driving
school after they had passed the driving test. We discovered a girl of
eighteen who did so a year after she had passed, and a man who had
set himself up as an instructor though he had failed five tests before
getting his licence. We asked the usual MPs to express shock and
horror. The law was changed. Now there are stringent tests.

We exposed religious racketeers in a series called 'The Faith
Merchants'. A typical *People* headline ran across two full-sized
pages: THEY CALL HAROLD WILSON 'SATAN'S AGENT' – BUT THEIR OWN
FOUNDER WAS A SHYSTER! We were not beyond having a go at humble
folk who made a good story. PULL YOUR WEIGHT, BASIL, we traduced
some unfortunate chap, adding in brackets (ALL 20-STONE OF YOU).
Peter Brodie, Assistant Commissioner (Crime) at Scotland Yard,
thanked us for smashing a drug ring. Spike Milligan wrote his life
story, from dinner with the Queen to the horrors of his period in a
mental hospital. He thought he had been in it for years and they were
giving him old papers to convince him he had not. A bright
psychiatrist cured this by turning on the BBC radio news which gave
the date. Milligan had the most original 'next week' line I have seen.
'Next week,' he wrote at the end of his second instalment, 'Monday,
Tuesday, Wednesday, Thursday, Friday, Saturday, Sunday.' We
had the first picture of Christine Keeler with her new baby son on
page one. It looked suspiciously like a *Daily Express* front page.
More traditionally, we had THIS AMAZING PICTURE apparently of a
ghostly monk kneeling before an altar. IS THIS THE FACE OF CHRIST?
Similar variations featured regularly in Sam's *People*. The films on
which these unearthly manifestations appeared were invariably sent
to a laboratory for tests and emerged immaculate. In 1967 I started a
book column by John Braine, followed by Tom Driberg, a sign of my
confidence because sales were an all-time record. (For July to
December 1968 they were higher still at 5,607,670. Today they are 3
million.) Ken Gardner, the chief reporter who later deserted Fleet
Street to run a pub, received the British Press Award as News
Reporter of the Year for an exposure of old people's homes.

The paper broke new ground by interviewing a judge about
controversially severe prison sentences he had imposed on Mick
Jagger and Keith Richard for drug offences. 'Any reason why we
shouldn't?' I asked our wise old lawyer Hugh Davidson. 'No reason
at all,' said Hugh. Then he added, 'Send a gentlemanly fellow.' I sent

an ex-naval lieutenant Bob Taylor, whose public school manners disguised his skills as a tough reporter. Sure enough, he produced an unprecedented talk with the judge, Leslie Block, defending his sentences which were later reversed on appeal, and talking of much else besides. I was delighted. 'How did you do it, Bob?' I asked. 'It was simple,' said Bob. 'I knocked at the door of his country house and he opened it himself. "Sorry to call on you unannounced, sir," I said, "but I had the privilege of serving under you aboard HMS ..."' and Bob named the aircraft carrier the judge had commanded. 'Of course, he invited me in,' Bob continued, 'but before I stepped inside I added: "I have to tell you that I also represent the yellow press."' Newspapers now frequently seek to interview judges. They seldom succeed.

Bob Taylor covered the first ever attempt to row the Atlantic by John Hoare, a twenty-nine-year-old weekend sailor, and a thirty-four-year-old journalist, David Johnstone. I inherited the contract for their story from Sam Campbell, and full of fear for them tried to talk them out of it. Then I was told that two army parachutists, Captain John Ridgway and Sergeant Chay Blyth, were also making the attempt with official backing. This eased my mind and I bought them up, too. 'Everyone currently rowing the Atlantic is under contract to the *People*,' I joked. Hoare and Johnstone perished in a storm not far from Ireland. Their unsinkable craft, designed and built by experts on the Solent, survived upside down.

Ridgway and Blyth became national heroes and personal friends. We gave a banquet in their honour at the Hyde Park Hotel. Years later, becalmed alone in a round-the-world race among ice floes in the Antarctic, Ridgway wrote me a postcard. He told me when, slightly to his surprise, he had survived and come home, that he had sat down to write to the people he had met he really liked. This was one of the nicest things said to me in my career as a journalist, and I rebuked myself for thinking that with his steel blue eyes and incredible courage he was incapable of such warmth. On a hot summer evening I tied up my thirty-four foot motor cruiser against a vast, trim racing yacht in the crowded harbour at Yarmouth, Isle of Wight. The rugged, professional crew viewed me coldly until Chay Blyth emerged from a hatch and I became instantly welcome. You get to know people as a newspaper editor. 'Mr Editor,' Ted Heath always called me at the Royal Southern Yacht Club. He is bad at remembering names.

In 1968, the *People* won another Oscar. David Farr became News Reporter of the Year for an exposure of fruit-machine rackets. His next assignment was on strip-crazy Britain. When Enoch Powell made his famous and not unprophetic 'rivers of blood' speech, which probably had the support of a majority of readers, I wrote that 'he ought to be sacked, but probably won't be.' To my surprise he was, that night. The editorial began: 'This column, as you may have noticed, is called "Voice of the People". By that we mean the voice of this newspaper – the editor's opinion. But it's nicely ambiguous. It could be taken to mean the "Voice of the Public". We hope it often is. ESPECIALLY THIS WEEK.' We received 130 letters, all but three against us. The following week I wrote: 'The emotions unleashed by Mr Powell were just a little too unBritish for comfort.' A fortnight later, as the storm about Powell's speech raged on, I published a remarkable picture across two pages of 50 coloured men and women of 47 different nationalities at a hospital in Essex, under the headline: DEAR ENOCH POWELL, IF YOU EVER HAVE TO GO INTO HOSPITAL, YOU'LL BE <u>GLAD</u> OF PEOPLE LIKE THESE . . .

Later the same year we hit upon an extraordinary police racket. A minor crook told us he had been blackmailed on threat of prosecution into setting up a robbery at a bank in Surrey. We fitted him up with a hidden tape-recorder and played back conversations he had with a detective-inspector, detective-sergeant and detective-constable plotting the crime, which they had suggested, nominating the bank at Ashtead railway station. The motive of the police, apart from any benefit of sharing the reward, was succinctly explained by the detective-sergeant on our informant's tape: 'It looks good for us to catch a bloody bank team. Obviously we can't keep setting up bloody banks all over the place, but it looks good when they say, "Oh, well, the Mitcham squad brought a little bank team in." They say it looks as if we are doing our bloody jobs, then.' A well-hidden cameraman photographed the police officer handing our informant a convincing toy replica of a Luger revolver and a Squeezy bottle filled with diluted ammonia with which criminals induced to rob the bank would terrorise its staff. We decided it would be wildly irresponsible for us to let the robbery take place – the police stooge would conveniently escape – and to what must have been the considerable surprise of the three policemen we published the story complete with the picture and their names. Surprisingly, such was the state of Scotland Yard at that time, they survived for a while, escaped prosecution and later left the police after issuing libel writs they did not pursue.

Meanwhile we discovered another raid, this time on a post office in Rotherham, also entirely set up by the police putting pressure on a minor criminal to persuade acquaintances to commit the crimes, in which one man inveigled into it had been sentenced to five years and another to two years. A detective-constable even lent his car to the conscience-stricken stooge who, after reading our account of the other planned raid, told us what had happened. It was his turn to wear the tape-recorder. 'By golly, listen,' the detective's voice said loud and clear, 'if our gaffer had known that I'd used my car he'd go mad.' Our informant obviously had a reporter's skill for steering the conversation along lines that would produce good copy. The detective produced some kind of moral code for tempting criminals into robberies they had not even contemplated. 'We never set a bloke up unless he's – how can I put it? – he's bang at it,' he said, 'and if we didn't do it he'd do summat else. I wouldn't set up a bloody innocent bloke.' Our informant presumably then asked if he had any further projects in mind. 'The only thing I can fancy,' said the detective, 'is that tobacco warehouse. I'll have a look at it tomorrow.'

The actual raid on the post office had many elements of farce, apart from the getaway car belonging to one of the arresting officers. It was arranged that our informant should loosely tie up the elderly postmaster, who had been let into the secret. Though the postmaster knew there were police hidden everywhere, he shook badly. 'I am afraid I'll have to stuff some paper tissues into your mouth,' said the police accomplice. He in turn was knocked flying when a policeman burst in from a back room. 'Hurry up and get the hell out of here,' cried the policeman. One of the criminals was caught when his case carrying the loot got stuck in the door. Our informant found himself being pursued down the road by a detective. As we reported: 'He did not know whether to stop running in order to join up with friends in the police, or to carry on in order to keep up with the pretence of being a robber. His dilemma was resolved when the detective shouted, "Keep on running".' This produced one of my favourite headlines, across the obligatory two pages: KEEP RUNNING THE POLICEMAN TOLD THE ROBBER.

The judge, not knowing that the police instigated the crime and that the postmaster was forewarned, said, 'It must have been exceedingly unpleasant for a man of 64 years of age. He did not know what is going to happen to him.' The case went to the Appeal Court. Lord Justice Winn, the same man who had given the *Daily Express* city editor, Fred Ellis, such a hard time in the Bank Rate Tribunal, gave his verdict on what we believed had become a widespread practice: 'It is a horrible and repulsive experience for any

judge to find that justice has been prevented in this fashion ...
Justice was blindfolded. Let us hope to God it does not happen
again.' The two men were freed. Jim Callaghan, the Home Secretary, set up an inquiry in every police force. Eventually the Lord
Chief Justice ruled against set-up crimes.

Early in 1970 the *Cleveland Plain Dealer* in America published the
story of the Pinkville massacre. Manny Shinwell, created a baron
that year, said that no doubt in the heat of war British troops had
committed similar atrocities. I wrote a leader saying that he should
either produce evidence to sustain that charge or withdraw it, and
not unshrewdly added that if any reader knew of any such incident
we would investigate it 'to the ends of the earth'. Thus emerged the
story of the killing in cold blood by British troops of twenty-five
Malayan villagers in 1949. One of the soldiers involved read the
leader and went to our Manchester office. The village was suspected
of harbouring terrorists. The women and children were herded
together and led away. Then the men, also grouped together, were
told to walk towards a river. On the orders of a sergeant they were
machine-gunned in the back. It turned out they worked in a small
local factory or were elderly. None were terrorists. Everybody who
had taken part, including the sergeant, confirmed the story, deeply
regretted their actions and swore affidavits for us. We interviewed
their former C.O., who expressed shock and denied complicity. All
the soldiers had told their wives. They had sleepless nights and were
glad to get it off their chests. The reporters who persuaded them to
do so were our award-winning chief reporter Ken Gardner and Bill
Dorran, who later became news editor.

I published the whole story under the front page headline HORROR
IN A NAMELESS VILLAGE in the most unusual and, I think, best edition
in the history of the *People*. We dropped the usual narrow columns
and ran the soldiers' testimonies across several pages. The editorial
said, conceding Shinwell's case, 'A newspaper has a simple duty to its
readers which is best summed up in the biblical phrase "Ye shall
know the truth". The truth in this case illustrates – as at Pinkville and
elsewhere – the corrupting and fearful effect of war on otherwise
decent men, and what can happen when the highest standards of
discipline are allowed to fall. That is the lesson, and it can never be
taught too often.'

We were severely attacked for our report by people who ought to
have known better, but to my surprise by only a few of our readers.
Jeremy Thorpe, whom I later protected over the Norman Scott
affair, said I should be prosecuted for criminal libel, and in the same

10 Princess Anne thanks *Sunday Mirror* editor for record sum raised for the Save the Children Fund.

11 *Sunday Mirror* retirement party for Hugh Cudlipp, Mirror Group supremo (centre), with Marje Proops in full battle order.

12 Bob Maxwell and friend at one of the Mirror chief's many press conferences.

13 Fleet Street gossip with well-known photographer.

14 Mrs Thatcher in the Mirror lions' den. Also present: Richard Stott (second from left), now editor of the *Daily Mirror*, and leader-writer Joe Haines.

15 All is perhaps forgiven. At Buckingham Palace with the CBE received from the Queen.

speech accused *The Times* of trial by newspaper over its *People*-style exposure of crooked policemen. The *Guardian* backed us. Denis Healey astounded me at a No. 10 party given by Harold Wilson when he got me into a corner and said my behaviour had been 'disgraceful'. Presumably as Defence Minister and a former major he thought that damaging the reputation of the British Army outweighed the virtue of telling the truth. And it was Labour who had sent the troops to Malaya. I defended the paper the week after our sensational but calmly presented report by asking if the *Cleveland Plain Dealer* was wrong to have exposed the Pinkville massacre. Nobody sued us. No questions were asked in the House of Commons. The country was shocked, I felt, but wanted the matter quietly dropped, and that is what happened.

Meanwhile, I continued to edit the *People* along more traditional lines. I revived Arthur Helliwell's famous column, complete with his 'titfer' under the more modern but less effective title 'The Arthur Helliwell Show'. Why change 'Follow Me Around'? Helliwell was a gentlemanly person, deferential to his editors, who became extremely offensive and articulate in drink, something I have often encountered. His alcoholism combined with his paranoia made him an extreme nuisance at times. One day I had to attend several parties, two given by Hugh Cudlipp, and ended up very happily at the pub favoured by the *People*. Helliwell was at the bar. I got very drunk and did not remember the rest of the evening. Next morning several members of the staff who were there showed more familiarity than usual. 'My God, Bob,' said one, 'the things you said to Tony Helliwell. I've never heard anything like it. You tore him to shreds.'

This was a man I was critical of because of his habit of leaving the office for a drink at regular intervals throughout the day on the pretext of getting cigarettes, and I feared he was going to put his arm around me. The internal phone went after I had received further congratulations. 'Helliwell here,' said the voice. 'May I come to see you, sir?' I imagined I would have to grovel. He came in looking as he frequently did at that time of the morning. 'I've no idea what I said to you last night,' he said, 'but whatever it was I am sorry. I was drunk.' Immensely relieved that he was unaware of everything I had said, I forgave him in true Christian spirit. Over drinks some time later he told our mutual friend Terence Lancaster that I had only started up his column again to get rid of him.

The fun went on. We had a page one picture of a naked girl standing outside Buckingham Palace in a stunt for a film, with a good piece of social observation: 'We wouldn't have published this picture

18 months ago.' We ran another picture of a happy looking man who swapped his wife for the car he was somewhat ostentatiously polishing for our photographer. A sensational series exposing cruelty to British dogs exported to Japan led to a march against us in Tokyo and a march against the Japanese in London.

We found there was corruption right at the top in Scotland Yard. A reporter was sent to Amsterdam to discover how pornography got to Britain. A pornography merchant, when the reporter pretended he wanted to buy some, said he would never get it through customs without the help of James Humphreys, an old lag who had cornered the market. The pornography merchant said that Humphreys was a friend of the head of Scotland Yard and had even been on holiday abroad with him. The reporter could not believe that Sir Joseph Simpson, the Commissioner, was a crook. He rattled off the names of other Scotland Yard chiefs. The one the pornographer remembered was Commander Frank Drury, head of the Flying Squad. Scarcely believing it possible, I sent a reporter unknown to the London police from Newcastle to Cyprus where Drury and Humphreys were supposed to have stayed with their wives. Sure enough, Drury had signed the register at one of the hotels. Humphreys's name was above his, and the manager told our reporter he had paid the bill. We ran the story on page one under these headlines:

POLICE CHIEF AND THE 'PORN' KING

A GRAVE QUESTION IN THE PUBLIC INTEREST

WAS IT WISE FOR COMMANDER DRURY OF THE
YARD TO GO ON HOLIDAY WITH THIS OLD LAG?

We listed Humphreys's criminal record, which included six years in Dartmoor for office-breaking. The judge had described him as 'a hardened and dangerous criminal.' I had heard of him before. John Trevelyan, the film censor, when we were having lunch at a Soho restaurant, told me he often entertained police friends in a private room below. 'He has scores of them round his swimming-pool at the weekend,' Trevelyan further revealed. The *News of the World*, confronted by the sensational story in our first edition, got its crime reporter Peter Earle, who was always photographed with a cigarette in his mouth, to phone Drury. In its later edition the *News of the World* referred to the filthy lies published in an unnamed rival and, under headlines as large as ours, said the reason for Drury's trip was because Humphreys had had a tip that the missing train robber Ronald Biggs was in Cyprus.

If this was true, we faced colossal libel damages and I was ruined. I saw the *News of the World* headlines at breakfast and rang the news editor, Laurie Manifold. 'Please tell me, Laurie,' I said politely, 'why I shouldn't worry about the *News of the World* story?' 'Sir,' said the incomparable man, 'if you are going to Cyprus to catch a train robber you take a sergeant with you not your wife, and a crook does not book the trip three weeks earlier on a package holiday.' Unbelievably, Drury was not instantly dismissed. He resigned shortly afterwards and put it about that Humphreys was a 'grass' who shopped his fellow crooks. This infuriated Humphreys, who in turn shopped Drury for taking bribes. Drury was gaoled for five years. It was a stunning example of a newspaper rooting out what Sunday papers in their off moments call a rat. 'Rat of the Week' was one of Cudlipp's favourite headlines. Like me, he has never taken the profession too seriously.

The circulations of all the popular newspapers, except the *Sun* with its page three girls, endless series with ill-clad girl models on how to make love, and its adoption of the Bartholomew formula for the *Mirror*, were falling, largely because bad managements were increasing prices twice a year ahead of inflation in deference to chapel demands. The *Sunday Mirror*'s had fallen far more than the *People*'s, and rather peremptorily I was posted there at Hugh Cudlipp's suggestion by the editorial director, Sydney Jacobson. Michael Christiansen, whose paper had become increasingly odd, was offered the sack or the deputy editorship of the *Daily Mirror*, which he chose. During my editorship I had changed the name of the *People* to the *Sunday People*, which I thought had more appeal to the young. It was changed back fourteen years and four editors later. I was sorry to leave the paper, which I still felt had Sam Campbell's ghostly hand lightly on its tiller. The staff gave me champagne and yet another inscribed silver beer tankard to add to my collection.

At least the *Sunday Mirror* was read by many of my friends though it was a far less worthy and crusading newspaper. I brought in a former *People* news editor, Graham Gadd, published several more news pages, strengthened the political coverage and devoted much attention to page two editorials that sometimes took the whole page. Possibly the most famous picture the *Sunday Mirror* has published was of the streaker in 1974 at a rugby international, who was decorously covered by a helmet skilfully placed by a gloriously camp-looking policeman, while a humourless, earnest man was running up behind carrying an open raincoat to protect Princess Alexandra from the appalling sight of the naked figure. I moved it from the back sports page to the front under the headline, WELL IT WAS A ROYAL OCCASION. It appeared in *Paris-Match, Life, Oggi, Stern*, and all over the world.

On a tour of Africa with John Graham, the political correspondent, I arrived in Ethiopia as the world learned of starving tribes in the north of the country. Because soldiers were blocking all the roads, Oxfam asked us (in the same hotel where Robert Maxwell hired his mercy-mission suite years later) if we would fly two gas cookers to a camp it had set up, without which food that had got through was inedible. Eventually in a tiny Cessna plane we flew over a 10,000 foot mountain. The man we had persuaded to take us was the chief training pilot of Ethiopian Airways. He looked like Fats Waller and told us that the klaxon we had heard on the last ridge over the mountain top was a stall-warning device. My deputy led with my report until a better story came in.

In February 1974, I totally supported Labour in the general election and backed the argument that the miners were a special case by printing 7,768 crosses on the centre pages, each representing a miner killed in the pits since nationalisation in 1947. Nobody had totted up the figure before. Later that year we got close to putting our finger on the alleged MI5 plot against the Prime Minister, Harold Wilson. IS THIS THE WORK OF A DIRTY TRICKS DEPARTMENT? was our headline to a report by our crime correspondent, Norman Lucas, on a series of break-ins at the office of solicitors involved with Wilson, including Lord Goodman.

We had our fun. 'The dossier to end all dossiers' is how we described a series by Donald Zec on 'This Permissive World'. '*Playboy* wanted it. The *Sunday Mirror* has got it,' someone wrote on another occasion. 'Miss World – The Naked Truth. Today on the centre pages the *Sunday Mirror* presents the most sensational Miss World picture ever taken.' It would hardly be sensational today. I edited the *Sunday Mirror* for thirteen years, longer than anybody. Among my deputies was Nick Lloyd, present (at the time of writing) editor of the *Daily Express*. David Montgomery, who succeeded him brilliantly as editor of the *News of the World* and now edits *Today*, was a Saturday casual. Which paper did I most enjoy editing? I am often asked. Them all, is the answer, including the *Evening Citizen* in Glasgow. But the *People* was the most exciting.

15
ROYAL
LOVE TRAIN

'Well,' said my friend the Special Branch man, while we were waiting for our respective guests at the Kennel Club, 'bang goes your K, old man.' He was talking of my sensational refusal to accept the Palace denial that Lady Diana Spencer had met Prince Charles on the Royal Train. I thought he was also hoping I would let slip a clue about our informant. Since Mrs Thatcher's elevation of John Junor, Larry Lamb and David English, many friends and colleagues assumed that long-serving editors like myself confidently expected knighthoods, as is the automatic lot of senior civil servants and diplomats. As with the Special Branch man, I was subject to much jolly banter following the Royal train story, in my local in the country as well as in the office and Fleet Street. In fact, any editor who had one eye on Downing Street and the other on Buckingham Palace would very soon be unfit to hold his job. He would soon be suppressing or toning down stories for the worst of all possible reasons. Falling foul of the Palace is one of the perils of editing a popular newspaper. It happens to us all.

My first experience of it was in 1964. The impressive Commander Richard Colville was the Queen's press secretary. Princess Anne was still at school. The subsequently notorious 'paparazzi' freelance photographer R. Bellisario had taken some quite splendid pictures of Princess Margaret, then the leading sex symbol in the endless Royal soap opera, water-skiing in Sunninghill Park. One of the pictures showed, as the Palace later complained, 'a photograph of the Princess dressed for swimming'. Another showed her 'dressed for water-skiing' with the Queen 'reclining on the ground'. A third, I was told, was of the Queen Mother sitting, also on the ground, with a bottle of gin next to her. This was not used, but if it had been it would have added to her even then enormous popularity. As Prince Charles demonstrated again quite recently, when he changed his mind about allowing TV to show Princess Diana by the family pool, the Royal Family do not like their womenfolk to be photographed in bathing costumes. Mr Bellisario added to the offence by taking his world-beating pictures from his customary position inside a bush on private land. They were published in the *Sunday Express* and the *People* and every newspaperman or woman looking at them, harmless though they were, instantly knew they were taken under the dodgiest of circumstances and totally unauthorised. That is when I should have been on my guard.

As editor of the *Daily Express*, I was on duty on the Sunday the pictures appeared. I should have told the picture editor not to attempt a repeat performance by sending one of our own photographers on hands and knees along the same track as Bellisario. It is the job of the picture editors to succumb to temptation and the job of editors to restrain them. Without telling me, because he thought it best I should not know, the picture editor sent one of the greatest photographers of the time, Robert Haswell, on the perilous journey that ended, predictably, with him being found by a searching forester hidden in the undergrowth. He was lying on the ground with his camera trained, as Commander Colville later complained, 'on the hut where Her Royal Highness was changing her clothes.' Haswell, and a freelance photographer who was with him, and had presumably shown him the way, were taken to the deputy ranger of Windsor Great Park, of which Sunninghill Park and its lake form a part, and escorted off the private property. The Palace had an open-and-shut case and asked the Press Council to adjudicate. John Junor, crawling suitably on behalf of the *Sunday Express*, said Mr Bellisario gave an assurance that all the pictures had been taken from a public footpath. He observed: 'If, as would now seem was to be the case, we have been misled by Mr Bellisario, it would be a matter of great regret to me and I would like to express my apologies to Her Majesty and Her Royal Highness.' Sam Campbell, the less highly principled editor of the *People*, went even further. He said that 'had he thought the photographs had been taken surreptitiously, by trespass, he would have regarded the act as intrusion of a particularly unpleasant kind.' Neither editor could possibly claim they thought the Royal Family were aware of the pictures being taken, firmly though they believed Mr Bellisario had stood on a public footpath, happily unobserved. Haswell and I rated a brief mention in the Press Council's findings: 'Mr Robert Edwards, editor of the *Daily Express*, expressed his regret and said Mr Haswell had been "over zealous". Mr Haswell, who did not take any pictures, sent a written apology for his action.'

I was fond of and admired the gentlemanly Bob Haswell, who

later left the profession to set up a fishing tackle business. So on the day before we published the suitably severe Press Council adjudication, I called in the picture editor, Frank Spooner, and said I wanted to show it personally to the photographer. 'Bit of a problem there,' said Frank, who as is customary was notably evasive when defending his staff. 'Why?' I asked. The conversation continued like this:

'He's not available just now.'

'Where is he? On a job?'

'No, he's not on a job.'

'Holiday then? Come on, Frank.'

'No.'

'Tell me, for heaven's sake.'

'Well, sir, if you must know, he's in hospital.'

'All right, Frank. I'm sorry to hear it. What's wrong with him?'

'Broken arm.'

'How did that happen?'

'Fell out of a tree.'

'Where?'

'Benenden.'

I often found it a heart-stopping moment when the news editor rushed in to tell me he had a great world exclusive story. It almost always meant trouble, whether it was Laurie Manifold on the *Sunday People* telling me that Commander Frank Drury, head of Scotland Yard's Flying Squad, was a crook, Graham Gadd on the *Sunday Mirror* reporting that building workers had found some extraordinary papers in an attic involving Jeremy Thorpe and someone called Norman Scott, or Graham's successor P. J. Wilson telling me that Lady Diana Spencer had twice secretly spent several hours with Prince Charles on the Royal train. Fortunately I had always taken care to have first-class news editors. None of them were chancers. They knew their job was to get the story right and that I was as concerned about avoiding Press Council rebukes as I was about libel and contempt of court. It is relevant to the famous (or infamous) Royal train story that almost certainly I had fewer Press Council censures than any other long serving editor, including the editors of *The Times*, *Observer*, and *Daily Telegraph*. In my last ten years as *Sunday Mirror* editor we broke all records for a national newspaper with no rebukes at all. This did not mean, as some journalists will suspect, that we were too cowardly to print 'hot' stories. It meant that our reporters were well-trained and honest. They knew that all the pressure at the top was against stories being bent to get sensational headlines. All the same I had that familiar sinking feeling as the excited 'P.J.' told me that Jim Newman, a freelance journalist in Wiltshire, had evidence from what seemed an impeccable source that Lady Diana had visited Prince Charles in a local sidings at dead of night. Newman had previously given us a story, which I subsequently learned came from the same source, that an army officer had committed suicide because the army's Special Investigations Branch were investigating his sex life with a male warrant officer. The story was interesting because the army officer was a gossip column peer known in Royal circles. It was strongly denied and obloquy was poured upon us. Later it was totally confirmed.

Because no sane newspaper would publish the Royal train story without knowing the source, Newman had told P.J. in the usual confidence. As a general rule, it is best for editors and news editors not to know such a thing. This avoids the painful necessity of going to jail rather than reveal it on the orders of a High Court or Tribunal judge. The gallant reporter is then left to his lonely martyrdom. In this case the source was not as good as the Chancellor of the Exchequer, Dr Hugh Dalton, in the famous budget leak that cost him his job, but since it is unlikely that Prince Charles himself would be anyone's informant it could scarcely have been a better one. Not only did he claim he knew Lady Diana was coming to see the Prince, he said he saw her very clearly at close quarters. She was instantly recognisable. Her picture had been on TV and all over the papers every day in a frenzy of speculation.

Had he simply made a mistake? Had he made it up? That last possibility seemed highly unlikely from what we knew of him. If we published the story and then became convinced he had lied, we might no longer feel obliged to protect him as its source. There was no question of any payment either from us or the freelance Newman, the crafty device some newspapers use so that they can tell the Press Council with hand on deceitful heart that they have paid no money to an unsavoury person. Newman was a country reporter with the same sort of contacts that I had had on the *Reading Mercury*, nice people who should not perhaps tell you but do, because that is human nature and you can be trusted. His source had a proper concern for fellow human beings. The reason he first mentioned to his friend Newman the Royal train's secret resting place – secret for security reasons and to avoid sightseers – was because he was shocked that members of its staff had to clean up under it in the morning. Little piles of sawdust seen later by one of our reporters seemed to confirm that the toilet arrangements on this train are as primitive as on any other. (Sam Campbell once ran an unsuccessful campaign in the *People* against the railways' disgusting habit of discharging human waste on to the line, which explained to a few million readers for the first time why they were asked not to use the lavatory while the train was standing at a station.) When the source went on to mention Lady Diana's visit, Newman knew he had a great story and persuaded his friend to let him use it for the simplest of all reasons given by reporters in such a situation. This can be summed up in two words, why not?

I told P.J. there was no way we could publish the story simply on the word of a freelance journalist, however trustworthy he had proved, and from a source, admirable though he may be, we had never met. And we needed convincing supporting evidence. 'Of course,' said the highly professional P.J. 'I am sending Wensley Clarkson with Newman to check it all out.' 'Get the source to confirm it to Wensley,' I said, 'so that we know Newman hasn't gone off his rocker and made it all up.' Wilson knew I trusted Clarkson totally on difficult stories like this. He met the by now somewhat worried informant at a social evening fixed up by Newman. In the briefest of conversations, the source confirmed when no one else could hear that he had seen Diana enter the Royal train. He wrote his name and address in the reporter's notebook as a gesture of good faith. Clarkson believed him absolutely. The process of checking what he had told Newman began.

Everything he had said about the movements of the train was confirmed to another *Sunday Mirror* reporter, Steve Bailey, by railway workers, villagers and a farmer's son, who said the police had kept a mobile caravan on a site overlooking the sidings, as the source had also told Newman. The son pointed out the exact position of the train as he had seen it the first day. There were the tell-tale patches of sawdust to back him up. A railway worker told Bailey that a Post Office engineer had rather indiscreetly asked him where the Royal train of Prince Charles was stopping so that he could instal a telephone line. Unfortunately it was put in the wrong place. Bailey saw it, still in position, and presumably another was installed hurriedly where the train actually stayed. So the source had told us where the train had been and he was right. No one later disputed this, though there was an attempt to deny the train had stayed as long as we said in the same spot on the second night. Another clue the informant gave Newman was the number of Lady Diana's car. I said to P.J., 'That doesn't prove much. You would expect that people whose job is involved with the Royal Family might conceivably know it.' 'Aaah!' said the news editor, in a Sherlock Holmes manner as though talking to a dense but attentive Dr Watson, 'that's the whole point. The number he gave us wasn't Di's car at all, and we had a job checking it out. It was her mother's car, Lady Shand-Kydd's. We found it outside Di's flat in Kensington. Her VW was pranged and she borrowed her mum's Renault. Simple as that.' It seemed to us that if the source was inventing Di's visits he would have given us the number of the car he would have expected her to use, in the unlikely event that he knew the number at all.

By now there seemed no reason to doubt the story, but the checking continued. According to the source, Di had visited Prince Charles's friends the Parker Bowles at their country home before making the short journey to the sidings on the second night, when the guests had left the official dinner Charles had given as Duke of Cornwall. The source said he knew that Prince Charles had telephoned the Parker Bowles's number that evening because all calls were recorded for security reasons and he had seen it, but he did not know whether the Prince spoke to Diana. When P.J. told me this I thought it had the hallmark of truth. If the source was a liar, why not say the Prince had called up Lady Diana? Clarkson telephoned and asked for Mrs Parker Bowles. She was out and when he called later she still had not returned. Tactfully questioned, the nanny then confirmed that Lady Diana had spent the evening in question at the house and had left very late. Had she got it wrong? That was inconceivable. Was the reporter lying? I trusted him absolutely. All my colleagues, including my deputy Nick Lloyd, who became editor of the *Daily Express*, and the *Sunday Mirror* lawyer Tom Crone, were as sure as I was that we had done everything by the book and the story was true.

One thing that did not occur to any of us handling the story, as far as I know, is that it meant that Prince Charles and Lady Diana had behaved in a way that almost no one in the country would regard as scandalous with any other young couple. When the Queen's Press Secretary Michael Shea fulminated in his first letter: 'Grave exception has been taken to the implications of your story,' I thought, well, at least that was not in my silly mind. Nigel Dempster, the *Daily Mail* gossip columnist, who had the gall to criticise me day after day for publishing the story, got into trouble at the time for saying on London's Capital Radio that Prince Charles had 'sowed all his wild oats' and was 'now down to virgins'. My thoughts were altogether less crude and offensive. Like millions of others, to me Lady Diana was a very old fashioned girl and I totally accepted the image she innocently projected. She seemed an ideal bride for the heir to the throne and there was not a breath of scandal about her. I just hoped, as many others must have done, that they were actually in love as well as being ideally suited to each other. Her escapades down to the Royal train, if true, to me proved up to the hilt that they were in love, and that, I was sure, would be the public's reaction. It was true romance. We would have a smashing front page. The nation, the world, would be delighted. And, I thought, she has got high spirits too.

But I knew the Palace would be far from happy. They liked to decide what the public should be told. They did not like newspapers to find out for themselves. We decided not to phone them because the news desk feared they might issue a general statement. You get like that when you have a big exclusive. Everyone, Scotland Yard or even the Palace press office, is deeply distrusted. Worse still, they might issue a denial, and we would have to run one of those coded stories: 'Despite official denials, reports persisted last night that Lady Diana Spencer . . .' the coded message being it's true, folks, they are lying through their teeth. Either it was true or it was not. We were sure of it. Publish and be damned.

There was a stylish front page: a small heartshaped picture at the top with a Cupid's arrow through it and a secondary headline CHARLES AND LADY DIANA SPECIAL. The main headline seemed inevitable: ROYAL LOVE TRAIN, and beneath it a third heading SECRET MEETINGS IN THE SIDINGS. There was a small crown next to the first three lines of the report. No one was striving too hard for originality. The report that was to cause such enormous eruptions read in the staccato manner of popular tabloid newspapers:

> The Sunday Mirror today can reveal two late night meetings between Prince Charles and Lady Diana Spencer – the girl many believe will be the next Queen.
>
> The couple met secretly aboard the Royal train as it stood in secluded sidings in Wiltshire.
>
> The Prince's interludes with Lady Di happened during a West Country tour.
>
> We can reveal the fascinating details of the Royal rendezvous on both nights.
>
> Lady Di made a 100 mile dash by car from her London home to be with the Prince.

Under cover of darkness she was ushered through a police road block to the waiting train.

The 19-year-old spent a number of hours in the carriage normally used by the Duke of Edinburgh.

Lady Di then left Charles in the early hours of the morning to drive back to London.

The train came to a stop at a well-established Royal resting place near the village of Holt on the nights of November 5 and 6.

The first meeting was after Charles had visited Duchy of Cornwall estates in Somerset.

The carriages halted on a track running beside a narrow country lane called Station Road.

Lady Di arrived at a checkpoint manned by plainclothes police near the end of the lane.

A detective accompanied her in her blue Renault car down to the deserted siding, then escorted her aboard the Royal train.

It went a short distance up the line to Bradford-on-Avon junction near the village of Staverton.

Then followed hours alone together for the couple whose friendship has captured the country's imagination.

Later Lady Di emerged from the coach and drove back to London.

The following evening Charles entertained Duchy tenants in Bath.

Meanwhile Lady Di travelled from London to the nearby country home of the Prince's close friend and confidante, Mrs. Camilla Parker Bowles, where she got the phone call which sent her dashing once again to the same lonely siding.

And for the second night running she stayed with the Prince until the early hours.

A member of Mrs. Parker Bowles' staff said yesterday: "Lady Diana stayed for a few hours and then went out very late.

"But I dare not say anything more about this."

The rest of the report was about how villagers knew the Royal train was in the sidings, with Prince Charles aboard, though it was supposed to be a secret. The rest of page one was a large picture of Miss World headlined WHY I DID IT. What she did I have forgotten. After the first edition was published Wensley Clarkson phoned the Buckingham Palace press office and asked if they would care to

comment. The duty press officer handling this hot potato replied
that there would be no comment. So far, so good. It was the
following day that the fan was hit. The Palace issued an official
denial. I was on the phone repeatedly to P.J. and Clarkson at their
homes trying to knock holes in our story in case we had got it wrong.
Clarkson said later that three times he had tried to hammer a nail in
a wall and each time he had been prevented by a call from me. The
story remained, as far as we were concerned, impregnable. When I
returned to the office on Tuesday a letter awaited me from Michael
Shea, the Queen's press secretary. It said:

BUCKINGHAM PALACE

<u>Not for Publication</u>   17th November, 1980

Dear Mr Edwards,

I am writing to protest in the strongest possible terms about the
totally false story carried as the major front page item in yesterday's
edition of your newspaper. You will know that I have since gone on
record as saying that, with the exception of the fact that The Prince of
Wales was in the West Country and used the Royal Train on the two
nights in question, any other suggestion made by you is a total
fabrication. For your information, the only guests on board the train
on either night were the Secretary of the Duchy of Cornwall, his
successor and the local Duchy Land Steward. Grave exception has
been taken to the implications of your story and I am writing to ask
you for an apology which we would require to be printed in your
newspaper in a prominent position, at the earliest possible opportunity.

I look forward to receiving your reply.

Yours sincerely,

Michael Shea

Press Secretary to The Queen

'Totally false story ... total fabrication ... grave exception ...'
how soundly my stomach had warned me with that sinking feeling
when P.J. had first bounded into my office. The obvious reaction to
Shea's letter was that clearly, with the best will in the world, we had
got it wrong, so why not apologise? But how could we have got it
wrong in view of the supporting evidence we had obtained ourselves
from what the impressive source had told Newman? I discussed the
letter with Tony Miles, then chairman and editorial director. As any
sensible editor would, I had told him the previous Saturday that I

was publishing the story and had given him all the background to it. The editor is responsible, but he may as well have the boss on his side. Tony was as sure as I was that we had got it right and so was our lawyer, Tom Crone.

I was influenced by an extraordinary experience I had had with the Palace some years earlier. Robin Ludlow was then the Queen's press secretary. He asked to see me and sought my advice about how he could stop all the speculation in the papers that Princess Anne would marry Captain Mark Phillips. 'Well, they are going to marry, aren't they?' I replied, reflecting the belief of every Fleet Street newspaper. 'No, they are not,' said the pleasant Mr Ludlow. 'They are not in love. They have a mutual interest in horses. That's all.' I was still not convinced. 'Let's get it straight,' I said. 'You are here off the record but officially?' Robin said he was. 'And they know you are here?' I added without specifying who 'they' were. 'That's right,' said Robin. That was enough for me. I said I would do my best to help. That Sunday we led our gossip column with an authoritative story denying the marriage rumours under the pretty good headline, I thought, NEIGH! NEIGH! Not long after the engagement was announced. Robin Ludlow later gave me permission to tell this story. He had been as taken in as I was. Presumably he had been asked to plant the denial in an attempt to stop reporters and photographers hounding Princess Anne and Mark Phillips wherever they went. Another editor, Geoffrey Pinnington of the *People*, was approached by Ludlow at the same time. He was better informed than I was and did not fall for the story. Years later he told me one of his reporters had seen Anne and Mark kissing in a horse-box.

Aided by the lawyer, I sent a 'holder', as we call it in the trade, to Michael Shea while Newman and everyone on the staff involved in the story sat down to write memos so that every detail was on record. Sleuths were despatched and another reporter found a signalman who was able to give an exact description of the Renault our report said Lady Diana had used. The holder read:

Dear Mr Shea,

Thank you for your letter of November 17th.

Certainly we never knowingly print anything that is untrue. Needless to say we were absolutely certain when we published it that our report was true. It came from an excellent source and we made extensive independent checks that confirmed the details we had been given.

In view of your denial of our report, I am having further enquiries made and will get in touch with you shortly.

In the meantime I note with some surprise that "grave exception" has been taken over the report. Certainly we did not intend to imply that anything improper had occurred, nor do we consider that the report carried any such implications.

Yours sincerely,

Robert Edwards

Three days later Tom and I wrote a further letter.

Dear Mr Shea,

I have made extensive further enquiries into the matters raised in your letter of November 17th 1980, as a result of which I am placed in some considerable difficulty.

As I have already made clear to you, we do not publish our reports wantonly and recklessly; we take great care to get our facts right. You will also know that if, despite our best efforts we err on an important matter of fact, we are always willing to apologise and put the correct facts on record.

In this case I am faced with (for me) the unprecedented situation of a denial from Buckingham Palace of a report the accuracy of which I was satisfied about at the time of publication and, after further intensive enquiries, remain as convinced about its truth as anyone can be who was not there himself. Obviously, you will not expect me to divulge sources, but I hope you will accept my word that I do have strong evidence and that I do honestly believe we were right. You will, of course, appreciate that the professional reputation of two journalists as well as that of the Sunday Mirror is involved in this matter.

I could be wrong, of course, but I believe on all the evidence that our report in all essential matters was true. I am also satisfied that it in no way reflected badly on Prince Charles or Lady Diana.

It is not for me to speculate about the basis on which you have seen fit to describe our report as "totally false" and a "total fabrication". It was, however, my unfortunate experience at the time of the impending engagement of Princess Anne and Captain Mark Phillips to have published a report based upon an off the record suggestion by one of your predecessors only to find it to be totally inaccurate – with the result that the Sunday Mirror was made to look very foolish. I refer to the incident merely to illustrate that the Press Office itself can on occasion be mistaken.

Your letter to me was marked "Not For Publication". If, however, you wish to issue an official denial on the record, I will, needless to say, publish it in full, though I reserve the right to inform our readers of the Sunday Mirror's position.

In the meantime, in view of the above, you will appreciate that though my judgment may turn out to be at fault, I cannot publish an apology while I believe we are right.

Yours sincerely,

Robert Edwards

It was a Friday. We had to have a story the following day for Sunday's paper. I sent the letter round by hand. Shea replied the same day:

Dear Mr Edwards,

Thank you for your letter of 21st November. I have no idea, and would not wish to know, who your "sources" are. I can only reiterate that, apart from the fact that The Prince of Wales was indeed on the Royal Train at the relevant time, there is no truth whatsoever in your story published last Sunday.

You say that the "professional reputation of two journalists as well as that of the Sunday Mirror is involved". You will appreciate that the reputations of others also are involved, and I would therefore be grateful if my letter of 17th November could be published, as you suggest, in full.

It is of course for you to decide what to include as editorial matter in your newspaper. If, however, your stated intention to 'inform your readers of the Sunday Mirror's position" means that you intend to repeat allegations made on the basis of statements from anonymous informers, I trust that you will print this letter as well. Your readers would then be able to form their own views as to the value of a story which has been denied on the express instructions of those most closely involved at Buckingham Palace, whose veracity you would thereby be impugning. In those circumstances I would have to consider what further action should be taken.

Yours sincerely,

Michael Shea

Now what did we do? In Tony Miles's office on the ninth floor, he, Tom Crone and I discussed the problem. The office has a panoramic view of the City of London. It was dark outside and the atmosphere was suitably theatrical. Tom came up with the solution. 'Why not publish the whole correspondence, yours and his?' he said. The idea was brilliant. Not only did it give both sides as fairly as could be but, starting on page one, there would be two pages of compulsive reading. I rang Michael Shea. I said there would be a few linking paragraphs and that was all. 'No further comment?' he asked. 'None,' I said. He agreed at once and I admired his decisiveness. Thus the readers had the unusual experience of reading on the front page a letter from Buckingham Palace marked Not for Publication, and the rest of the correspondence displayed with equal prominence on page two. I imagined that most readers would accept the Palace denial. They would assume I was honestly mistaken and honourably defending my staff. Others would think I was potty not to take the Palace's word for it and say I was sorry.

It was such a trifling matter, really. What if the madly in love Diana had dashed down to see her Prince after his dutiful but no doubt somewhat tedious dinner with the Secretary of the Duchy of Cornwall, his successor and the local Duchy Land Steward? People in love want to be together at every possible opportunity and not be alone, pole-axingly bored, in a train in a sidings in some God-forsaken spot in Wiltshire. What if she did, as the nanny told us (or didn't, if the Palace denial was correct), leave late after visiting the Parker Bowles's the following night and see the Prince again? And what if, as I consoled myself when Mr Norman St John Stevas, then Leader of the House of Commons, morally rebuked me, Prince Charles had told a little white lie at breakfast that Sunday morning at Sandringham where Lady Diana was a guest? That would have been far from dishonourable if everyone was going to be so stupidly shocked about two journeys as romantic as the highwayman's famous trip in a ribbon of moonlight. And then I imagined the Queen saying to Michael Shea the modern equivalent of 'Off with his head.' I knew he had total faith in his denial, just as I had in our story. I was not impugning anything against anyone, though the word was being flung all over the place.

I vaguely wondered whether I should suggest to Shea a private, off-the-record meeting with Prince Charles ('Look, Michael, if he would just tell me face to face that it isn't true, I will believe him of course ...') but that was fantasy. I was just the editor of a popular Sunday rag, even if Prince Philip had once at our suggestion written a very good article for us, and even if (after what I thought was a vetting lunch with the Lord Chamberlain) I had once had lunch with the Queen, at which Frank Chapple had impressed me beforehand by saying in a loud voice to a footman, 'Where's the toilet?' – and where I was much struck by Princess Anne. Tony Miles, the chairman, was rock solid in my support when uproar followed the agreed publication of the letters. The *Sunday Times* had someone hound me as I was supposed to have hounded Lady Diana. It was quite a good piece. And the *Daily Mail* had its revenge. It ran an editorial suggesting I should be fired. The *Guardian*'s diarist reported about that:

DEAR DAVID HITS BACK

Revenge is sweet and the editor of the Daily Mail, Mr. David English, was lapping it up yesterday by the serving spoonful. A fierce editorial in his paper lambasted Mr. Bob Edwards the editor of the Sunday Mirror, over a story about Prince Charles and Lady Diana meeting secretly at night in a railway siding.

Buckingham Palace has vigorously denied this fantastic, though romantic, yarn and the Mail described how Mr. Edwards was "wriggling" over the matter with "nauseating hypocrisy". How Mr. English must have chortled as he penned the lines – remembering Mr. Edwards's patronising "Dear David" editorial of May 1977.

That followed the Daily Mail's hideous embarrassment over Lord Ryder and the forged Leyland letters – and Mr. Edwards accused Mr. English of allowing his strong dislike of the Labour Government to cloud his judgement. Dear Davids, undoubtedly, are not easily forgotten when they can become Dear Bobs with knobs on.

Peter McKay, one of the best of the gossip writers, from whom no one is safe, said to me at a party, 'The moment I saw the Palace denial I knew the story was true and she was going to marry Charles.' I was not so pleased a few years later when, in his London *Evening Standard* column, he rebuked me (unnamed) for not accepting the Palace denial and for standing by a story that was obviously false. At the editors' monthly lunch with Sir Alex Jarratt, the Reed chairman, the loyal Tony Miles asked me to explain why I had refused to back down over our report. I did so, and nothing more was said. Full marks to Alex, I thought. A report appeared in the *Daily Express* that fascinated me. It quoted Col. Parker Bowles interviewed about the story, which he denied, saying that Prince Charles had phoned him from the sidings to fix a hunting date. So the information we had that the Prince had telephoned the Parker Bowles's home was true.

Editors meet royalty from time to time. I was in the first group to be introduced to Prince Charles at a Press Club party shortly after his marriage. Miss Anne Hope, former woman's editor of the *Daily Telegraph*, said, 'This is Mr Robert Edwards, editor of the *Sunday Mirror*.' The Prince then had the usual polite, brief conversation with me that he does with managers of brick works or clothing factories. The next person talking to me was Michael Shea. 'He didn't mention the Royal train,' I said jovially. Michael replied with a smile, 'Well, he did on the way here.'

Only one person protested to the Press Council about my disgraceful refusal to accept the Palace denial and apologise. He was a former Pole with the MBE who lived at Wimbledon, and like many immigrants was a true patriot of his adopted country. He had mistakenly thought the offending paper was the *Daily Mirror* and had clearly read neither our original report nor our handling of the correspondence. Still, there it was. The Press Council was landed with a complaint. I thought the last thing they would want was to pursue it without a nod of approval from the Palace, and wondered whether I should not myself ask the complaints committee to investigate, as editors are entitled to do. I discussed with Tom Crone volunteering to give details of the informant's status to a small sub-committee provided it was sworn to secrecy like my own staff. Under Press Council procedures, a complainant has first to write to the offending newspaper. If he is dissatisfied with the reply the complaints committee will then decide whether to investigate. Tom and I composed a long reply to the Wimbledon patriot. It was pretty good, I thought, and my secretary took the office car to deliver it to him personally. She thought he was a pleasing, rather lonely chap. A Press Council friend told me that having read my explanation he rang the Palace for guidance. They said they had no wish to pursue the matter further. The complaint was dropped.

It was pleasing for me in 1986 to be recommended for a CBE by a Tory Prime Minister, Mrs Thatcher, whom I had attacked down the years; just as in 1979 Jim Callaghan had recommended Charles Wintour, editor of the Tory *Evening Standard* for twenty years. In the Palace quadrangle after the investiture Michael Shea came out of the crowd to congratulate me. One in the eye, I thought, for my friend the Special Branch man. It is nice to be forgiven, and how awful if I was wrong about the whole silly thing.

16
STRICTLY LIBEL

I have had a lot to do with lawyers, and have never regarded them with the contemptuous indifference they are accorded by some editors. Newspaper lawyers, many of them rather hard up doing part-time stints like printers from the union pool, are usually placed in some remote part of the big news room as if they are not really welcome. In the *Daily Mirror* newsroom, they are tucked behind a pillar within shouting distance of the night editor, but invisible. Most of them, unlike journalists, are from public schools, and these in my experience are usually the best. The others tend to get caught up in the excitement and missionary zeal of news editors and reporters, and say things like 'that will fix the bastard' about their quarry instead of, 'I take it we have a witness for that statement, old man?'

Their job, on properly conducted newspapers, as well as reading galley and page proofs, is to read through potentially dangerous stories direct from the news desk before they are handed to the sub-editors, and in their traditional green ink mark lethal sentences either with queries or straight deletions. The best of the lawyers, usually from the full-time staff, get involved with reporters when they are actually constructing what could be time-bombs costing the paper even more than the chairman's salary. Their job is not to kill good stories but to defuse them. Or to agree with the editor, if the editor has the sense to get interested in such matters, that a libel writ might well follow but the paper has a 99 per cent chance of winning or will be covered in glory if it does not.

'How much could it cost?' Sam Campbell used to say on the *People*. The lawyer, Hugh Davidson, would give his assessment. If it was worth it, in it went. Hugh was Fleet Street's most legendary libel lawyer and a frustrated yellow journalist. He was straight out of a Dickens novel, tall, thin, stooping and ancient. Libel writs rained on him and his editors throughout his services to the paper. He broke the rules I have outlined above and frequently led the pack in pursuing a wrong-doer, particularly if his or her sins made good copy. He would come into my office after I had succeeded Sam Campbell and say in his gentlemanly manner, 'I say, I think we have been far too gentle on this chap. "Blackguard" is the word I suggest. Or "rogue" if you prefer.' But unlike most lawyers who wished they were editors, his judgment was sound.

Officially, this remarkable character never entered our office and played no part in the paper's production. Because he was counsel whom we consulted when we got into trouble, the pretence was that the office lawyer had vetted the paper. Thus, hilariously, after the expected libel writs had arrived, the editor and the office lawyer, who had probably been playing golf on the Saturday when the offending words were approved, would troop off to Hugh's chambers in the Inner Temple for his independent judgment as a QC on the merits of the paper's case. Our solicitors, an outside firm, were also represented at the conference, and they also never admitted to the knowledge that Hugh had actually passed the words on which he was now bestowing upon us his dispassionate and lordly judgment. With great solemnity, after studying the documents that had been placed before him via the solicitors, he would give his verdict that we were right to publish and had every chance of winning. Such was the charade, we would emit an audible sigh of relief.

The paper did not always win even when it was certain it was right. There were riots at Notting Hill because of alleged harassment of blacks. Full of crusading ardour, I unleashed a team of *People* reporters, including a black freelance journalist, Lionel Morrison. Freed from the restraints of working for Beaverbrook, I had moved the paper sharply to the Left. Sam Campbell would probably have contented himself with the familiar comment, a sure-fire winner with prejudiced whites and racist policemen, that blacks should not expect preferential treatment and must be punished as severely as anyone else if they broke the law. To emphasise the point, he might have had some blurred snatched pictures taken of young blacks selling cannabis in Portobello Road. It seemed to us that the troubles all centred round the behaviour of one policeman who, deservedly or not, had become a hate figure and symbol of persecution. I published in large type on page one the headline THE GOOD POLICEMAN PULLEY. This, for the *People*, sophisticated headline based on the classic book *The Good Soldier Schweik*, was meant to indicate that while PC Frank Pulley was doing his earnest best to apply the law even-handedly he was making as big a hash of it as the good-natured but bumbling Schweik. It also meant, although the guardian angel who has served me so well did not alert me on this occasion, that we did not have anything like the evidence we required to go hard against the unfortunate Mr Pulley. Hugh Davidson, after talking as usual to the reporters, did not on this occasion incite me to greater boldness, which should have disturbed me.

Backed by the Police Federation and his chiefs, PC Pulley threw the book at us. There was the usual procession to Hugh Davidson's office, and after the usual deliberation he concluded that we were soundly advised to publish the story. Eventually we consulted Mr James Comyn, the senior counsel who was to lead for us in court, with the elderly Hugh sitting behind him somewhat ludicrously as his 'junior'. Hugh was always treated by judges with great courtesy because of his knowledge of the laws of defamation, but he was not a good court performer. Mr Comyn, who was to become a High Court judge, having studied our evidence, was far from confident. He gave us at best a fifty-fifty chance. I thought he was a nice man but too cautious. 'How about the headline?' I asked as a point in our favour. He advised me not to mention it on the grounds that what it really meant, which it did, was that he was a bad policeman. Or, as we say in Fleet Street, for up read down.

The case lasted a week and was well reported. Counsel for PC Pulley, Mr Brian Neill, also became a High Court judge. It was like a TV drama as he cross-examined our reporters with ferocious forensic skill. 'You claim this black youth told you this terrible story,' he would say in a voice that indicated total disbelief. Since he had seen all the documents, he would continue confidently, 'Can you please produce his name and address from your notebook?' The reporter could not, of course. Otherwise Mr Neill would not have asked the question. I was cross-examined by him for over four hours. 'You did very well, congratulations,' Mr Comyn was kind enough to write afterwards. Mr Neill did better. 'Is this not a case,' he said eventually, 'of willing to wound but afraid to strike?' It was the first time I had heard the phrase. We argued for several minutes, and eventually the judge Mr Justice Bean awarded him game, set and match. 'Would you not say, Mr Edwards,' he said in a kindly voice, 'that what you really meant is that there is no smoke without fire?' Since this was blindingly obvious, I decently conceded.

Mr Comyn made the best of a bad job in his summing up for the paper. The jury awarded Mr Pulley £5000 and each of them shook his hand. He was totally vindicated and went on to high rank at Scotland Yard. Lionel Morrison was praised by the judge and became vice-president of the Race Relations Board. Back at the office Hugh

Cudlipp summoned me up to the ninth floor, offered me a drink and a cigar, and said in his best Raymond Chandler manner, 'You lost the case. Now forget it.' Years later I met Brian Neill at a wedding party in the penthouse suite at the Carlton Hotel. 'Why didn't you question me about my headline?' I asked. Brian replied, 'That would have been in your favour. The Good Soldier Schweik was a nice chap.' It was the only libel action I lost.

I have noticed down the years that those who hit the hardest sue the most. Randolph Churchill became our hero at *Tribune* when, in a ferocious assault on the press barons with the notable exception of Lord Beaverbrook, he described the then Lord Rothermere as the Pornographer Royal. The basis for this attack was the endless fictional series published by Charlie Eade, editor of the *Sunday Dispatch*, about Lady Hamilton and other legendary ladies. Fiction does not normally sell newspapers, but these articles were the most daring any newspaper had published, laced with sex, sin and sadism. The *Sunday Dispatch* was a poor sister paper to the *Daily Mail* and a fifth rate competitor to the *Sunday Express*, but Eade's desperate formula worked, along with bathing beauty contests, at which he liked to be judge, comic cartoons, the stars and a collection of other trash. Dog did not eat dog in those days, and Churchill's speech went unreported until Michael Foot made up for the deficiency by publishing it in full in *Tribune*. It thus became the talk of Fleet Street, where *Tribune* had its highest readership, and was deeply embarrassing to Lord Rothermere. After other attacks by commentators like Woodrow Wyatt, whom I put up to it, Eade was eased out and replaced by an altogether worthier editor, Walter Hayes, who took the paper rapidly up-market with such disastrous consequences that within a few months it was closed down. The readers Eade had garnered were baffled by the sudden onslaught of good journalism and fled. Hayes moved to a public relations job at the Ford Motor Company and eventually became one of the company's chiefs. Once you have blown a paper in Fleet Street you seldom get another.

Thus Randolph had the distinction of destroying a newspaper that did no good but little harm. He also won another notable victory, a libel action against Sam Campbell, editor of the *People*, whom Randolph had also attacked for publishing the scandalous memoirs of Errol Flynn. (A more serious form of pornography in the *People*, which Churchill had not spotted, was that Sam exploited a morbid interest in war atrocities by serialising for as many as sixteen consecutive weeks the various books on the subject by Lord Russell of Liverpool. Cyril Kersh's joke in the office was that when Sam had wrung every sickening word out of each book he would keep it going for another week or two by starting again at the beginning.) Sam hit back at Randolph in a typically venomous leader in which he described his assailant as 'a paid hack'. This, to Fleet Street's surprise, was considered worth £5000 in damages by the libel jury.

Shortly after I had arrived at the *Sunday Express* as deputy editor, Randolph appeared on one of those off-peak programmes in which celebrities 'face' the press. In this case, he was the celebrity and when someone tried to pin him against the wall over his links with Beaverbrook, and possibly spurred on by a gin or two in the hospitality room, he said, 'I'm not a hack like some of these editors are. Who do you think I am? Do you think I'm a sort of Bob Edwards who's taken away from *Tribune* and put on the *Daily Express* at ten times the salary to write exactly the opposite opinion that he wrote before?' Normally I would not have objected to being called a hack. Most of us in Fleet Street had previously regarded ourselves as hacks, some better than others. Anyone witnessing an intelligent writer thumping out a leading article on a subject that is not of the slightest interest to him or possibly anyone else would regard 'a drudge (esp. at literary work)', one dictionary's definition of hack, as an almost sympathetic term. But Churchill's libel victory had given it an altogether different interpretation, and on the TV programme he had spelt out exactly what he meant, in case anyone was in any doubt. A libel writ was issued against Churchill that day which we announced to the Press Association to let him and everyone else know that I was in earnest. This was duly reported to Lord Beaverbrook by Tom Blackburn, the joint chairman, on 2 July 1957: 'Bob Edwards is issuing a writ against Randolph Churchill and the BBC because of Randolph's references to him on television. He took this action on his own.'

This was a risky thing to do with Beaverbrook. As the father figure he liked to be consulted on such dramatic matters, especially since on the same programme with Malcolm Muggeridge, then editor of *Punch*, George Scott, then editor of *Truth*, and Francis Williams, then editor of *Forward*, Churchill announced his resignation from the *Evening Standard* because some of his articles had been killed. For a few days my relationship with Beaverbrook seemed the same. John Junor encouraged me to throw the book at Randolph. Then Beaverbrook's manner changed abruptly – I heard later because Winston Churchill had appealed to him for help on behalf of his son.

Nothing I wrote was any good. He shouted at me over the telephone, as I heard him do to others whom I regarded as despicable for putting up with it. He gave me no support against Churchill. So on *Sunday Express* notepaper I wrote him a resignation letter:

Dear Lord Beaverbrook,

In my considered opinion, you are behaving contemptibly over my libel action against Randolph Churchill.

I am astonished at your complete lack of stamina and shocked at your disloyalty to someone who has served you well. My affection for you is clearly not matched by any feeling of affection by you towards me.

I am attacked, in the most painful way, before millions of people and you will not stand beside me (I am referring to moral, not financial, support).

Instead, at a period of great difficulty for me, you behave in a way which is clearly intended to make my life as difficult as possible.

Under the circumstances, I feel compelled to resign my post and give you notice accordingly.

I did not consult my solicitor before delivering this letter. He would have cautioned me against such folly, I am sure. And Beaverbrook's advice was known: 'Never resign.' Seething with rage and self-pity, but aware that there was some careful calculation in what I was doing, I drove in a rainstorm that I thought was singularly appropriate to Arlington House, dropped my letter through the letter-box at the flat, hoping the Old Man would not emerge as I did so, and went home.

I could not imagine what would happen next. It was John Junor who telephoned. He had clearly been charged with getting me back and he did so brilliantly. 'Well done, Bobby boy,' he said, clearly delighted. 'Come on back. The Old Man can't possibly let you go after writing a letter like that. He wouldn't dare. His reputation would be mud. You're in a very strong position, but come on back.'

Next day I wrote another letter in an altogether different tone unscrambling my resignation.

Dear Lord Beaverbrook,

I deeply regret the letter I wrote to you yesterday and wish to apologise both for the tone and the words used.

I wrote to you in a moment of great depression. It seemed to me I was being made to stand alone against Churchill whose allegation against me is just about the most serious and certainly the most damaging that could be made against any journalist.

I now know that my impressions of how I was being treated are false and I do ask you to forgive me for my altogether outrageous behaviour.

If you do not, I shall most certainly understand.

John Junor assured me everything was fine. He said Max Aitken had phoned in a tone of astonishment to read him my first letter. No more pressure was put on me over Randolph Churchill and later he wrote me a letter expressing his regrets in terms I found acceptable, despite its typically pugnacious beginning:

> Stour
> East Bergholt
> Suffolk
>
> 3 April, 1958

Dear Mr Edwards,

My solicitors, Messrs. Oswald Hickson, Collier & Co., have been sending me a lot of vexatious letters and correspondence and pleadings emanating on your behalf from your solicitors. Since you did not reply to my letter dated 4 July 1957, it has become difficult for us to settle this matter in private, but I would still hope for such a solution. I am not litigious by nature and if I have done you a serious injury, I only desire to rectify it.

I very much wish that in referring to you as I did on television on 28 June 1957 I had not used the expression of which you complain. I have never had the pleasure of meeting you, and many common friends assure me that you are a most agreeable person whose friendship I would enjoy. In these circumstances, I am glad to express my regret that I ever used such words about you. You may, of course, print this if you will.

Yours sincerely,

Randolph S. Churchill

A brief announcement was put out via the Press Association. On the day it appeared in *The Times* and elsewhere Randolph rang me from East Bergholt: 'I hear you are a jolly fellow and have a pretty wife. Come down for the weekend and we can go through your file and laugh about it all.' It was a wonderful weekend. Randolph had no money and we had to go in increasing circles before a pub landlord could be found who would let him have some whisky and gin on tick. The BBC, who also apologised, paid my costs and I was able to carpet the upstairs of my house with second grade, wall-to-wall Kosset.

There was a period when I seemed to be issuing threatening writs as frequently as Robert Maxwell in my fifteen months with him on the Mirror group, when he dispatched them all round the wicket like Ian Botham scoring sixes. Even the most loyal journalists get a kick out of bringing bad news to the editor: how he reacts makes a good topic over drinks later at Poppins (*Daily Express*) or the Stab in the Back (*Mirror*), and the story is utterly distorted within an hour or two and becomes another legend. At least half a dozen colleagues came to me in January 1962 clutching copies of the *Spectator*, doing their best to hide their excitement over an astonishing, wildly defamatory attack on me by Peter Forster in the guise of an article about Jimmy Edwards, the comedian. I was aggrieved not only because of what Forster wrote but because, contrary to his belief, it was Beaverbrook and not I who wanted him sacked as *Daily Express* book critic, and I had fought a rearguard action for several months, until the fateful article on Scrooge I have described elsewhere.

Still, it was sweet revenge but altogether too damaging, and I had the pleasure of consulting the witty, wise and vastly calming Arnold (now Lord) Goodman. He prescribed an instant writ and I decided to continue the action after I was sacked a week later from my first editorship of the *Daily Express*. This can be the road to disaster, as Derek Jameson demonstrated in his famous case against the BBC, but although we were up against a most formidable team of legal adversaries it was Forster in the end who turned out to be the clown. For those who enjoy reading the delightful legal language of apology, which totally disguises the true feelings of the defendant, here in full is the settlement as reported in *The Times* law report the day after it was announced in the High Court the usual eighteen months later:

EDWARDS V. FORSTER AND OTHERS
Before MR JUSTICE MELFORD STEVENSON

The settlement was announced of this libel action by Mr Robert John Edwards, of Danehurst, Leverstock Green, Hemel Hempstead, Hertfordshire, acting editor of the Daily Express, against Mr Peter

Forster, of Carisbrooke Cottage, Wadham Gardens, N.W.3, journalist, and The Spectator Ltd., proprietors and publishers of The Spectator, in respect of an article in the issue of The Spectator for January 26, 1962 under the heading "Clown Edwards, by Peter Forster".

Mr J. T. Molony, Q.C., and Mr F. P. Neill appeared for the plaintiff; Mr David Hirst for Mr Forster, and Mr Colin Duncan, Q.C., for The Spectator Ltd.

Mr Molony said that the action was brought in respect of a television critique written by Mr Forster. The first paragraph of this article purported to be a criticism of a recent television series, but was in fact a thinly disguised and defamatory attack on the plaintiff. So far as the second defendants were concerned the plaintiff accepted that, at the time of the publication of the words, they neither knew that the words were intended to refer to the plaintiff nor that they could be understood as so referring; moreover, after it had been brought to their attention that the words had been so understood they published an apology to him in The Spectator and made an immediate offer of amends under the Defamation Act, 1952. Mr Forster recognized that, quite apart from considerations of good taste, the publication was improper and unwarranted and designed to cause damage to Mr Edwards's reputation and he, too, had published an apology to the plaintiff in The Spectator. In these circumstances the plaintiff had accepted a sum offered him by the defendants by way of damages which he regarded as sufficient to mark the gravity of the matter, and had accepted their offer to compensate him for any further expense to which he had been put.

Mr Hirst said that on Mr Peter Forster's behalf he (counsel) endorsed everything that Mr Molony had just said and repeated Mr Forster's apology to Mr Edwards for ever having published such an unjustifiable and inconsiderate attack on him. Mr Forster also wished to repeat his sincere apology to the second defendants, who had no knowledge of the circumstances in which the article was written and he never expected it to have consequences involving The Spectator.

Mr Duncan said that he, too, on behalf of The Spectator Ltd., endorsed everything that had been said on the plaintiff's behalf. His clients very much regretted that they ever published this unfortunate article concerning the plaintiff, a journalist of ability and unquestioned integrity, and were relieved to know that the plaintiff accepted that such publication was so far as they were concerned, entirely innocent.

Solicitors – Messrs. Goodman, Derrick & Co.; Messrs. Field, Roscoe & Co.; Messrs. Oswald Hickson Collier & Co.

By this time I had returned from my pleasing period in the Glasgow wilderness and was back in charge of the *Daily Express*. I was now able to carpet the downstairs of my house at Leverstock Green with best quality Wilton.

Another nasty blow to my pride, or honour, occurred shortly after Forster's outburst, in the wake of my departure from the *Express* when apparently I was down for the count. An anonymous columnist in the *Observer* put in the boot as follows:

> In the last few weeks those lucky people who work in Lord Beaverbrook's paper palace in Fleet Street have been living dangerously . . . one by one Express men disappeared. One of them, Anthony Lejeune, no sooner went than wrote an article in About Town called 'The Lid Off Beaverbrook'. Peter Forster, the plump book critic, went – and wrote in last weekend's Spectator a television column entitled 'Clown Edwards'. At the end of the paragraph it emerged that he was writing about Jimmy Edwards. Staff remaining by this time were almost afraid to walk the corridors. There were cruel jokes about the Sack of the Express. And then, last Thursday, authority, real authority, roused itself. Edwards went.

Cruel stuff, so cruel that I detected a personal motive, which emerged when I learned that the author was Ivan Yates. He was a fellow Labour supporter and I thought a friend. I decided he had been very embarrassed when I saw him in the humbling role of assistant to Lord Beaverbrook, and this was unconscious but devastating revenge. Once again Arnold Goodman took the reins and the following Sunday the score was settled in a prominent apology which said, in the splendid style of such things, that 'unfortunately' the paper's comments 'have been misunderstood to reflect upon Mr Edwards.' The legal humbug was further compounded in the traditional manner: 'The allusions to Peter Forster's article and remaining staff being "almost afraid to walk the corridors" were made in jocular vein, and were in no way intended to be taken literally.' Game, set and match to Goodman, but no new carpet on this occasion.

The most shattering moment I have had in a libel case involved *Private Eye*. I had decided while editor of the *People* that if they ever wrote anything really damaging and untrue about me, I would sue until they cracked. An article appeared accusing two of our reporters, Hugh Farmer and Dennis Cassidy, of taking a notorious anarchist whose confessions we were about to publish to a Glasgow brothel, where he performed with a prostitute while they drank in another room. I suspected it might be true, especially since the report was believed to come from Paul Foot, then working on the *Daily Record*, who does not usually get things wrong. The news editor, Laurie Manifold, himself an investigative reporter with an impressive record, was unshakable. 'No,' he said, 'neither would do a thing like that. Dennis is quite a puritan even though he likes a drink. Hugh is a dedicated family man and devout Catholic. He just wouldn't.' I said that being a devout Catholic did not usually dissociate people from sin, rather the opposite, and called in the reporters individually. To each I said, 'If this story is true, I will smite you with a feather. If it isn't we will back you all the way to the High Court.'

Dennis and I often drank together at The Stab. Hugh I did not know. Both were adamant: it was a lie. Writs were issued. Several months later I met Richard Ingrams at a party where the only drink was vermouth. I felt he was lucky to be a teetotaller. He shuffled across. 'You should drop your action,' he said, genially enough, 'we are going to smash you.' I told him that we were certain we would win. He should apologise and that would be the end of it.

The case was far more exciting than any TV soap opera. The anarchist gave his account, the reporters theirs, and we were confident of winning against the word of a man who had admitted lying on a grand scale, to General Franco and his own mother of all people. Then came the bombshell. The reporters had detailed their movements on oath. They had been with the anarchist in a pub near the BBC in Glasgow until closing time. Then all three went to a restaurant, where they had intended to eat before going to a BBC studio in time to see a pre-recorded programme featuring the anarchist, but the restaurant was full. The reporters went into some detail about the restaurant, and how they settled for fish and chips elsewhere instead. It was at this time *Private Eye* said they were at the brothel. The producer of the programme, an impressive and independent witness, testified that they were at the pub until closing time and then throughout the whole programme at the studio. After much flurry in court, the defence lawyer announced with great drama that the restaurant so graphically described as overcrowded by the reporters, which was normally open seven days a week throughout the year, was on that single evening closed for repairs. He questioned Cassidy, who was still in the witness box, and his explanation that he must have made a mistake and someone must simply have told them the restaurant was full, delighted the *Private Eye* staff next to me in the public gallery.

All seemed lost, but Mr Justice Bean, who was sitting without a jury at *Private Eye*'s request, found for the reporters principally on the grounds that there was undisputed evidence that Hugh Farmer's small car had a permanently fixed baby seat. The anarchist had claimed that he, the reporters and a prostitute picked up in the pub had gone to the brothel in this car. The judge ruled that there simply was not room for all four. It occurred to me years afterwards how the reporters came to make their incredible 'mistake'. The clue was that by everyone's account they stayed in the pub until closing time. Even the landlord had sworn to this. I presumed that, in fact, they had stayed long after closing time until the programme was due to start. No decent journalist would ever shop a landlord who let him continue to drink. The reporters were each awarded £500, which I thought was exactly right, but the costs were horrendous as usual. A concert was held at the Albert Hall to pay for the case. The Curse of Gnome was put on the judge and myself. The judge died soon afterwards.

17
DECLINE AND FALL

I recall the exact moment I knew for certain the skids were under the newspapers in the Mirror Group. Mr (now Lord) Don Ryder, our new overlord, had just appointed the former civil servant Alex (now Sir Alex) Jarratt managing director of IPC, which then included our newspapers. The immensely successful Sunday paper the *People*, with the now mind-boggling sale of nearly five and a half million copies a week, and with its cheap, highly efficient, trouble-free printing plant in Covent Garden, was about to be transferred to the Mirror complex in Holborn Circus alongside its then traditional chief rival the *Sunday Mirror*. Our type was to be set at the Mirror, the pages made up there and moulded in the foundry. Then the plates would be taken round to Associated Newspapers and printed on the *Daily Mail* plant.

There was no advantage whatsoever to the *People* as a newspaper. There would be no love for us either at Associated Newspapers or the Mirror. We would have to go to press earlier because of the delay in getting the plates from the Mirror foundry to the Mail. There would be fewer editions, which meant a reduced news and (worst of all) sports service, and the cost of the whole operation would be vastly higher. The *People*, despite its huge sale, would probably run at a loss, a situation that no newspaper management in its right mind would ever contrive, because naturally the cost of contract printing on AN's plant was far higher than on our own, which was paid for, as was our building, for which our total outgoing apart from rates was a ground rent of £5,000 a year. Despite the failure of the *Daily Herald*, due to the TUC's stultifying influence, and the appalling subsequent wreck of Hugh Cudlipp's *Sun*, which it became, Odhams Press was comparatively well run, even following Cecil King's successful takeover when he was the Mirror boss. We did not have the vast army of loafers that filled the *Sunday Mirror* publishing room on Saturday nights, with the one hour on, one hour off racket they had been given in return for accepting automatic tying, labelling and movement of bundles. No doubt we had more than we needed, but our plant did not seem full of people who clearly had nothing whatsoever to do. The relationship between editorial and craftsmen in the composing room was so good that I, as editor, and my wife were guests along with the managing director, Harry Rochez, and his wife at the printers' annual Christmas party at a restaurant in Piccadilly Circus. To reduce costs at these jolly affairs, wives, including Harry's and mine, were expected to smuggle in half bottles of spirits in their handbags. They might as well have carried them openly, since the bottles were strewn all over the place when we left. Among the amenities available to Odhams Press workers were three excellent pubs and a first-class fish and chip shop, where I ate most Saturday nights, and for the journalists with their expense accounts the Soho restaurants were within walking, and sometimes for the return journey, staggering distance.

We would have preferred our building to be in Fleet Street, because there is nothing journalists like better than talking shop with their own kind, but otherwise our situation was sublime and our paper was read by something like 14 million people every Sunday. Now it was to be gravely damaged, and all because Reed International, into whose hands IPC had been delivered, saw a vast profit in selling our own freehold. No proper newspaper proprietor would have done that. When Alex Jarratt made his first visit to the building where this no doubt to him strange and alien newspaper was produced, loved though it was in every Coronation Street in Britain, I stopped him as we walked down the main staircase. 'Alex,' I said, 'I beg you. Do not turn us into an unprofitable newspaper. Postpone the move and look into it all yourself. You will see that it is madness. No one with the newspaper's interests at heart would do it.' He was not hostile, but I could see that I was making no impression. He was in no way responsible for the plan. He had no ink in his veins. How could he be expected to reverse something that made sense to the accountants at Reed House and no sense as far as its biggest selling newspaper was concerned? It was then that I knew.

Would Marks and Spencer move a highly successful store to an unprofitable site in order to sell the building? That was the parallel. It only added up, in crude financial reckoning, if Reed International regarded its ownership of the Mirror newspapers as short-term. Acute paranoia set in among the journalists. We were to be milked dry and sent to the abattoir. On a couple of austere occasions the Mirror editors were invited to join the Reed directors at their Christmas party. There was no resemblance to the printers' parties at Piccadilly Circus, or indeed any Fleet Street party. I remember Don Ryder standing on a chair to address his sober acolytes and their wives. One wife, possibly emboldened by her second gin and tonic, told us she would not have the *Daily Mirror* in her house. Several directors made it clear that they found the ownership of such vulgar Labour newspapers distasteful and difficult to explain to fellow Conservatives at the golf club. We would return to the office with our wives for a stiff drink and curse the managers who had delivered us into such hostile hands. The parties were voted the worst we had ever attended.

You never knew what would hit you in Fleet Street. When Cecil King ruled over us on the ninth floor of the Mirror, his probably illegal coal fire sending up its papal smoke to the top of the great building he had conceived, it would not have been possible to imagine the ultimate control of these highly successful newspapers for the masses being entrusted to manufacturers of quality wallpaper, emulsion paint and Twyford lavatory systems, with no love whatsoever either for us or the black art. I liked Cecil as a boss. He was suitably vain and slightly dotty, suffering from the delusion most of us shared that he was invulnerable, a de Gaulle in the Street of Shame. Had he not, after all, snatched Odhams Press from under Roy Thomson's acquisitive nose, with the several successful magazines it owned as well as the *People*, the *Sporting Life* and their ailing but important sister paper the *Daily Herald*? Had he not acquired so many other magazines, including even *Horse and Hound*, that in IPC he had created the biggest publishing company in the world?

As editor of the *People* in the last three years of his reign I found him no trouble at all. The *Daily* and *Sunday Mirror* were his principal interests. Like (I suspect) Hugh Cudlipp he regarded taking over the *People* as a regrettable consequence of thwarting Roy Thomson's bid for Odhams. He regarded inheriting the editor Sam Campbell as even more regrettable. Unlike most editors in a takeover situation, Sam had bravely opposed being swallowed up by the Mirror. King was too good a newspaper boss to fire him. Why get rid of the best man for the job just because he was a rather disgraceful fellow? That has never been held against an editor in properly run establishments. Jack Nener, the most celebrated *Daily Mirror* editor, was not a person the fastidious would have had in their homes. His language was legendary. He is alleged to have fired three reporters and three sub-editors every Friday, and he was totally respected by his staff as a master of his craft. Joe Grizzard,

my excellent deputy on the *Sunday Mirror* for several years, whom I
called the Israeli commando (he was, apart from being devoutly
Jewish, a first-class pistol shot), was night editor under Nener. He
was considerably influenced by his former master. His 'regimentals'
when some wretched sub had written a headline that bust or a
picture had been badly cropped were something to behold. I once
heard the head printer, Len Walledge, protest at his character
reading of a stone-sub who had marked the wrong type on a piece of
copy when the paper was running late. The printer himself was not
known to be mealy-mouthed. Sam Campbell was a gentle editor. It
was his total commitment to the truth that was in question.

My impression was that if Cecil King ever did read the *People* he
held it with a pair of tongs. Occasionally he sent for me, I imagined
after saying to his chief henchman Cudlipp, 'Well, I suppose I ought
to see Edwards. He is, when all is said and done, one of our editors.'
The ritual, as I recall it, was always the same. The appointment
would be for something like 12 o'clock. He was as good at time-
keeping as a Harley Street specialist confident of his BUPA payment
and I was never kept waiting for more than a minute or two. Then it
was into his vast office, now occupied by Bob Maxwell, across the
great expanse of carpet to where he sat, a true Harmsworth, behind
his enormous desk. A moped would have cut the journey time
considerably. No doubt I would have that shy smile on my face that
in my *Express* days some commentators had mistaken for cold
ruthlessness. He would rise to his absurd height and shake hands. It
was very grand. Nothing about his manner or surroundings indicated
that his principal role in life was to head three yellow papers strictly
aimed at the servants' quarters, with the exception of the *Sunday
Mirror* which might catch the mistress's eye if she happened to see it
lying on the kitchen table. Never once did he refer to the *People* or
mention that its sales were an all-time record, greater by a few score
thousand than even Sam's best. Possibly, since he was very civil with
me, he felt that I had fallen upon hard times to become editor of the
People and the decent thing was not to refer to it. In fact, of course,
like any editor, I was intensely proud of my paper.

As always seemed to be the case when Labour was in power, the
country would be staggering through a financial crisis. King,
knowing of my liking for Harold Wilson that had been part of my
undoing at the *Express*, would invariably say, 'And what do you
think of your friend now?' He would then, like a slightly weary elder
statesman, list all the Prime Minister's personal as well as policy
failings, as if the Utopia to which King had committed himself by

flying the red flag on his Rolls-Royce during the 1964 election was being denied us by the hopelessness of this one, as he called him, silly man. The reason for King's disdain for Wilson, apart from the familiar state of the nation, was difficult to discern. Maybe, as has been written, it was because he was not offered some immensely important job. I think it arose from a genuine conviction that if he were at No. 10 himself we would move rapidly towards the paradise Wilson had lost. Such delusions are regarded as megalomania in anyone except a fellow politician.

Cecil King never expected his monotonous recitation of Wilson's shortcomings to be translated into editorials in the *People*. It was obvious he was saying the same thing to anyone who would listen. One Saturday, however, Cudlipp summoned Michael Christiansen, editor of the *Sunday Mirror*, and myself to join him in King's office. That had not happened before. Since we were not on the Board, we scarcely met King even during the week and regarded Cudlipp as our editorial chief. There had been a run on the pound for several days. The Bank of England, of which King was a director, had spent a huge amount of its reserves trying to prevent its collapse. Wilson had given him the job in a forlorn attempt to satisfy his craving to serve the country, and doubtless also with an eye on the *Mirror*'s continuing support. He sat in his armchair and with great solemnity told us, 'There is nothing left.' We knew what he meant.

He continued his mournful tale. The Bank had spent its last penny. It could no longer shore up the pound. The country was broke. I was deeply impressed, went back to my office in Covent Garden and called up the city editor at his home. He did not come in on Saturdays and worked part-time for us. His column took less than half the space of Dr Goodenough's advice to the ailing. Without revealing the source I told him the dreadful news and said, 'You can take it from me this is gospel. It has as good as come from the Governor of the Bank of England himself.' Although the city editor was better equipped to advise readers in a few paragraphs how to invest their little nest-eggs than write on such weighty matters, he and an experienced splash-sub did their damnedest and our main headline appeared in end-of-the-world white on black type the following morning: BLACK WEEKEND. That was my contribution. No other paper, I noticed as I scanned the rivals that evening, had a whiff of the magnitude of the crisis, and the following Monday in the City is not remembered by anyone who worked there because nothing in particular happened. The run on the pound continued, and the Bank of England propped it up as usual with money, if

King's advice to his two Sunday editors was sound, that no longer existed.

King had become a Mirror director in 1929. Nobody could say he was not steeped in the business. He had terrible battles with Harry Guy Bartholomew, the creator of the modern *Daily Mirror*, who in the last five years of the 1930s transformed it from a limp Conservative picture paper for ladies into a rough, vulgar and brilliantly successful champion of the masses that looked as if it had been brewed every night in a mix of whisky, beer and strong tobacco. 'Bart', an exceedingly common man, emerged from some humble role in the picture process department. As Vera Lynn was the Sweetheart of the Forces in the war, the *Daily Mirror* under his direction became their voice, and for all Churchill's threats to close it down over Cassandra's incomparable column and Zec's famous cartoon it probably did more for morale than even the BBC.

When Maxwell took over the *Mirror*, what he remembered of its wartime contribution, like millions of ex-servicemen, was the Jane strip cartoon, and as an early example of his non-interference in editorial matters demanded its restoration. He also had the more inspired idea of putting sculptures of Cecil King, Cassandra (Sir William Connor) and Hugh Cudlipp in the refurbished front hall, but uncharacteristically not one of himself. I said his generous tribute to past eminences would be incomplete without a bust of Bart, and suggested he sought a second opinion. Later he asked Mike Molloy, 'Who was the true creator of the *Daily Mirror*?' Mike replied instantly, 'Bartholomew.' Bart now gazes rather benignly at everyone who enters the front door of the Mirror building, but without the whisky flush on his cheeks. At the opening ceremony I asked Connor's widow, Lady Megan, what she thought of the artist's impression of his former boss. 'Too kind,' said this nice lady. Bart was not loved.

In 1950 Bart committed the unpardonable folly of sacking Hugh Cudlipp, who had been editor of the *Sunday Pictorial* (now *Sunday Mirror*) for three years after his extremely successful period as a colonel who was editor-in-chief of army newspapers during the war. Cudlipp also edited the 'Pic' for three years before the war, to which job he was appointed at the startlingly young age of twenty-four. Generally billed as Fleet Street's best tabloid editor, Cudlipp was in fact a national newspaper editor for only a total of six years. He was not, as many believe, editor of the *Daily Mirror*. As an editor, therefore, he is pretty small fry compared, say, with Geoffrey Pinnington, who edited the *People* for ten years and Sir Larry Lamb, who was in the hot seat at the *Sun* for a total of nine years from Murdoch's takeover in 1969. Larry raised the circulation from 700,000 to 4 million, before he was fired, then went via Australia to the *Daily Express* and ended up the way of all flesh on that paper. And I edited the *Sunday Mirror* for thirteen years.

Editors, in fact, are lesser mortals than Cudlipp became. It was as editorial supremo that he made his incomparable contribution to the *Daily Mirror*. In 1951 the Wykehamist King won his battle against, by all accounts, the appalling Bart, who was the only inky apart from Caxton and Levy, who took over the ailing *Daily Telegraph*, to make it to the top in the business. Bart was fired as chairman. King took over, and a year later retrieved Cudlipp from his backwater as managing editor of the *Sunday Express* under John Gordon and made him editorial director. It was a legendary partnership. There was no competition from the pitiful *Daily Sketch*, later the *Daily Graphic*, which showed none of the *Sun*'s flair a few years afterwards against the *Mirror*. When the *Sketch* was once put up in price ahead of the *Mirror*, it was Cudlipp who coined the phrase on the *Daily Mirror*'s front page that this was 'the only known case of a carbon copy costing more than the original.'

The enormous profits of the *Daily Mirror*, *Sunday Pictorial* and *Reveille*, a weekly magazine in newspaper form for the simplest in the land that had been founded by the renegade W. R. Hipwell, enabled King to indulge in altruistic empire-building in Africa. He created a Nigerian newspaper chain, beginning in Bart's reign, of considerable merit, apart from one paper which reported court sex cases in such detail that even the old-style *News of the World* might have been shocked. This was the only one of our Nigerian papers read regularly at the Mirror. Several of the British managers King recruited for Nigeria later graduated to Fleet Street. Some shone, like Frank Rogers, *Daily Telegraph* director and chairman of East Midland Allied Press, and Percy Roberts, who became Mirror Group chairman. They were known as the Afrika Corps. The papers were eventually sold to Nigerian interests. Their technology was far in advance of anything we were allowed to use in this country.

King's desire to contribute to the common good showed itself in other ways. At his instigation the Mirror organised a series of meetings at the Café Royal in London. The dullest journalists on the heaviest papers in Europe, plus their counterparts on British newspapers, eagerly attended these conferences that lasted several days, complete with interpreters behind glass barriers and all the paraphernalia associated with a session at the UN. The purpose, it was stated, was to further international understanding. Others said it was simply a mad ego trip by Cecil. In his best de Gaulle manner, he would open the conferences with a ten-minute address written for him by the distinguished former *Guardian* journalist, John Beavan, later Lord Ardwick. It came as a surprise to his visitors that he would then stride out immediately, not to be seen again until the vote of thanks to him was moved at the end of the final session, in a speech again written by John and delivered by an English-speaking political commentator on some foreign paper with an unpronounceable name.

Naturally, the *Daily Mirror*, which seldom devoted more than a few paragraphs to major debates in Parliament and none to sessions of the United Nations, was scarcely able to print a word of these proceedings apart from, as the night editor would shout to the chief-sub, passing on instructions to the editor from Cudlipp, 'five pars for Cecil, page 2, column seven, from the top.' Though they searched in vain for reports of their speeches in the serious newspapers delivered with the *Mirror* to their suites at the Savoy, King's guests from abroad enjoyed his bountiful hospitality. This included visits to the theatre, concerts, the best restaurants and several cocktail parties. The conferences were brilliantly stage-managed by Tommy Atkins, the *Mirror*'s publicity director, and as they switched idly from one language to another on their headphones, trying to pair the voices with the pretty interpreters in their glass cages, *Mirror* journalists were gripped by tedium almost beyond endurance.

The suffering of Reg Payne, then my deputy on the *People* and former editor of *Titbits*, was pitiful to behold. At the last of these affairs, I left shortly after Cecil made his customary exit and returned to my place in good time for the vote of thanks to him on the final day. John Beavan, who had skilfully culled the delegates from all over Europe, and in one instance Soviet Russia, gave every impression that he felt the interests of mankind were being measurably advanced at each session. He confided to me recently that he was excruciatingly bored. Working for Cecil King made me appreciate that as a portrait of a newspaper baron Citizen Kane, if anything, was an understatement.

King's mistake was that he did not own the papers. I was shocked by his bombshell dismissal, though the amazement of *Mirror* editors in no way matched his when the company secretary, who was either a brave soul or too cowardly to refuse, arrived at his house at breakfast-time while he was cleaning his teeth to hand him a letter from his fellow directors telling him he was fired. I tried to imagine the directors, most of them pipsqueaks in our reckoning, telling their wives in the suburbs the previous evening and the sleepless hours that followed. Supposing something went wrong, Cecil rose up in wrath, and they were fired instead. I wrote to King saying I was horrified, and vaguely wondered whether he would publish my letter (he did not).

My dismay for him was balanced by joy that Hugh Cudlipp, his reluctant assassin, had taken over as chairman of the IPC colossus. My first meeting with Hugh after I had left the *Daily Express* for the second time set the tone of our future relationship. He did not have a job for me then, but I remember it well. 'Drink?' he said, taking the well-worn track to his wine cupboard. After genial chat about what it had been like working for Lord Beaverbrook, whom he did not admire, he offered me a cigar, found he had only one left in the box of Havanas in his desk drawer and pressed a bell. This brought my first sight of Ted Lucas, King's and later Cudlipp's butler, who struck me as splendidly out of place in the headquarters of such plebeian newspapers. He had a deferential stoop, wore a white coat, and was reputed to own a yacht in the west country. His face had a pleasingly ironical look bordering on insolence. The following brief conversation took place:

'Sir?'

'Get me some cigars, Ted.'

'How many, sir?'

'A whole box, of course.' Pause. 'Why, what have you heard?'

Working for Hugh was fun. The same could not be said for Cecil. The excuse for not telling him face to face that the empire he had built no longer required his services was that he had once moodily talked of ending his life and might have thrown himself from the ninth floor window. He could just as easily have strolled across the road from Cheyne Walk at high tide into the river. There must have been such occasions, but I cannot recall visiting Hugh in his office without having at least a glass of wine but usually half a bottle. Sometimes it would be too absurdly early. He would look at the clock and say, 'I don't think it would do any harm if we had a couple of beers.'

Lunches were seldom with fewer than six or seven people and, before he became supremo with his own dining-room, were usually in private rooms in Italian restaurants in Soho. Both his favourite restaurants have since closed, presumably because they no longer had his patronage. At one, Pinnochio's, the private room was in a basement that resembled a disused tunnel on the Underground. Reg

Payne was usually the victim of Hugh's wicked baiting. He played the court jester's role with quiet resignation. Malicious stories were told, re-told and constantly improved about Fleet Street personalities past and present. Vast quantities of Chianti were drunk. It was very Mafia-like. There was much banter with the restaurateur and we would arrive back at our offices, flushed, at about four o'clock, just after our deputies, equally flushed, who knew with immaculate timing how much longer they could linger after hours in their favourite haunts when we had lunch with Hugh.

I was the victim of his vitriol at the lunches only twice. The first time, as King did in a far gentler fashion, he went for me at Pinnochio's over my personal liking for Harold Wilson. This was a surprise since I thought he was a founder member of the Wilson supporters' club and both of his honours came from him. Was he under pressure from King, and this simply a better scripted replay of his master's voice? In fact, Hugh takes a pretty jaundiced view of most people who put themselves above fellow-members of the human race, and his stories as the wine flowed of the weaknesses and foibles of the great were hugely entertaining.

The second time I was furious. It was a year or so earlier, concerned about falling sales, that he had appointed me editor of the *Sunday Mirror*. Mike Christiansen, my predecessor, was offered the deputy editorship of the *Daily Mirror* or the sack. Within a year sales had risen by three hundred thousand to over 5.3 million, and I was modestly pleased with myself. The *putsch* had taken place, Cudlipp was chairman and his chief guest at lunch was a son of Sir Frank Packer, the Australian newspaper magnate. Suddenly, with Ted Lucas in attendance pouring Cudlipp's favourite Château Latour, Hugh stared at me with eyes that can be remarkably cold and said he was totally baffled by the success of the *Sunday Mirror*. He could not understand why the sales had gone up so dramatically. He continued on this theme for some time. My fellow editors looked on with, I thought, some sympathy. Packer was riveted.

As Beaverbrook would have said, I was too sensitive as usual. Next day I was due to lunch with Cudlipp again. He got to the office to find a letter from me saying I thought it best under the circumstances that I should not come. 'I don't mind you attacking me in front of my colleagues,' I wrote, 'but in front of the privileged son of another newspaper proprietor is too much.' The chairman's red light flashed on my intercom first thing. 'Come and see me,' said Hugh. As I went into his office, he walked towards me, hand extended to shake mine. 'Sorry Bob,' he said. 'Sorry, sorry. Sorry, sorry, sorry,

sorry.' Then he added: 'All right?' It was indeed. All my enormous warmth for him flooded back. 'I think we could manage a couple of beers,' he said, glancing at the clock. He completed the healing process by inviting my wife, Laura, and myself for Sunday lunch at his Sonning home beside the Thames. We arrived in our boat through the ice at Sonning Lock, which appealed to his sense of the dramatic, and stayed on for dinner. On another occasion we were invited to a fancy dress party. Among the guests was Lew Grade. We wore clothes provided by Hugh's friend, Monty Berman, the theatrical costumier. As I recall it, we were in medieval dress. I wore something humble. In Cudlipp's domain, real and imagined, I felt it was important to know your place. He was a cardinal, I think.

Hugh's house at Sonning was built on stilts so that the river in flood could swirl safely around it. He had another building nearby, designed as a pub, with all the usual equipment including dart-board. He had an ocean-going motor yacht of much charm but no great seaworthiness and a Chinese junk he had bought on a visit to the Far East. This merely went as far as the White Hart in Sonning, to boisterous lunches. Not surprisingly, he was known to his inti-mates as The Captain. He was a pleasing sight, with wind against tide rounding Cap Barfleur in a Force Five, skipper's cap firmly wedged on his head, a badly-chewed enormous cigar from Lew Grade clamped between his teeth, glass of red at his side, peering through the spray for the next buoy. These voyages invariably ended at some delightful small restaurant in northern French towns like St Malo, Deauville or Le Havre, which were often the rendezvous for new members of the crew carrying bundles of the latest newspapers and gifts for the boat.

If I concentrate on the conviviality of life with Hugh, it is because that was the major part of my relationship with him. He said when he took me on, 'You're the kind of editor who likes to be left alone. I will leave you alone.' He did, on both Sunday papers, and when he retired reminded me that he had kept his promise. He twice sugges-ted that I should run two pages every week in the *People* on crime around the world, but I thought it was a bad idea and sidestepped it. He did not like some of the pictures of naked girls we published in the *Sunday Mirror*. I agreed with him but thought my colleagues might have a better idea of the dimensions the readers wanted. 'Choose them yourself,' said Hugh. 'You've got much better taste.' Editorials were of major interest to me. Sydney (now Lord) Jacob-son, editorial director and formerly political editor of the *Daily*

Mirror for many years, read through them and I recall being talked out of publishing only one.

Hugh, Sydney, the Sunday paper editors and our deputies would lunch quite frequently on Saturdays. These lunches went on until alarmingly late and I wondered what kind of madness was going on in the office. I should have had more confidence. Some editors are blasé about such matters, but they don't usually last as long. There was much banter about keeping each paper's 'world exclusives' from the other, but Cudlipp was so amused by one of my 'splash' headlines he asked permission to disclose it to my rival if he solemnly undertook not to pinch it. It was PRINCESS MARGARET: TIME FOR A STATEMENT. The page one editorial called on the Princess to say whether or not she and Tony Snowdon were to be divorced. Cudlipp liked such brash impertinence. It was a headline guaranteed to get the paper off the newstands. Lord Snowdon forgave me. Later we became friends.

One of Hugh's great talents was as a mimic. In a public relations exercise organised by Lambeth Palace, the key figures of the Mirror newspapers were invited to meet the Archbishop of Canterbury, Dr Michael Ramsey, for a full and frank discussion about the Church of England. Several were Jewish, including Marje Proops, Donald Zec, the top showbusiness writer, and Sydney Jacobson which struck us all as amusing and a typical Cudlipp touch to bring them along. We arrived on a hot summer day in a fleet of office cars. With suitable gravity we talked of the Church's relevance, and otherwise, to contemporary society. The only lasting benefit was Cudlipp's masterly imitation of Dr Ramsey, like Mike Yarwood's parody of Harold Wilson, his best, that followed.

Hugh seemed to show no real interest in being the publishing tycoon he had become. He was not merely the boss of the Mirror Group, drearily called 'the newspaper division', but of scores of magazines and other publications in IPC. Instead of a Rolls-Royce, the dull company chairman's symbol, he had the more stylish Bentley version, and continued to devote his chief attention to the *Daily Mirror*. The reason he is mistakenly thought to have been its editor for years is that he dominated those parts of the *Mirror* that gave it such clout and importance. The Welsh wizardry of his page one leaders, turning to page two (and never mind the huge story everyone else was running on the front pages), his 'shock issues', campaigning stories and flair for headlines (DON'T BE SO BLOODY RUDE, MR K) are the reason he is rightly recalled as a newspaper genius. On budget days and other big news occasions like royal weddings and state funerals he took over the running of the paper.

Downstairs on the third floor The Editor Who Wasn't made sure the paper came out on time and looked after the parts that did not interest Hugh Cudlipp. Most of the time when I worked for Hugh the editor was the patient, much-loved Lee Howard. He had a bottle of whisky on his desk from the moment he arrived and stayed, like all good daily newspaper editors, until late every night. Everything would be brought to him; copy, layouts, page proofs, pictures, features, cartoons, libel writs. He had two conferences a day and every senior executive shunted in and out of his office to get his nod of approval. He never seemed drunk. His bottle of whisky, which he alone drank, was replaced at least once a day. His colleagues were allowed to help themselves to whatever they wanted from his drinks cupboard without asking permission. Even the raw material from Hugh's genius on the ninth floor had to go through this Clapham Junction. Lee called everybody who worked for him 'darling'. He grew alarmingly larger and larger and finally had to go. When my wife Brigid and I visited him and his wife Madeleine shortly before he died, he was as benevolent as ever. He could no longer get into a suit and wore a kaftan instead.

King had been gone for two years when the next shock wave hit the Mirror building. Its impact was almost physical. Totally unheralded, as these things always are, the editorial executives and management were summoned without notice into Ted Pickering's office on the fourth floor. He was chairman of the newspaper division, although Hugh on the ninth was the real boss. With Pick in his office was Percy Roberts, the managing director, as usual in his shirtsleeves and wearing braces. Intriguingly, large, florid-faced Percy was feeding documents into a shredding machine. Another document, later handed to us, was being run off on a duplicator. There was an electric atmosphere but no sign of Hugh. Pick could take the drama out of the parting of the Red Sea. In flat tones he announced the extraordinary news that Reed's, a partly owned IPC subsidiary producing newsprint and corrugated paper in its own mills, was to become the controlling company of IPC with Don Ryder, someone most of us had scarcely heard of, as chairman. It was hard to comprehend what had happened, but Dennis Hackett, the highly talented former *Nova* editor who was the *Mirror*'s publicity chief, got to the heart of the matter. 'It's a reverse takeover,' he said, in words that everyone who was there remembers. 'No, it's not,' said Pick, glumly, and I immediately wondered whether Dennis's days were numbered. They were, and it was. Ryder was the chief, who the hell was he?

We all moved under the umbrella of Reed International Ltd. Hugh remained chairman of IPC and became deputy chairman (editorial) of Reed. The humiliation for us was almost as great as we imagined his to be. Jarratt was moved in from the civil service to become managing director of IPC above Percy Roberts. Reed's balance sheet was now what mattered. The long-term interests of the Mirror group and its famous flagship the *Daily Mirror* were far from paramount. We had come a long way from Cecil King and it had been downhill all the way. What is now called Cudlipp's *Sun*, previously the *Daily Herald*, had been a disastrous flop, and after King's departure the failure had been compounded by selling it to Rupert Murdoch. Some weeks before this was announced Cudlipp told me in confidence, as editor of its sister paper the *People*, that it was to be closed down. I thought about this overnight and the following morning asked to see him. The original *Sun* was the result of considerable market research. Its advertising slogan claimed it was 'born of the world we live in', but judging by its shocking failure that is manifestly what it was not. The *People*'s sales were at record level. I suggested the *Sun* should be linked directly with the *People* and the Sunday paper used as its principal means of promotion. The *Sun* would have to be changed dramatically to appeal to *People* readers and I volunteered for the job. 'You want to be editorial director?' asked Hugh, his manner hostile I thought. 'No,' I said. 'Editor.' 'It would damage the *Mirror*,' he said, dismissing the idea.

I had hoped to put half a million on the sales of the *Sun*. Murdoch increased them by 4 million. But then I would not have thought of the Page Three Girl, the most famous newspaper institution since Pip, Squeak and Wilfred in the pre-war *Daily Mail* and Jane in the *Daily Mirror*. Dennis Hackett also volunteered to edit the *Sun*. He bravely put his objections to selling the paper to Murdoch in writing.

Another great shock was to follow three years later. The ownership of the papers was a matter for ribaldry and regret, but at least we still had Hugh in total charge of the editorial side on the ninth floor. Except at Christmas, we did not see the wallpaper manufacturers, as he called them. The wine continued to flow. Sydney Jacobson said one morning, 'Can you pop down to see me at 12 o'clock?' He said the same to the other two editors. There was a bottle of champagne and five glasses on a small table and some dry biscuits. I had never seen them before in his room. Cudlipp was there. He told us he would retire and leave the company completely in a few months when he was sixty. His public announcement said he had always proclaimed that young people should run newspapers and it would be an 'unpardonable vanity' for him to continue.

The farewell parties for Hugh are now part of the Fleet Street legend. A river steamer was hired to take almost the entire *Daily Mirror* staff to a banquet at Greenwich. By the time it arrived most were drunk on champagne. Buns and insults were hurled, but the marvel today is about the money that was spent. I decided, for Hugh's sake, to make the *Sunday Mirror* affair at the Café Royal a little less boisterous. The lunch was at 12.45 for 1.00 p.m. instead of the customary 12.15 for 1.00 p.m. and I told the executives, 'Everyone can get as pissed as they like afterwards but they are not allowed to throw buns.' A large replica of his boat faced Hugh at the far end of the room, and he sat next to me giving his character reading of various colleagues. There were Board parties, IPC magazine parties, and parties in Manchester and Glasgow. If the total cost was less than £50,000 I should be surprised. It was not just a lot duller and less dangerous when he had left. The *Daily Mirror* was a lot less important.

Alex Jarratt was the first of our odd new breed of chairmen, but the nicest of men. He had been Secretary to the National Board for Prices and Incomes from 1965 to 1968, Deputy Under-Secretary of State at the Department of Employment and Productivity for two years after that, and then reached his zenith as Deputy Secretary at the Ministry of Agriculture until Ryder persuaded him to leave his promising career in the civil service. He busied himself, I imagined, with tedious management meetings. The editors saw little of him during his year in office except at occasional lunches where he drank one, sometimes two, whiskies with water in a lager glass, which seemed the right thing to do with editors. The only dramatic moment was when we were asked, one by one, to agree to a policy of non-automatic replacement of staff in all departments of the newspapers. This was the first attempt to do something about outrageous overmanning and Fleet Street's famous Spanish customs. It failed totally. Every day the Mirror's cash flowed through Reed International. Reed was not willing to have its milch cow run dry, possibly for months, in a stoppage. By the time Maxwell took over in 1984 the usually sensible journalists' chapels had also won the right of automatic replacement, even of layabouts who were useless (as distinct from useful) drunks or mad and had mercifully reached retirement age.

In 1974 Michael Foot and I were chatting as freely as we always do. He was worried about whether the links between the Mirror newspapers and Labour would continue to be as strong as in the days of King and Cudlipp. 'Well,' I said, 'you could always offer Don Ryder the chairmanship of the National Enterprise Board. He is a brilliant business man obviously. If anyone can make it work, he will.' Michael put the idea to Wilson, Ryder got the job and became Baron Ryder of Eaton Hastings. Jarratt became Reed chairman and we had a journalist again, Edward Pickering, in the big office on the ninth floor, but this time he was chairman of the newspaper division only and not IPC. We had lost a lot of clout. Pick retired in 1977 only to re-emerge five years later as the executive vice-chairman of Times Newspapers and a Murdoch trusty. Before Pick left, Jarratt took each of the editors to lunch in turn to seek our views on a successor. He told me that Tony Miles, the editorial director who had edited the *Daily Mirror* for three years after Lee Howard, had said he would understand if he was not appointed at this stage of his career. I said Tony was wrong and nominated him first, out of loyalty, and myself second out of conviction. I said, unasked, that I thought Percy Roberts would be a mistake. He was a manager. We needed charisma, leadership, excitement and a good public image. 'But he is so good with the unions,' said Alex, who made him chairman, Tony Miles deputy chairman and put all three editors on the board.

Percy spent his three years bravely seeking a place in the hall of fame as the man who brought New Technology to Fleet Street. He succeeded, but unfortunately the concessions to the unions to win their agreement were so great, the lack of aptitude of former hot-metal printers for the less skilled, but more delicate, art of photo-setting by computer so catastrophic, and shop floor management so abysmal, that no jobs were saved, which was the purpose of the operation. The papers had to start earlier instead of later, there were countless misprints and 'pie-ups' and our costs were startlingly up instead of down. *Sporting Life*, once as dependable as the Queen Mother's presence at Ascot and the guinea-pig paper for the change-over, failed to appear for several days because the system of full-page composition sold to the Mirror by the American Linotype Paul company could not be made to work at all. The paper was restored to hot-metal and continued to employ hundreds of printers for another ten years. 'Cut and paste' was substituted for full-page composition for the three national newspapers. There were no visual display units for journalists, so that they were unable to see instantly what was happening and make corrections, and no direct input for them to feed in their own stories. But at least the unions, and more importantly the powerful chapels, had accepted New Technology and that battle no longer had to be fought. Until Percy had a go at it no one in Fleet Street thought it possible. He deserved a red badge for courage if not, as it turned out, for performance.

Percy's board meetings were often stormy. He enjoyed a scrap. The editors would complain about having fewer and fewer page changes and ever-earlier start-up times, wrong editions going to key football areas, bloody-mindedness in the composing-room and lack of money to promote their papers. The publicity chief Felicity Green, one of the first women journalists on a newspaper board, did her best to keep the peace. Percy allowed no say in the contents of the papers. That was Tony Miles's job as editorial director. Then he became chairman and was allowed no say in the management of the company. That was the prerogative of Douglas Long, the chief executive, who reported directly to Reed's. Every night the production and labour relations directors would meet in his office to discuss this or that threat to the papers from the 57 fathers of the union chapels. They were deeply relieved on the rare occasions when not a single dispute imperilled production.

The power of the FOCs was enormous and irresponsible. They, not the managers, decided who worked for the company in the majority of departments and were the real gaffers on the shop floor. I asked one of the editorial drivers whom he regarded as his boss. 'My FOC,' he replied, immediately. The impression was further enhanced because the FOCs were not expected to do the work for which the company paid them and were given their own offices. Restrictive practices and rackets were rampant. FOCs had been conditioned to believe their mission was to get as much as possible for their members for as little as possible in return. It was very difficult for compositors working with a couple of friendly journalists on page one to be told by a tyrannical FOC or committee man well past the edition time to take their 'blow' before the paper was away, thus leaving only a skeleton crew and making the paper even later. No journalist would ever think of leaving the floor for his break at this crucial time, and most printers were just as dedicated. But the FOC was boss, and the worst of the FOCs got their kicks out of being little Hitlers and bullying weak managers.

To my surprise Douglas Long was head-hunted out of retirement to be the manager of the *Independent*. Freed from Fleet Street's madness he set up model printing arrangements. They worked brilliantly from the start, with only one slight hitch on the first day in one of the printing centres he had contracted to print the pages composed with the latest technology and minimum manning in the *Independent*'s own offices. I thought he was merely the best of the bunch after Percy Roberts retired. I misjudged him. It was clearly impossible for him to manage as he would have liked without the backing of the people at the very top at Reed House.

In the years between Cecil King and Robert Maxwell there was a supreme example of an opportunity missed. The *News of the World*'s circulation had fallen and the *Sunday Mirror*'s risen. All that was required was a small nudge to push the N.O.W. off its perch as number one for the first time in history. The 'heavies' now all had colour magazines, but not one of the popular newspapers. The *Mail on Sunday* had not yet been conceived. I suggested the *Sunday Mirror* should have one and this was enthusiastically supported by Brian Downing, the marketing director. The advertising department was sure that with our good profile of younger, affluent readers they could raise the necessary revenue. The circulation manager was equally sure a magazine would give us the greatest circulation triumph in the paper's history. The company dithered. Months later the *Sunday Express* launched its colour magazine, and then the *News of the World*. There was no longer enough revenue available for us to run one at a profit. The advertising department gave the thumbs down. The Mirror Group's two Sunday newspapers became the only ones without a magazine. We soldiered on.

In 1983, we were told the astounding news that the Mirror Group was to be floated off by Reed International, or cast adrift as we felt it to be. Somebody most of us had never or only vaguely heard of, Clive Thornton, was to be chairman because it was believed he would appeal to City investors when we were put on the market. The fact that he knew nothing about running newspapers and as chairman of Abbey National had no experience of industrial relations did not deter Reeds from appointing him. He was the top name on a list submitted by Tony Miles, and he in turn got the name from Bob Head, the *Mirror*'s extremely able city editor, but not so able (I felt) nominator of newspaper chairmen. Apart from Douglas Long, the chief executive, none of the editors or other directors knew what was going on. It was as much a surprise to us as to the nice Indian doorman who invariably said when he saw me coming into the office, 'Good morning, gentlemen' or 'Goodnight, gentlemen' when I left. It sounded all right when I was with somebody else.

The Thornton era filled me with gloom. Unlike his too diffident predecessor Tony Miles, who moved down a rung to be deputy chairman, he was the greatest egotist we had had since Cecil King.

He certainly knew how to put himself across to the City and boasted openly of his ability to plant stories that would help him to get his way. Behind his back colleagues mocked his ignorance of newspaper life. They stifled their yawns at endless board meetings. To keep him happy, Tony Miles had a dummy designed and printed of his favourite project, a new London evening newspaper. Since it was edited by Peter Thompson, then deputy editor of the *Daily Mirror*, and Roy Foster, art editor of the *Sunday Mirror*, it was bound to look good, and Clive was pleased to show it around. But it was a pure pipe dream since there had been no market research on the likely readers of such a paper and no serious discussion on how it would be printed and distributed and what advertising revenue it would earn. Meanwhile the serious business of producing a prospectus for the flotation of the company on the stock market was coming unstuck because of the failure to find printing facilities for the two Mirrors in Manchester. Thomson, who owned a vast, ramshackle plant in Withy Grove running at a severe loss, had given us notice. A viable solution had to be found before we could go on the market. Thus, to Reed's intense annoyance, the flotation was postponed. This gave Maxwell his chance. The short reign of the kindly but cruelly appointed Thornton was all but over.

18
CAP'N BOB

Working for Maxwell, I found people tended to look at you as if you were a street accident victim. 'What's he like?' they would say. 'It must be awful.' I was at an impressive French Embassy affair with most of the Royal Family, Lord Snowdon and Bob Maxwell. Maxwell went immediately to a raised dais, where lesser mortals who like him had not been invited to the preceding dinner thought it was presumptuous to tread. Nevertheless he was not spotted by Snowdon who had heard he was there and was with the common herd. 'Where is he?' he asked me, affecting great excitement. 'I must see him.' There was no need to ask who. 'I will introduce you,' I said. But he was not interested in that. 'I just want to look at him,' he said, and hurried towards the dais.

How do you explain a man who at all his personal offices is invariably served his coffee or tea in cups larger than anyone else's and engraved 'For a Very Important Person', and who one Christmas sent all of his staff, some of them highly intelligent, a book on the triumphs of Oxford United containing sixteen photographs of himself and even more numerous mentions? Do these examples mean that he has a great sense of humour about himself, as I often suspect, or a lack of one? The Louis XIVth Restaurant was closed for the night at The Imperial Hotel, Blackpool, so that he could give a private dinner for his staff after the Mirror Group's traditional party at the Labour conference. Maxwell took a large cigar out of his pocket. 'Is that your red wine?' he asked my wife, Brigid. She said it was. Without asking whether she wanted to drink it, he reached across the table, took the glass and dunked the end of his cigar in it. Then he lit the other end. My wife, understandably, was amazed. To do such a thing in reverse was unthinkable. It seemed an unbeliev-ably hostile and aggressive act.

I was greatly amused, since editors are taught by experience to fear no man except policemen in patrol cars late at night. The same thing had happened to me to my equal surprise at lunch in the office,

215

because I was sitting as I usually did on his right hand. 'Did you notice that?' I said to one of the editors afterwards. He had, of course. Put into a newspaper soap opera on TV most critics would regard it as over the top. No offence was meant on either occasion, of that I would swear to any libel jury. But what does it tell us about him, except that he ruins his cigars and other people's wine, although they could always order more?

My wife, who is an illustrator of great ability, but also a non-practising Jungian psychotherapist, says it would take five years of analysis to sort out my true feelings about Maxwell. Possibly, I might say in my first session on the couch, I feel guilty because I like him, or think I do. He is so acquisitive, so dominant, so forceful in his endless pursuit of success and fame, is this a character weakness on my part? Do Michael Foot and I have some deep-seated personality flaw because we both loved Beaverbrook, another despot? Does Maxwell have any real, close friends, or does he consciously or otherwise cultivate relationships with people like Lord Elwyn Jones, the former Lord Chancellor, Harold Wilson, the former Premier, and assorted trade union leaders including Clive Jenkins and Ray Buckton, because their presence at his table is a compliment to him and assists him on the path to glory?

I felt I was used by him much more than he gave in return. After Labour's victory in 1964 he asked me if I would edit a daily newspaper he was seeking to launch in conjunction with Mr Jack Diamond, a rich and respected MP, George Brown and other leading socialists. In view of Brown's notorious disloyalty to his leader, I checked with Harold Wilson at No. 10 that he would not regard such a paper as a threat to him. He did not, and I attended what was meant to be a secret meeting at Maxwell's office, then in Fitzroy Square. We stood or sat around waiting and waiting for Labour's deputy leader. He was supposed to take the chair at lunch.

Eventually some minion must have persuaded him to leave whatever bottle he was drinking from, and he arrived almost blind drunk at ten minutes to two. Pushing his plate away from him, almost slumped over the table, he said over and over again, 'Are we agreed? When I say go we go? When I say go we go? Are we agreed?' That was all he was capable of saying. Though an alcoholic, George was a formidable figure in those days when Labour's stature was at its peak. The rest of us exchanged resigned glances, but nobody remonstrated with him. It was not a propitious start for a great Labour newspaper. The project withered and died faster than any state in Marxist mythology, and so far as I recall no further meetings were called. The damage to me must have been considerable. With the incomparable news sources of the *Daily Express*, it was inconceivable that Max Aitken failed to hear of the meeting. Besides, what a piece of gossip. Maxwell and the editor of the *Daily Express*, as I was at the time, plotting to start a socialist paper!

Even then Maxwell was a figure of speculation and, regrettably, fun, not least because of his silly habit of retaining his relatively low army rank of captain, something usually only the most inadequate do, which was still more amusing in the eyes of the prejudiced because of his foreign origins. Such was this prejudice I was told by several people, including a newspaper editor who should have known better, that Maxwell had invented his Military Cross and no one of his name had received one. The last point may have been true, since to save him from summary execution if he was captured, because he was both a Czech and a Jew, Maxwell changed his surname at least three times during the war, including once to du Maurier because he liked the name on the cigarette packet. This again demonstrated a great sense of humour or total lack of one. Like Sydney Jacobson, the Mirror Group's editorial director for many years, the young Maxwell received his MC for an act of stunning bravery. It was pinned on his chest personally by Montgomery.

The picture of this proudest moment is modestly displayed in the vast wine cellar at Maxwell's home in Oxford, instead of, as one would expect from someone so hilariously immodest, in the drawing-room blown up as large as a portrait of Lenin in Red Square. My wife was shown the picture by his daughter Ghislaine while I, the other editors and Joe Haines were in some supposedly serious discussion with him about the economic future of Britain. In fact, we were having a pleasantly relaxed gossip while boffins led by Bernard, now Lord, Donoughue completed a blueprint for the *Mirror* they had been slaving over for two days on how to end unemployment. When copies of the completed document were finally handed to us, none of us including Maxwell could bear even to glance at it. (Joe Haines had the misfortune to have to read it later because it was his job to write a summary for the then dwindling number of *Mirror* readers.) Maxwell has never shown me the picture of Montgomery and himself, nor referred to his award. He does tell how he executed a German soldier whom he had just seen deliberately kill a British trooper in cold blood after the Germans had waved a white flag of surrender. Maxwell tells the story as a matter of regret, though his act was totally justifiable.

Another little chore I did for Maxwell was to advise him in two or three telephone conversations about his bid for the *Observer*. I suggested he should say that his distinguished publishing company Pergamon Press, whose works are primarily for university scholars throughout the world, and the *Observer*, with such a high proportion of intellectuals among its readers, were natural bed-fellows. He listened, which I found him singularly unable to do after he took over the Mirror, and used my suggested form of words almost verbatim. He had intended that his British Printing and Communications Corporation (BPCC) should bid for the *Observer*, but switched the bidding to Pergamon when he saw the force of my argument. It seemed to me that Maxwell would be a much more suitable proprietor for the *Observer* than the equally buccaneering but right-wing Tiny Rowland with his embarrassingly affluent investments in impoverished Africa. In fact, after his initial scuffles with the editor, Donald Trelford, he has turned out to be an ideal press baron, with an obvious love for newspapers and an uncharacteristic ability to allow his editor to pursue policies he must sometimes abominate. The late Lord (Roy) Thomson, to everyone's surprise, also fulfilled nobody's worst fears and was an ideal newspapermen's boss.

In the run-up to the 1983 general election Maxwell had the idea of running a daily newspaper for the Labour party throughout the campaign. There did not seem too much of a problem about printing it. He had recently added the Odhams plant at Watford to his new BPCC empire and was now the biggest printer in Europe, if not in creation. Reed's had sold the plant to Maxwell, Les Carpenter told me later, because they thought he was the only person who could solve the problems of over-capacity and over-manning in the industry, which did not say much for Reed's labour relations skills. How he did this is worth a study on its own. He had a series of face-to-face meetings with the workforce and succeeded where Reed's had failed in forcing through massive redundancies. Reed's had passed the buck and to Maxwell it was a gold mine. It is one of the strange contradictions in him that he should emerge from the smoke and flame of this battle, deeply wounding in the short term to many families, once again as a Labour champion. The Mirror chairman Tony Miles gave me permission to help the newspaper project and Maxwell wanted me to edit the paper while it lasted. But it seemed to me one of his madder notions. Where would we find sufficient journalists, many of them politically aware, for the duration of an election? Bill Keys, general secretary of the printing union SOGAT '82 and predecessor of Brenda Dean, was summoned by Maxwell to join us for lunch at his BPCC headquarters, quaintly named Maxwell House, yet another example of his sense of humour or lack of one. Depending on the state of industrial relations between the two of them, Keys was either locked in battle with Maxwell or locked in an embrace. We talked over the possibilities. There were none. 'Not on, is it?' said Maxwell after Keys had left. It never was.

He rang me at home one Wednesday to tell me he was making a bid for Mirror Group Newspapers. It was not much of a confidence, as I learned later, because he had telephoned the same news to Les Carpenter of Reed's at his home the previous Sunday. 'I am offering £80 million,' boomed Bob, 'but I will probably go up to £100 million.' I knew that the reaction at the Mirror would be one of total horror. The printers would fear he would sort out their outrageous mal-practices, or hard-won rights as they preferred to imagine them, and the journalists more altruistically would dread interference in the editorial content. (Earlier in 1984 Maxwell had come close to buying Express newspapers. Nobody speculated at the time that he would have turned them into Labour papers, in accordance with his beliefs. Maxwell as boss of the hard-nosed Tory *Sunday Express*, then edited by Sir John Junor, would have been even odder than my editorship of the *Daily Express*. It is possible on the *Daily Express* to pursue some editorial policies that are sympathetic to Labour and the unions. Beaverbrook favoured high wages and full employment and would have backed huge public investment in housing and utilities to keep people at work. He would have opposed Mrs Thatcher's trade union legislation, sound and fair though much of it has been. But to have switched the *Sunday Express* in line with Maxwell's devotion to the Labour cause would have been the equivalent of steering the Titanic into its iceberg in broad daylight, in wind Force Two with a visibility of 32 miles.)

I gave Maxwell some good advice on the phone when he told me about his bid for us. 'Whatever you do,' I said, 'don't attack the Mirror papers. Say they are first-class with good editors. If it looks as though you are going to start telling them what to print they will fight you flat out.' Maxwell duly praised the papers and concentrated on his strong point, effective management and vast financial resources. If he had not, he would have had all his editors in London and Glasgow publicly against him, including me. The strange silence of the editors during the takeover battle was, I think, due to my sound advice to Maxwell. A letter in *The Times* from all the Mirror editors opposing him as a sole proprietor of socialist newspapers with the powers of a dictator might have exerted more influence on the

vacillating Sir Alex Jarratt than the pressure of Reed investors with
no other concern than profit.

My own feelings were mixed and troubled. Having Maxwell as
something of a friend for twenty years was one thing. Having him as
an autocratic boss, which I knew him to be, was not how I wanted to
end my Fleet Street career. One Beaverbrook was enough for me,
much though I liked him. I suspected I would like Maxwell a lot less,
and besides he had no journalistic, as distinct from publishing, skills
though with his usual bravado he was convinced of the opposite. His
very pleasing family, and his clever and talented French wife,
Elisabeth, who took her degree at Oxford in her middle years and
went on triumphantly to get her Ph.D., have thanked me for
'standing by' Maxwell during his blackest period, the Pergamon
Press upheaval, when the Board of Trade inquiry made its famous
and manifestly wrong judgment that he was unfit to run a public
company. One of them recalled my Christmas card on the mantelpiece when scores of his professional friends had stopped sending
them, presumably because they thought he was done for and of no
further use.

I would, in fact, have sent Bob Maxwell a Christmas card if he had
ended up in Pentonville, which was where some notably prejudiced
people wanted him to be. Unlike the bigots and humbugs who
ceaselessly condemn others, I try to follow the divine and familiar
guidance: 'He that is without sin among you, let him cast the first
stone . . .' As someone who has committed most sins except violence,
sending my Christmas card expressed no judgment on Maxwell's
business methods, good or bad. The phone call forced me to make
one decision. If I could choose between having Bob Maxwell as a
boss and not having him, I would choose not. But since I had to
choose between Maxwell and Thornton, whose flotation of the
company was delayed and floundering badly, I thought that at least
with Maxwell we would make a good profit again, the papers would
be secure, and my relationship with him was surely an advantage
from the point of view of pure self-interest. I thought that if we went
public under the amateur Thornton, the unions might stitch him up,
the firm might collapse under the weight of debt and chaotic
production, and heaven knows what the future would be of the *Daily
Mirror*, *Sunday Mirror*, *Sunday People* and the *Sporting Life*.

I was being forced to choose, but I wanted neither. To me the guilt
of Reed International for allowing this situation to occur was
colossal. To most journalists, owning national newspapers that
fulfilled such a vital role in the political mix of the country was almost

a sacred trust. They should have sorted out our management problems and made the papers viable, but they funked it just as they ducked out of their commitments to Odhams (Watford). Why blame Bob Maxwell for charging in to prove that where they had failed he would succeed, as indeed he did? Why blame him for forcing Reed's to swallow its public pledge that they would never allow the Mirror Group to fall into the hands of one person?

I did not fancy the role of spy or double agent. When I arrived at the office after Maxwell's call, the news was already out. I was able with a clear conscience to tell Tony Miles he had phoned me. There were several more phone calls between us. Maxwell does not phone anyone to pass the time of day. I think I played a fairly key role in how he played his cards, but good manners and less noble motives prevented me from saying I regarded him merely as the lesser of two evils. I knew that he would soon be yearning for the halcyon days when the managers, with little support from Reed's, were in a state of constant battle with little tyrants in the union chapels, the wine flowed, and Tony Miles presided benignly over newspapers that were far from discreditable and allowed to run themselves. In Fleet Street you never knew when you were well off – as many redundant printers who will never again be in the big pay league must ruefully concede. When it would really have counted to keep the new breed of hard-faced, non-editorial press barons outside the gates, they conceded nothing. At the last minute of the eleventh hour, several unions offered Thornton a no-strike deal. It was too late.

One small service to Maxwell I withdrew during the take-over battle. He had the habit of phoning me on Saturday nights to discover what had appeared about him in the first editions of the Sunday papers. This became too time consuming, so I arranged for someone with little to do to scour the rivals and read over any mentions to him. This sometimes took half an hour or more. The news desk journalist with this chore had a voice that could be heard across a crowded room. He seemed to presume that everyone on the end of a telephone was deaf. Some of the articles and snippets from gossip columns were the usual witty or offensive stuff people write about Maxwell. The news desk man ploughed on fearlessly, to the delight of those around him. Before I delegated this task, Maxwell would occasionally ask me if anything was going on. Once I had the impression someone was in the room with him. I told him the night's big news and he immediately suggested a headline. It was a very bad one. A frustrated newspaper boss, I thought, who wanted to show off to his friends that he had editors in his power. 'This service had better be discontinued for a while,' I told Maxwell, after he had phoned me about his bid. 'You are supposed to be the enemy.'

The Maxwell bid was announced on 5 July 1984, and Thornton was actually filmed for TV being telephoned the shock, horror news. Like the man who supplanted him, he enjoyed being on camera and had allowed a documentary crew to accompany him to a meeting of trade union representatives in Manchester. He was interrupted to take the dramatic call after he had told them how well plans for the flotation were proceeding. Reed International said they had no intention of considering the Maxwell offer. Then they considered and rejected it. They said they still believed the interests of MGN and its employees would best be served by it becoming an independent company with a wide range of shareholders. They did not add that its interests would have been served best of all if the flotation was scrapped and they fulfilled their responsibilities by managing it properly. Maxwell typically denied that his bid had been rejected. 'They have not turned down my offer, they can't turn down my offer,' he said. That was the language of money power, and he was right. Reed's obligations to the big investors carried more weight than Sir Alex Jarratt's pledges to his staff. Maxwell set up his headquarters in the Ritz Hotel opposite Reed House in Piccadilly and fired his salvoes of ever-increasing millions. He found time to say to Peter Sissons in a TV interview, with a solemnity that would soon become familiar, 'I would certainly hope to make a small contribution with the help of these newspapers, if I became pro- prietor, to halt the retreat of Great Britain.' Bully for you, Bob, was supposed to be the reaction.

I waited around the office on the evening of 12 July, but there was no news from the front-line except of much to-ing and fro-ing by bankers, lawyers and other minions across Piccadilly. At 11.30 p.m. I was in bed with my wife in our London flat. At 12.10 a.m. on Friday the 13th the phone rang. It was Maxwell. 'We have lift-off,' he exulted from his Ritz Hotel bunker. 'I am your new proprietor.' I was standing naked, talking to the boss on the telephone at an absurd hour, just as I had done with Beaverbrook. His first orders I found vastly amusing. He asked me to call Ken Hudgell, the company secretary, and get him to haul all the directors out of their beds for a board meeting to be held at 1.30 a.m. at Maxwell House. 'Get there at one o'clock yourself,' said Maxwell, 'we'll have a drink.' 'Certainly,' I said. I phoned Ken Hudgell, an unflappable, excellent man who had seen just about everything in his forty years at the Mirror. 'You're pulling my leg,' he said. 'No, I'm not,' I said. 'It's par for the course with newspaper proprietors. They're all like this.'

Outside in heavy rain a taxi conveniently dropped a neighbour. I arrived at 1.00 a.m. on 13 July in the dreary, aptly-named Worship Street in the City to find Maxwell House in darkness. I pressed various bells. There was no answer. Standing under an umbrella in the pouring rain I reflected on my future with the man who had so unexpectedly thrust himself into all our lives. I decided the chances were that my role in the developing drama would be similar to that of the music critic friend of Citizen Kane, played by Joseph Cotten, whose newspaper was taken over by Kane and who became a disillusioned employee swamped in drink and self-pity. Since I liked Joseph Cotten and he was in the right, the thought was not displeasing as I gradually became illuminated in the shadows by the approaching headlights of Maxwell's Rolls-Royce. Out of it jumped three of his incredibly loyal, and usually jolly, sometimes fed-up female staff. Earlier Ken Hudgell had telephoned my wife because several directors had told him I was obviously pulling his leg. 'No, he's not,' said Brigid. 'He's got dressed and gone off in the rain.' One of the Maxwell ladies ushered me into the car. 'He was driving past the Mirror and couldn't resist the temptation to go into the building,' she said. 'He sent us down here to pick up anybody who had turned up.' And I had thought he had sent the car specially to fetch me.

With Joseph Cotten still in mind, I got into the Rolls and when we arrived at the back entrance of the Mirror was confronted by bright lights and a microphone thrust under my nose. 'Can you make a statement please?' said an eager young TV reporter. He did not, I thought, know I was one of the editors taken over by Maxwell. 'This is not my normal mode of transport,' I said in my best Joseph Cotten manner. Not a bad joke, I thought. It did not make it on Breakfast TV.

There was an atmosphere of great drama. The paper was printing, as seen on the movies, and many of the publishing room hordes had given up any pretence that they had anything to do, and were watching the comings and goings with far greater interest than they ever watched the machines tying the bundles, labelling them and delivering them to the vans. Maxwell's sudden decision to enter the building meant there was no one to welcome him. He had taken the lift to the third floor where he was doubtless surprised to find how few editorial staff are visible at that time of night. Word spread instantly to the ninth floor where Mike Molloy, the *Daily Mirror* editor, was with Douglas Long, the group chief executive and others. Tony Miles, the editorial director, had gone home in a fury that Reed's had sold out to Maxwell. He had been persuaded by colleagues to return in his own best interests and was on his way back with Anne, his sensible and supportive wife. Mike, who was understandably well tanked up that night but coping well, said to Long, 'He is the owner, I ought to go and welcome him.' In a few minutes, accompanied by Mike, the massive frame of the new boss made its triumphant entry into Douglas's office. Maxwell saw the wine cupboard was open, seized a whisky bottle and said, 'Anyone care for a drink?' They were his first words to the Mirror top brass.

It was the surest way to make friends in Fleet Street. I arrived shortly afterwards, and moments later Maxwell faced his first industrial crisis. A print manager told him one of the major chapels was demanding a statement, the implication as ever being that they would not work without it. 'They shall have one,' said Maxwell, and he dictated a bullish, placatory declaration to his office director, Jean Baddeley. She ran off dozens of copies for all the chapels in all three offices. The crisis was over. 'What a good thing I decided to hold the meeting this morning,' Maxwell said to me. By 2.15 a.m. all but one of the directors had arrived from their beds and probably the only board meeting of Mirror Group Newspapers to be held at that hour began.

I went back alone with Maxwell to his office in Worship Street. 'What shall I do today?' he asked as he drove the short distance from Holborn Circus. 'Give the editors a splendid lunch,' I said. 'Make them feel the good days are here again.' 'In the office?' 'No, somewhere really good.' We talked for a few minutes in his surprisingly small and tastefully appointed office overlooking Liverpool Street station. 'What would you like from me?' he asked. 'Tell me what you want and it's yours.' 'Nothing,' I said, virtuously. 'Oh, come on,' said Citizen Kane, 'Editorial director?' 'You should keep Tony Miles,' I replied, 'but if he decides to go, fair enough.' Maxwell, as he frequently does in takeover battles, had worked almost round the clock for more than a week. He had a bed in the office. 'How will you get home?' he said. I replied that any newspaperman could find his way home at that time of the morning. 'I will walk with you until you get a taxi,' he said, and came with me as far as Finsbury Square. 'Go to bed,' I said. 'You must be shattered.' He clasped my right hand with his left one and murmured his affection for me. I no longer felt the least bit like Joseph

Cotten. Perhaps my premonitions of unhappiness to follow were wrong.

The lunch the next day was exactly as I had suggested. It was at Claridges in a private room, and only the editors and Tony Miles were invited. Maxwell said to me, 'I'll come in your car.' His attitude to the driver was extraordinary. 'Go to the left,' he would cry. 'Nip in front.' 'Jump the lights.' He instructed the driver, Roy Tween, from the start of the journey to the finish. Roy, a former SOGAT FOC, was something of a wreck by the time we arrived. His hands were shaking, which I thought sad. And we had gone the worst possible way. It made me wonder whether it was true, as legend had it, that one of Maxwell's drivers, pushed to breaking point by his endless barracking, had got out of the car at traffic lights, said, 'All right, if you're so good, you drive,' and left him for ever. Maxwell had laid on Buck's Fizz, the champagne and fresh orange juice drink I had introduced him to years earlier, as an aperitif to please the editors. A nice gesture, I thought. 'I'll have gin and tonic, please,' said Tony Miles, which struck me as churlish since on my advice Maxwell was trying hard. He was visibly offended. We had cheese soufflé that could have won an award. The rest I have forgotten and we were a little late back at the office for the second board meeting within thirteen hours of Mirror Group Newspapers under its new proprietor.

The entire board who had opposed Maxwell – with myself thought to be his sole supporter – were now playing suitable court to him around the oval table in Clive Thornton's former office. (Clive had left, as those at the very top invariably do, with wheelbarrow-loads of money shortly to follow, having found Maxwell sitting in his chair behind his desk first thing that morning.) Then followed a pretty good comedy sequence. 'Would someone please move that the resignation of Clive Thornton as a director of this company be accepted?' he said. Somebody moved. It was a formality. 'Next,' said Maxwell, 'would someone move that I be appointed chief executive of this company.' Eyes shifted to the young, thrusting, able but not over popular Roger Bowes. 'We have a slight problem here, chairman,' he said, smiling calmly, for which he moved up several notches in my esteem. 'What's that?' said Maxwell. 'Well,' said Roger, 'until this moment I was chief executive.'

How will the old rogue cope with that? I thought. 'Is anybody managing director?' he asked. Since the answer was no, Maxwell continued: 'You are now managing director. Is that all right?' Bowes sportingly conceded. 'There is also a slight problem with me,' said

Douglas Long. 'I am group chief executive,' which would have put him above Maxwell. 'You can be deputy chairman,' said Maxwell. 'That's no good,' cried the editors defensively, 'he's deputy chairman,' and we pointed to Tony Miles. 'Any vice-chairman?' asked Maxwell. No vice-chairman. 'All right?' he said to Douglas, who had nothing to lose since he was due to retire shortly. Douglas smiled. Ken Hudgell was jotting down the new titles. He had another one to note in a few moments. 'I also am chief executive,' said Vic Horwood, who has a long, rather funereal face, 'in Scotland.' In Maxwell's next breath he became managing director, Scottish newspapers. Vic's doom-laden appearance disguises a person of far greater wit and ability than is usual among newspaper managers. It was customary at Mirror directors' meetings to bring grim tidings of trouble at mill. Vic, slow off the mark for once, had not taken on board that everything had changed in the past seventeen hours since Maxwell had handed over his cheque. 'There is something I should mention,' he said, having received his new title. 'The printers are holding a mass meeting at a cinema in Glasgow this evening and I fear we may lose the entire run.'

Such a threat would normally have produced much head-shaking and sorrow at the perfidy of the workforce, bitter words about this or that tyrannical FOC, tough talk that this time they had gone too far and would be smashed, coupled with the unspoken certain conviction in everyone's mind that as the deadline approached the company's negotiators would make whatever concessions were necessary to bring out the paper. On the madly logical grounds that they would have to work harder, these usually included overtime and delightfully named 'compression payments' to printers who had illegally held a disruptive meeting in the company's time, which needless to say they would not have done if the company had not behaved so disgracefully in failing to resolve their legitimate grievances.

Maxwell, endowed by his Maker with the ability to work without apparently flagging almost round the clock, a huge, menacing bulk that only the bravest can resist without trepidation, and a voice that seems to come from the depths of a volcano, eyed the gaunt Horwood with undiluted menace. 'In that case, chum,' he said, 'you had better leave this minute, get the first possible shuttle and tell them that if the *Daily Record* does not appear tonight it will never appear again. I will close it down and that's final.' Horwood sensibly rose to his feet. 'Is there anyone here who does not believe me?' said the new chief executive, chairman and publisher of Mirror Group Newspapers. 'I believe you, Bob,' I said. So, thanks to Vic

Horwood, did the Glasgow workforce. That night the *Daily Record* hit Sauchiehall Street in time for the late revellers as usual.

At this time in the Mirror's history the air was full of promises rather than threats. Reed International, having gone back on its declaration that no one person would have a controlling interest in the Mirror, issued a face-saving statement listing undertakings given by 'Pergamon'. It was obviously too embarrassed to say 'Maxwell', and I was interested that, as he had done on my advice in his bid for the *Observer*, Maxwell had linked Pergamon with us rather than BPCC. The pledges included maintaining the existing political stance and editorial independence, policies and practices of the newspapers within the Mirror Group; safeguarding and honouring the terms of employment including the pension rights of all MGN employees; and providing the opportunity for all Mirror Group employees to acquire shares in MGN 'as soon as possible'.

On Day One, after the lunch and board meeting, Maxwell held a press conference in the Mirror's Rotunda restaurant where his far from happy newly acquired acolytes were seated in a row, with him in the middle, to face the enormous interest of the media. He was in full flood before the TV cameras. He would start a new London evening newspaper by 15 September, as he had announced during the takeover. That, as we all knew, but he did not, was impossible. He would put one million on the sales of the *Daily Mirror* in two years and take it to its rightful place above the *Sun*. The two Sunday papers, he did not say which would administer the coup de grâce, would knock the *News of the World* off its perch as number one. It was heady stuff, no doubt bred of his buoyant self-confidence and aimed at staff morale, but either achievement in such a short time would have been miraculous. What would happen a couple of years from now? I wondered. Would Rupert Murdoch, his *Sun* and the *News of the World* have a ball, or just ignore us which was their policy and I felt should have been ours about them? Within less than a year nearly one million had drained away from the combined sales of Maxwell's three national newspapers, the fastest fall in their history. Fortunately there was no crowing from the enemy camp, though plenty inside it. Apart from the folly of acknowledging rivals, the one thing worse than bad publicity to an extrovert like Maxwell is no publicity. Murdoch just would not respond to the vitriol poured on him by the *Mirror*, and that was clever.

I doubt if in newspaper history there has been a phenomenon like the whirlwind months that followed Reed's cave-in to Maxwell. Out of it all emerged the astonishing industrial relations achievement, due partly to an incredible piece of luck, of reducing the total number of employees by a third without a stoppage. But the dynamism that deserves full credit for that also led to the catastrophic drop in circulations and revenue. If he had not been there the fall simply would not have happened to anything like the same degree. Maxwell's problem is that he has to run everything in areas that interest him, his self-confidence is total, and his lack of subtlety in projecting himself for what he believes to be the best interests of his newspapers is awesome. Like some previous newspaper barons he seems to believe that he and his newspapers are one, and held in equal affection by the readers.

It would be embarrassing for anyone but ebullient Maxwell to compare the number of column inches devoted to him in the Mirror newspapers, including the *Scottish Daily Record* and *Sunday Mail*, with the modest space allotted to Conrad Black when he took over the *Daily* and *Sunday Telegraph*, Murdoch when he acquired the *News of the World* and later the *Sun* and David Stevens when he became boss of Express Newspapers. There was no sales advantage in ramming home to *Mirror* readers, many of them Labour supporters and hostile to the cruder aspects of capitalism, that their newspaper was now to all intents and purposes owned by one man and subject to his giant ego and caprices. It was, in fact, a grave disadvantage. The paper is the thing not the owner, and instead of using his newspapers to put himself across as some kind of Wizard of Oz determined to distribute his bounteous gifts to all mankind, to the intense annoyance of some readers, it would have been commercially the right decision to have played his takeover concerto in a minor key and let the public judge his papers and not him.

I was led rapidly to the conclusion, as his name spread throughout the paper, from page one to Oxford United on the back, with no Mirror promotion, no international disaster, no coal strike, TUC. or Labour conference complete without his earnest and personal intervention, that the only fool this clever and in many ways meritorious man suffers gladly is himself. Would the editors, applying their normal standards of news judgment, have devoted so much space to him? The answer, of course, is no. It is in the city columns of the quality newspapers that he deserves and gets extensive coverage for his now acknowledged entrepreneurial and managerial skills. A period of becoming modesty from him in his own papers would have been the best policy. Instead, for the first few months of his ownership, he was almost a national joke. That could not be good for his newspapers and in particular the *Daily Mirror*, which because of its enormous influence, key role in elections, and outstanding record of campaigning journalism, was possibly the most important popular tabloid in the world. 'Don't spoil my fun,' he said to me almost pleadingly once when I earnestly tried to stop some wheeze or other. He was having a terrific time with the toy he had wanted for years. I think he was shockingly spoiled as a small boy in his humble home in the Carpathian foothills. Judging by early pictures of him, and by his own children, he must have been a beautiful baby.

I learned early on that Maxwell would prove a difficult man to influence. He told the editors at his first lunch with them that he wanted the slogan FORWARD WITH BRITAIN under each title. This was amended to FORWARD WITH SCOTLAND for the Scottish papers. Later, when he came down to see what my office looked like, I said I thought it was a mistake to put the slogan under the titles of both the *Sunday Mirror* and *Sunday People*. Readers regarded these as competitors. They often had both and many did not even know the papers were under the same ownership. 'Keep the slogan for the two Mirrors only,' I advised, confident that I would win. 'The *People* should be kept as independent as possible. Besides, having the same slogan for all your papers makes you seem a bit mad like William Randolph Hearst.' 'What shall I do?' he said. 'Very simple,' I replied. 'Just tell the editor of the *People* you have changed your mind.' The slogan and flag-waving, curiously a little redolent of the National Front, remained on all titles. Perhaps the thought of comparison with Randolph Hearst, the notorious American newspaper owner, pleased Maxwell. 'Bob thinks we are gangsters,' he said to Hugh Cudlipp one day. 'He's white Bob and I'm black Bob.'

One good piece of advice Maxwell did take. 'I want to launch some campaigns,' he said, 'How am I going to get them off the ground?' 'Mike Molloy can do whatever you want on the *Mirror*,' I said, 'but the one person you must have if you are to run good campaigns is a brilliant leader-writer. Joe Haines is possibly the best in the country' (since for years some people thought I was, I did not wish to concede entirely). 'He loathes you, told the chapel you were a crook and said that if you walked through the front door he would go out of the back. But he's the one.' 'Invite him to the Tuesday editors' lunch,' said Maxwell. 'Certainly,' I replied. 'But you will have to invite Terry Lancaster. He's Joe's boss, brought him into the company, and he's the political chief.' 'No, I don't want Terry,' said Maxwell. 'I want to please Joe. Terry's an old friend of mine. Have a word with him and do what you can.'

On Monday, after talking to Molloy, Maxwell did more than

invite Joe to the regular Tuesday lunches. He appointed him an assistant editor of the *Daily Mirror*. At the Tuesday lunch Joe made the good joke to Maxwell that instead of a cheap day return he was now buying a weekly season. 'You are on probation,' he said with his icy smile, which would have astonished Maxwell's managers in his other companies, who regard such bravado as the equivalent of diving into a water tub from the top of the Empire State Building. Terence Lancaster was far from pleased that he had been snubbed to please Haines. Thus began Maxwell's closest relationship with anyone on the *Mirror*. Joe is frequently to be seen whispering advice into Maxwell's ear, as he did into Harold Wilson's when he was press secretary at No. 10. He drafted some of Maxwell's missives to the unions and employees during the battle to reduce staff by one third. He was put on the board of the Scottish newspapers for similar services, and coined some of the better phrases used by Maxwell in white-heat situations. Each day he discusses his editorial with Maxwell as he did in the previous regimes with Tony Miles. Many of the ideas are Maxwell's but each of them has the authentic stamp of the *Mirror*. The faith has been kept. It is fortunate for both Labour and Maxwell that Haines did not, after all, walk out of the back door. It is also fortunate for the *Daily Mirror*. Without him the strong, consistent, editorial policy and powerful advocacy that had been handed down from the Cudlipp era would have been lost. A few score thousand intelligent readers who would not otherwise buy the *Mirror*, especially after Keith Waterhouse had gone, would have joined the others who left following Maxwell's colossal emphasis on himself.

19
PLAYING
THE GAME

At his first press conference as the new owner, Maxwell repeated the pledge he had given to Reed's that the editors in the group would be allowed to produce their papers 'without interference with their editorial judgment and freedom.' Whatever else that might mean, it certainly did not mean to him that the editorial side of his newspapers was forbidden territory. Whoever in his right mind would have thought otherwise? Within a few days, aided by Joe Haines and Terry Lancaster and with the willing compliance of the editor Mike Molloy, he launched in Cudlipp style an instant campaign to rid Labour of the Trotskyites and Militant Tendency. The first article appeared on page one under the headline FIGHT FOR THE LABOUR PARTY. On day two Lancaster was able to report KINNOCK FIGHTS TO WIN! And day three, when the Labour National Executive was to discuss the revolutionary idea that individual party members should be able to choose their Parliamentary candidates by ballot, became DAY OF DESTINY complete with separate pictures of every member of the NEC. As all good newspaper campaigns should, this one ended with Labour's enemies routed and the triumphant headline on day four KINNOCK VICTORY. Thus Maxwell emerged in his favourite role of saviour. I doubt whether most editors, exercising their own judgment and freedom, would have devoted so much space to the subject. Unfortunately the NEC vote in favour of the new concept of party democracy was later reversed by the wayward Labour conference.

Four days after his triumph, Maxwell launched his second campaign, this time to end the miners' strike. To the intense annoyance of Geoffrey Goodman, who had just received a Journalist of the Year award, and Terence Lancaster, he ordered the amalgamation of two articles they had written. They asked for their names to be removed. Thus the pseudonym Charles Wilberforce was revived, which the media instantly identified as the new proprietor. He (or Joe Haines, who largely ghosted the Wilberforce articles) described

231

Ian MacGregor and Arthur Scargill as 'the pig-headed identical twins'. Wilberforce, alias Maxwell, called on Len Murray and the TUC to get the miners back to work by assuring them that if they did settle they would be 'able to hold their heads high'. Then Maxwell the saviour had the idea of a miners' children's gala, a series of day-trips to the seaside for striking miners' families. Readers were asked to send their donations to him and thereafter his name appeared in the Mirror papers in several successive issues with much ballyhoo for the fund. Somehow this crusade lost steam. Only one day-trip, to Blackpool, was organised and the rest of the cash sent to the Miners' Solidarity Fund based in Sheffield with the stipulation that it was to be spent on children's holidays. This, when announced, was described as 'the way Mirror readers intended it. Once again, thanks a lot, folks.' A bit casual, I thought.

The decision to hand the money to the strike fund followed an off-the-record meeting between Scargill and his henchmen and Maxwell and his acolytes at a Sheffield hotel. We had sandwiches and coffee and talked for hours. Maxwell and Scargill were at their best, or on their best behaviour, but nothing we heard altered our view that the strike was totally flawed because there had been no ballot. More memorable for me than this civilised meeting between a press baron and an extremist trade union leader was the journey back to London in Maxwell's small, hired helicopter. It was waiting for us in a large recreation field on top of a hill overlooking the whole of Sheffield. A few people were taking an afternoon stroll. Maxwell and I both had the same problem, which I thought was insoluble. 'Is there a toilet somewhere?' he asked our driver, who pointed to a distant building. We were late as it was. Maxwell turned his back to us, faced the City of Sheffield, and reminded me instantly of Beaverbrook 'making water' in the middle of his lawn. It also reminded me of the last paragraph of an interview Logan ('Jack') Gourlay had with Billy Cotton at my suggestion. Billy told Gourlay that when he flew his own aeroplane before the war he had the habit of spitting over the side and saying to the populace below, 'Now share that among the lot of you.' I was fastidious in those days and cut out the paragraph.

The helicopter was brightly coloured, smart. Maxwell sat in the front passenger seat and Joe Haines and I in the back. It was hot. Maxwell cooled himself by putting his arm out of the window as if he was in a sports car so that the wind blew up his shirt sleeve. The noise this created was considerable. I hoped the pilot did not mind. We drank champagne and ate smoked salmon. As we approached the landing barge near Tower Bridge Maxwell exclaimed, 'Let's have a look at the Mirror building.' Banking steeply, we circled the vast newspaper monument to Cecil King employing 6000 (soon to be 4000) people, in which until scarcely a month earlier Maxwell had not owned a single share. We were light years from the struggling, lamentably misled miners. Maxwell was totally happy. Appropriately the Rolls-Royce awaited us. 'Office?' said the SOGAT '82 driver, and thereafter did not receive a single instruction.

Maxwell seldom discusses his ideas with anyone. He just does them. If he decides that someone has libelled him, he does not in my experience say to his lawyers, 'What do you advise?' He simply tells them to sue. If he wants to start a London evening newspaper, this time in earnest, he does not say to his editors, 'What do you think?' Or to the advertising director, 'Can you get sufficient revenue?' Or to the advertising and readership research experts, 'What market should we aim at, above the former *Evening News*, or below?' Or to his chief executive, 'Taking all things into consideration, including costs of production and the interest on borrowed money, will it pay?' He does not say it to his chief executive because he is the chief executive. He does everything, from my observation, by the seat of his large, well-cut pants. He seems to commune with no one except himself. His decisions are handed down unheralded to his careworn but stoical staff as if on Tablets of Stone, written in fire by Himself, and one can only marvel that anyone can be so totally self-sufficient. The person who marvels most of all at this phenomenon is Robert Maxwell himself. But, of course, it can lead to frightful mistakes, dwarfed as they are by his genius and colossal wealth.

He came down from the mountain and announced that his papers were to compete with the Express Group and have a £1 million prize game. This is the ultimate in newspaper madness. While initially, at vast promotional cost, it put half a million on *Daily Express* sales, this rapidly drained away to the previous total when sense prevailed over desire and the public realised the chance of winning was too ludicrously small. The vital question for the Mirror Group was not whether Maxwell could afford at least a £1 million prize and the horrendous cost of TV commercials and delivering a card to (allegedly) every household, on top of the parallel cost just spent on the newspapers' bingo card. It was, what sort of £1 million game would have the greatest appeal? The editors, top management and publicity chiefs were summoned to a Sunday morning conference on Maxwell's home ground in Oxford, the HQ of Pergamon Press at Headington Hall. Two rival advertising agencies were asked to present their ideas of the best games for *Mirror* readers. With something approaching a sinking feeling, I realised that Young and Rubicam were the certain winners when their managing director, soon to become chairman, John Banks, confidently smoking an enormous cigar and with no trace of shame on his sunny face, offered his company's suggestion that the game should be called Who Dares Wins and promoted personally on TV and in the Mirror newspapers by the man who in the minds of millions most typified that spirit, by a happy coincidence none other than Robert Maxwell himself.

We are sunk, I thought, we are sunk. Maxwell advanced like a cat on this vast bowl of rich cream. 'We are quite sincere about this,' said Banks. I looked at his face. There was no doubt he was sincere. He was convinced. So was Bob. Anyone who knew him would appreciate that he could not possibly resist such a challenge now that it had been propounded by one of the world's leading advertising agencies, who later invented the dreadful Sid to sell British Gas shares. I argued that what our readers wanted was bingo, and all we had to do was match the £30,000 weekly prize given by the *Sun*. Nobody listened. There was no point. Afterwards, when the defeated, or also-ran, advertising agency had left to very polite thanks from Maxwell, I said to him of the victor's triumphant presentation, 'It's an awful lot of money, Bob. Bingo would cost far less.' I wish I had also said, 'You will look like the man who sells turkeys in Norfolk' but, as with Beaverbrook, I treated Maxwell as if he needed to be protected from undue hurt.

I did not say either, as I should have done, that he would be selling the *Mirror* as John Bloom sold washing-machines. That would have been too wounding. The garage owner who puts his picture on half-page advertisements for second-hand cars, complete with his personal signature and the slogan 'The man you can trust,' always succeeds in looking the opposite. The turkey promoter does somehow overcome this hurdle, but was this the image the so recently created newspaper tycoon wanted? 'We have not had much time,' said the incomparable Banks, 'but we have done a couple of dummy runs.' Someone standing in for Maxwell appeared on the video. I could almost hear Maxwell's heart beating faster.

Afterwards several of us had lunch with him and most of his family at a long trestle table on the lawn. A couple of trade union leaders and their wives joined us. The Maxwells' splended Weimaraner, who earns his keep as a guard dog, bounded round the lawn. It was a pleasant day, and I noticed approvingly that my colleagues were quite taking to their new boss. But the idea of him saying, with his slight foreign accent when under stress – not as pronounced as Henry

Kissinger's but unmistakable – 'I promise that one of you will win a million pounds,' did not bear contemplation by a sensitive soul like me aware of the awful prejudices of the Great British Public. They would get the message all right, but they would not like the man who brought it to them. At worst they would regard his personal appearance as an act of vanity, wounding to his newspapers. At best he would be a figure of fun.

Like Mrs Margaret Thatcher, and indeed Neil Kinnock, Maxwell badly needed a Jeeves-like, Gordon Reece figure to advise him on his image. I was hopeless at it. He would not listen. And Sir Tom McCaffery, his director of public affairs, who said no to him as frequently as John Junor to Beaverbrook, fared little better and eventually left because he did not approve of Maxwell's style. His worst excess in my fifteen months with him was his exuberant belief that ceaseless, flamboyant self-projection and the interest of his newspapers coincided. After his unnecessary triumph against *Private Eye*, a sketch writer in *The Times* described Maxwell as having come across in the libel action as the school braggart and Richard Ingrams as the school sneak. Maxwell also has the reputation of being the school bully. Boastful he certainly is. When I was photographed being thanked by Princess Anne for raising what was then a record newspaper sum for the Save the Children Fund, I put neither the picture nor a report in the pre-Maxwell *Sunday Mirror*. That was going too far the other way. By contrast praise for Maxwell in the Mirror papers he owns has been far from sparse (a weakness shared by Beaverbrook, who at least showed more subtlety). I have seen him speak so harshly and threateningly to some of his top managers that if it had been me I would have walked out or written one of my resignation letters; but in my experience he was invariably patient and courteous with his editors, however many times he telephoned them in an evening.

Another side of Maxwell's character that he has succeeded in hiding totally from public view enables him to be an exceptionally able chairman of committees, the best in my personal experience. I served at his suggestion on the NSPCC centenary year media committee which he chaired. This was in 1984 before he took over the Mirror. I was much impressed. The Mirror Pensions Board consists of half management, half trade union nominees. Maxwell, as chairman, has the casting vote. The balance is therefore tipped, as it always was, in favour of the management, but his conduct of the meetings was impeccable in my experience as a board member. When he does not hold all the aces, he will listen, persuade and respond.

On the heady first day of Maxwell's ownership of the Group he repeated the undertaking he gave to Reed's to cloak their sell-out in a little more respectability: 'Under my management editors will be free to produce their newspapers without interference with their journalistic skills and judgments.' Editors who are sometimes summoned a dozen or more times a day must wonder what interference is, if it is not that. Yet they would also agree that he treats them well, and he obviously enjoys the company of journalists. He likes repeating phrases. 'The editors are on top, the management is on tap,' he has said over and over again. There is no reluctance to open the wine cupboard. His editors have better cars than ever before and are better paid. It was Clive Thornton, however, who gave me my biggest rise after some prompting by Tony Miles on behalf of the editors.

Maxwell's obsession in his first few weeks became the win a million game. Young and Rubicam, in conjunction with a firm that specialises in newspaper bingo and variations up or down market produced a contest so complicated that some of us (perhaps also because our heart was not in it) found it difficult to understand. It claimed to give every reader many chances every week to win £1 million. Each card, supposedly (but not as it turned out) delivered to every household had a different number. This was the simplest way of winning in the several variations of the game, and as it turned out the only one. All the potential millionaire had to do was buy or borrow copies of Mirror Group papers, or look at them in the public library, and if the same number against stupendous odds appeared in one of them, he or she was in need of urgent investment advice on how to handle a million. Some enterprising evening papers in various parts of Britain provided the service of publishing all winning bingo and other numbers. This enabled a sizeable number of people to collect every card dropped through their letter boxes, check each day whether they had won anything, but not actually buy any of the newspapers concerned, thus defeating the object of the huge expenditure. The national newspapers thought this a despicable practice.

A weekly accumulator offered the same glorious £1 million prize if crossing off the numbers led anyone to a frenzied full house on the last day, and if this was not sufficient to induce readers to switch to Mr Maxwell's papers another section of the game offered them a £50,000 prize plus a jolly chance to win the magic sum. That chance was at a ceremony presided over by Mr Maxwell complete with trumpeters from the Royal Marines. After a suitable blast on their instruments, a curtain would open revealing row upon row of boxes each with a different number, up to 51 in all. Inside all but one was a cheque signed by Mr Maxwell for the guaranteed £50,000. The exception had one for £1,050,000. A solicitor of unchallenged probity, on at least the first occasion, witnessed the placing of this cheque.

There were many such ceremonies, contributing generously to the coffers of the Royal Marines, but by whatever methods the contestants chose their numbers none had the good fortune to pick the box with the extra cash. Betting people tell me that 50–1 odds are very poor. I thought it must have been desperately disappointing to the readers, but they did not seem to mind. 'Congratulations,' Maxwell the self-made star invariably boomed, 'you have won £50,000!' Champagne was served in large quantities. A larger number of journalists than those actually covering the event invariably came to watch, possibly for that reason. It is said that a cork only has to pop inside the Holborn Circus headquarters of Mirror Group Newspapers for a considerable population shift to occur.

Maxwell, who usually drinks with moderation, is not censorious about such matters. In previous administrations, it was not uncommon for journalists with alcohol problems to be rebuked by executives similarly afflicted. It is a part of Fleet Street folklore that one of the Mirror's most respected chiefs was asked to warn a popular editor over his increasing lack of coherence after lunch and in the evening. The warning was delivered at length on a train journey back from a Labour Party conference, and since the senior man did not wish to appear prudish he ordered drinks. When they arrived in London, both men were too drunk to proceed and booked a room at the station hotel until they recovered. Each has told me this story on several occasions when we were drinking together. Their accounts differ as to who was the most drunk.

The business of composing the words to appear on the 25 million Who Dares Wins cards was something of a nightmare. Maxwell took personal charge and lifted from somewhere or other the vulgar slogan (again to those of delicate disposition): 'Do you sincerely wish to be rich?' He altered the wording and layout so frequently I was surprised someone did not attempt to get their fingers around his ample throat. Eventually after the umpteenth change he discovered in Ernie Burrington, later at my suggestion to become editor of the *People*, a man of infinite patience and tact. Ernie steered this frenetic and ludicrously prolonged task to a successful conclusion. Maxwell's picture appeared on the card wheeling a trolley carrying a million pounds in notes loaned from Coutts' Bank. The *Daily Mirror* reported: 'Mr Maxwell's pretty daughter, Ghislaine, 22, was on hand to see the cash in all denominations wheeled out under the watchful eyes of police and bank security staff.' The report went on to quote the undeniably pretty Ghislaine, 22, speaking in terms reminiscent of a member of the Royal Family: 'It pleases me to know it will make one of our readers very happy soon.'

Maxwell himself wrote an article in the *Mirror* extolling the virtues of his pet game. 'Each week,' he announced, 'there will be SEVENTEEN chances for readers of the *Daily Mirror*, the *Sunday Mirror* and the *Sunday People* to win our Magic Million. Readers of the *Daily Record* and *Sunday Mail* in Scotland can join in too.' He made another of his reckless boasts and said the new competition was 'the first powerful blow' to get the *Daily Mirror* circulation above that of the *Sun*, and the *Sunday Mirror* and *Sunday People* ahead of the *News of the World*. He also warned Dundee-based D. C. Thomson that he wanted his Scottish Sunday newspaper the *Sunday Mail* to top the sales of their best-seller the *Sunday Post*. Thus the great Publisher rammed home to his readers that each of his newspapers had more successful rivals, a considerable incentive for those who had not to sample these clearly superlative sheets. Maxwell did not let the opportunity slip to mention *Sun* bingo, pointing out that its weekly £30,000 prize 'is a fraction of the *Mirror*'s guaranteed million. Does that make you angry? It makes me angry too. There's a simple solution, I say: throw the *Sun* bingo card in the dustbin!'

As with its page three girl, the *Sun* is the brand leader in newspaper bingo. I doubt if there was a single person working so earnestly with Maxwell at that time who did not believe that matching the *Sun*'s bingo prize would have been a far greater and cheaper sales attraction than playing the *Express* game in the foothills of the lower middle classes. If the composition of the cards was a gargantuan task with Maxwell in charge, the job of explaining the game in his newspapers was still more taxing. Eventually it took a whole page in each issue, seven times the space required for *Sun* bingo. And we had to promote our own bingo, in which we regretfully believed, elsewhere in each paper. This reduced editorial space, and advertisements, by the equivalent of over two pages. In addition huge areas of page one were occupied day after day promoting the game. The dreaded *Sun* thus had an enormous advantage in selling the principal commodity of a newspaper.

There were pictures of Maxwell, the game's presenter, all over the place, and chunks of news pages throughout the papers were taken by famous people endorsing the game as the most brilliant imaginable, which they would certainly play themselves. Maxwell has a disturbing lack of confidence in the abilities of others. He took personal charge of the TV commercials in which he promised with great gravity that he would make at least one of the viewers a millionaire. Maxwell in the role of a Chaplin directing his own movie did not offend the philosophical young man appointed to the task by Young and Rubicam. He was well paid and content to let the world judge his creative skills, unaided by Maxwell, as director of the TV series 'Minder'.

Although many journalists fervently wish there were, there appear to be few laws governing newspaper games. The important one is that readers do not have to buy the paper. They can read it in the public library or telephone Sid, who does buy it. They can check the numbers in those caddish evening newspapers or, in the case of the *Sun* and *News of the World* when they were in Bouverie Street, find them displayed in the front office window as a further precaution to keep within the law. After that almost anything goes. The *Daily Mail* played its own version of a millionaire game for a while and had the good fortune not to come up with a single winner of the top prize. By an infinitesimal easing of the odds on the computer, the 'three ways to win a million' in the Mirror papers could actually have produced three millionaires or more in a week, to the consternation of the bankers who loaned Maxwell £60 million towards his bargain-price purchase of the Mirror Group. A computer adjustment the other way could limit winners to runner-up prizes as low as £1000.

There were plenty of winners in the last category, strewn through the paper ecstatically expressing their gratitude, in the early days of the win £1 million game. Maxwell's determination to hand a million pounds to a reader had one unexpected benefit. It unnerved the *Sun* management sufficiently for them to do the same. They multiplied the paper's bingo prize by more than thirty-three to match Maxwell's offer and, because they desperately wanted to announce their winner first, speeded up the game so that it was over in four days instead of the usual six. They had the good fortune to find someone who had not only kept the one card with the winning set of numbers on it when it dropped through the letter box, but read the *Sun* and meticulously checked the bingo results. 'Congratulations, David!' crowed the *Mirror* to the *Sun* winner. 'We're honestly happy for you. And we're even happier because without us you would never have become a millionaire.'

These tongue-in-cheek felicitations ('we're honestly happy for you') did not stop the *Mirror* joyously spreading the dirt, also on page one, that David had not told his wife, and was living with a girl-friend. Thus he obtained fame, fortune and notoriety in an instant. The *Sun*'s decision to rival Maxwell was reportedly taken by Bruce Matthews, News International's managing director when, for the first time, Rupert Murdoch had gone on a family mountain holiday in the United States in total purdah. This proved to Fleet Street that Matthews was the bravest of all newspaper managers, as well as the best. He decided to allow *Sun* readers one more million-aire, who emerged from one of the £30,000 bingo winners six months later in a knockout contest equivalent to drawing straws. Thus the paper repeatedly accused by Maxwell of meanness ended up by creating two millionaires, whereas the readers of the Mirror Group papers for all the ferocious publicity and endless commercials had to be content with a mere one.

When the *Sun* produced its first £1 million winner, Maxwell was anxious to follow suit rapidly. Day after day a winning number was published coinciding with one on a single card that had been sent out, but no one claimed. I was with Maxwell one Saturday morning when at last Jenkinson's number two Terry Sanders phoned him from publicity. 'You've got one!' Maxwell repeated, triumphant. Thus Maudie and her daughter's dog Thumper became the splash news. 'The Mirror Publisher broke the news to her personally,' the paper reported dutifully next day.

Maudie was just right for the *Mirror*. She was poor, hardworking and honest. She had a large family, only one of whom, as the paper felt obliged to reveal in case the *Sun* found out, had been in a spot of bother. In the usual way of newspapers, she was driven in a Daimler from one hotel to another to keep her away from the rivals, and must have been quite relieved when she was taken to Marje Proops's home for a quiet cup of tea and a highly professional interview. Eventually she, all the family and Thumper found themselves in suites close to Maxwell's at the Imperial Hotel, Blackpool. It was the week of the first Labour conference since he took over. Presided over by Maxwell, Maudie, her family and the dog were taken in a bedecked open tram to the town hall, where the Mayor and the Publisher handed her the cheque. Maxwell had eight mentions and two pictures the next day. Maudie did even better.

It took many more months before Maxwell could be persuaded to drop his pet game, but such were the odds and his good fortune there were no further claimants of a million pounds despite the constantly reiterated three ways of winning, or seventeen chances a week (as he had put it) in his combined national newspapers.

Another hard game to play, which Maxwell inherited, was the Snowball Bonanza. This went to the bingo prize winner who had some additional correct numbers on his or her card. If not, the snowball simply grew bigger. Eventually it became so large that the *Sun*'s weekly prize, which had been increased to £40,000, looked quite puny. Nobody won it, however, after many months and the *Mirror*'s bingo winners had to put up with the basic £10,000. It would have been won if the computer had been so instructed to ensure there were sufficient odds. The snowball was eventually melted down and added to prize money in another contest.

There is no doubt that what readers of popular newspapers like is so-called bingo with a guaranteed prize each week, the amount shared if there is more than one winner. I tried so hard to make the win £1 million game succeed in the *Sunday Mirror* we actually increased sales for a period by 250,000, about the same as we did with each new bingo card. 'Don't you think we've got too many pictures of Maxwell in the paper?' I said dubiously to my deputy Vic Birkin. 'We ran just as many of Max Bygraves when he did our bingo commercial,' was his unconvincing reply. The *Daily Mirror* shamelessly reported the reaction of one housewife who had won £50,000 but not, alas, £1 million. 'She turned to Mr Maxwell, gave him a kiss and said, "You are a wonderful man." ' Within a brief period the sales benefits of this costly exercise had vanished, and the plunge began.

Things happened at breakneck speed in Maxwell's first frantic months. The *Daily Mirror*'s price was reduced from 17p to 16p, thus removing a long-standing grievance of the *Mirror* staff that their paper cost a penny more than the *Sun* and the *Star*. The rivals then increased their prices to 17p and the *Mirror* crowed that the 'cheap imitations' now cost more than the original, only to put up its price again shortly afterwards. The Ethiopian famine again resulted in Maxwell's name appearing day after day throughout the paper. His appeal for money and mercy trip to Addis Ababa was the page one 'lead' on four days. The picture and story of him leaving London Airport on Speedbird 9041 loaned by British Airways was given more prominence on the front page than the murder of Mrs Ghandi. 'When we saw how quickly and effectively the *Mirror*'s publisher, Robert Maxwell, worked in saving lives, we realised he could use the foundation's resources the best,' a charity was dutifully reported as saying. While these laudatory words about Maxwell were appearing in the paper he owned, a new cartoon strip began in the *Mirror* starring Flook and for several days Robert Maxwell. Then came the news story, born of late night discussions in the office: 'The *Daily Mirror* is sending a squadron of light aircraft to Ethiopia to ferry doctors and supplies to remote famine-hit regions.' The mind boggled again at the thought of scores of Amy Johnsons and weekend pilots crossing the Sahara, led not on this occasion by Maxwell but the popular Fleet Street gossip columnist, Peter Tory, in his Chipmunk. Nothing came of it, and Maxwell fresh from his stay at the Addis Ababa Hilton and raising a huge sum for Ethiopia was soon preparing for further travels. The whole of page one on the first Saturday in January was devoted to an announcement that the *Mirror* was hiring a British Railway train to meet the people. 'Publisher Robert Maxwell will lead the crusade,' it said predictably, 'supported by a host of Mirror writers.'

Maxwell, who is given to making pledges, promised that 'all practical ideas' from the public would be acted on immediately. So far as I know, none were, because nothing worthwhile was suggested. The train, slow and often late, arrived to sparse attention at cities all over Britain. Huge halls were hired, but so few people turned up despite heavy advertising in local papers and enormous space in the Mirror papers that it became rapidly clear that there was no yearning to meet either the Mirror's new proprietor or even Mirror stars like Marje Proops and Claire Rayner (the incomparable Marje, I was warned by Mike Molloy, would probably quit if asked to appear on the same platform with her *Sunday Mirror* counterpart, which amused me because she is every bit as serene and gentle as she appears in the paper). I arranged that either Molloy or I would preside when Maxwell either tired of appearing at largely empty meetings, or was otherwise occupied, and I hugely enjoyed the three I took. The maximum number of people attending was about sixty in a hall that would have held many hundreds. They were very faithful *Mirror* readers and Labour stalwarts, with a sprinkling of Trotskyites and cranks. It was nostalgically reminiscent of my days as a Labour candidate with empty halls and earnest people. Afterwards, at the best hotel at whichever town we were visiting, I was invariably congratulated on being a much better chairman than Maxwell, who (I was told) hogged the meetings: his prerogative, of course.

There are always favoured journalists moaning in editors' offices, especially late in the evening when tongues are loosened. Mike Molloy had a stock answer when colleagues complained that Maxwell's dominance over the paper was damaging. 'It's not Bob who is interfering with the *Mirror*,' he said. 'It's me. He owns it.' The effect of his feverish dominance, apart from giving the unfortunate impression that he had bought the papers in order to get his name in them, was that altogether too much space was taken at the expense of traditional *Mirror* fare. The *Mirror* train occupied as many columns every day as a major air disaster. There were hopelessly dull profiles of the cities visited, complete with local fashion and pop reports, which were of no conceivable interest to the national readership and, judging by the small audiences, to the local readership either, who the following day were confronted by long reports of the meetings they had not attended.

Maxwell the saviour did his commendable best to bring both sides together in the mining dispute. Again a forest or two was hewn down to provide newsprint for the *Mirror*'s coverage for what would have rated no more than a few paragraphs if he had not been the owner. He may have thought his role as an intermediary reflected credit on the *Mirror*. In fact, it reflected credit on him but not on the *Mirror* because the paper had overdone the coverage. The space given to Maxwell's win £1 million game was ludicrous, and would never have been tolerated by press barons experienced in the newspaper craft. There was a half-page article attacking the *Daily Express*, with far fewer readers than the *Mirror*, and a whole page article attacking Rupert Murdoch and the *Sun*, with far more. Both were brilliantly done by Joe Haines, but Beaverbrook would have printed neither. The *Mirror*'s Ethiopian appeal would have been much better done in the name of the paper rather than in Maxwell's name ('I give my personal guarantee that nothing whatsoever from this magnificent sum will be spent on administration . . .') There were so many announcements of Maxwell-inspired activities on page one it looked like the front window of a down-market supermarket.

News became a side line. Normal news reactions on the third floor were constantly distorted by pressure from the ninth. Maxwell himself chose to ring the £50,000 winners of the win £1 million game ('the Mirror Publisher broke the news to her personally'), thus further annoying readers who thought the *Mirror* had become his personal publicity sheet. A 'Children's Mirror' was introduced in the Saturday paper, an idea that never fails to fail. There was a 'Welcome to YOUR paper' message signed by 'Robert Maxwell, Publisher,' and he moved so far into the editor's territory that a few days later the announcement appeared: 'Publisher Robert Maxwell is pleased to announce that Jimmy Reid, a regular columnist of the *Daily Record*, will be joining the *Daily Mirror* to write his own column.' That was not a notion that would have been likely to occur to anyone other than Jimmy Reid's old friend, and not many editors on their own initiative would have put his column about political and industrial affairs on page two in Saturday papers when the emphasis is necessarily on leisure, and that page is desperately needed for news. *Mirror* leader-writers traditionally work on Sunday for Monday's paper but never on Friday for Saturday.

Another contest suddenly appeared over half of one page ('Great news for all our family readers. WIN £100,000. It's the chance of a lifetime'). It was not the idea of a lifetime. Readers had to guess what Andy Capp was saying in a cartoon, which so overtaxed the sort of people who enter popular newspaper contests that it rapidly developed into a lucky dip. Almost the whole of page five was also devoted to this latest ill-planned bid for sales. About 200,000 entered compared with ten times as many checking their bingo numbers. The winner gave a dramatic account of how she was told. 'Then, when I realised it was Mr Maxwell on the phone, I nearly fell on the floor,' the *Mirror* reported her as saying. She was obviously not a regular reader.

Maxwell, showing his age, persuaded Molloy to run special issues every day commemorating the end of the war in Europe forty years earlier. For a whole week the front page was devoted to Elsie's War, Eric's War, Ivan's War, and so on. This was the equivalent of taking a large part of the *Mirror* for six consecutive issues in 1958 to commemorate the end of the First World War. On the Monday after the Bradford football stadium disaster every other popular paper led the front page with tragic and inspiring human stories of this cataclysmic news event. Maxwell the saviour's paper led with his personal launching of an appeal fund. One cannot fault that, of course, except as a journalist. Editors usually put the obvious idea of an appeal for victims on page one, column one, and do not invoke the proprietor's name, since that reminds readers that he could well afford to contribute a million or two himself. Somehow or other Neil Kinnock was persuaded into thanking the *Mirror* for rushing a life-saving machine to Bradford hospital. There was, of course, a picture of Maxwell with the hospital surgeon. 'SAVER,' the caption read. 'Mr Maxwell is thanked by Dr Sharper.'

Not long afterwards there was an enormous picture of Maxwell on page one with Prince Charles and Prince William. It was a charming photo put there by Mike Molloy, the editor, showing Prince William gazing up at the vast newspaper proprietor, but it would not have been used anywhere in the paper if Maxwell did not own it. The *Mirror* announced that he was to chair an appeal to raise money for the Red Devils, of which the Prince is colonel-in-chief. A small picture of them performing in front of the Princes and Maxwell appeared on an inside page.

It was at about this time that Maxwell made another of his many resorts to the law. (Asked on a radio or TV programme what he might have become if the Nazis had not driven him into the underground and out of his country, he replied with great effect and awesome gravity, 'A rabbi, probably.' I think he rivals Sergeant Bilko for forensic agility and would have been an often brilliant lawyer of highly erratic performance.) This particular excursion to the Law Courts, greatly benefiting the best legal brains acting for both sides, was because the *Sun* had announced, though not in these terms, that it was running what is called in the trade 'a spoiler' to reduce the impact of a *Mirror* series. The *Mirror*'s great exclusive was the oft-told tale, but this time by someone directly involved, about the world of Playboy from the nasty inside. A letter was sent to all newspaper editors, including Kelvin MacKenzie of the *Sun*, warning of the direst copyright penalties if they lifted any of the story. This inspired MacKenzie to do the traditional spoiler he had not previously intended, and thus the *Sun* announced on page one that it was to run (at last) the authentic, world exclusive, full story (as we say in the trade) about the bunny girl, murdered by her husband, who was the central character in the *Mirror* series. At the same time, as is also part of the ritual, the *Sun* warned its readers to beware of cheap imitations in other papers. A couple of reporters were given the thankless job of cobbling together the best they could from old newspaper clippings, and their meagre offering was supplemented by some material the *Mail on Sunday* had already published that the *Sun* bought for £750.

Spoilers are invariably inferior to the originals, but they can be presented with such skill and bare-faced deception that they look better. Unused to the wicked ways of Fleet Street in this sort of area, Maxwell rounded up his lawyers and called on the duty judge, Mr Justice Hirst, by all accounts a pleasant and hospitable man, late in the night at his home. The judge, as he naturally would, granted an injunction to prevent the *Sun* breaching the copyright laws by lifting material from the long published book the *Mirror* was serialising. The equivalent of this in criminal law would be for a judge to grant a householder an injunction against a burglar to prevent him breaking into his home. There can be fearful penalties for disregarding a judge's orders, and the *Sun*'s lawyers grimly ploughed through every word in the book the *Mirror* was to serialise to make sure none of it had got into the *Sun*'s version. Unfortunately, they did find nineteen words that had appeared in the *Mail on Sunday* material. Mac-Kenzie was told, and made the same decision as would any other editor to let them run in one early edition rather than endanger his paper's distribution, on the not unreasonable grounds that no one would notice such a trifling transgression; it would be an obvious mistake and who would care anyway about a mere nineteen words of little consequence.

He had not reckoned on Maxwell's motivation for vengeance. If not a rabbi, he would have been a memorable war lord. One of his equally dutiful and well-paid lawyers spotted the offending nineteen words, and I was astounded to hear he insisted on going ahead with contempt proceedings against the *Sun*, its editor, and its managing director, Bruce Matthews, whom he liked as much as I did. I also felt that since the law of the land allowed brief references from a copyright book on matters of public interest, surely a judge's injunction could not overrule that law? After a hearing lasting several days, Mr Justice Hirst took exactly that view. 'Such words as theft and kleptomania were used,' he said of a violent *Mirror* editorial attacking the *Sun*. 'The very virulence of this attack, when considered in the light of the evidence in this case as a whole, leads me to think that the proverbial caution to people who live in glass houses is not entirely inappropriate.' He dismissed the case against the *Sun* and ordered Maxwell to pay its costs. Outside the court Maxwell said with the pomposity with which he frequently fails to grace himself, 'I came to Fleet Street to eliminate the kind of artificial and undignified rivalry mentioned by the judge. In my opinion, the judgment today could no doubt be interpreted by the *Sun* as meaning it is lawful for the *Sun* to spoil, steal, cheat – and lie to its readers – in the interests of waging its war against the *Mirror*.'

No editor worth a light would have advised Maxwell to waste his company's resources over such a puny infringement, which transpired to be not even that. He did not ask my opinion. He seldom asks anyone's opinion. He employed Lord Cudlipp as a consultant during his first two years and he had some influence, particularly over the appointment of editors, but known or unknown to Maxwell, Cudlipp consulted me as well as using his own judgment. In a brilliant note to Maxwell, Cudlipp tried to staunch the flow of mentions of Maxwell's name in the Mirror papers. He said that every man, woman or child in the land who was not an imbecile must by now be aware that he was the Mirror's proprietor. Maxwell circulated a summary of the note. There was a brief respite before his papers were again as full of him as he is of himself. Hot on his court débâcle, he launched a fund for victims of the Brussels football stadium riot, followed in fairly quick succession by MAXWELL MAKES PRINTING HISTORY (he placed a record order for German colour printing presses: the headline could have been MIRROR MAKES PRINT-ING HISTORY); MAXWELL SAVES SINCLAIR ('I have a great page one splash story for you,' he told the deputy editor of the *Mirror*, who took the hint, though it turned out later that Maxwell was unable to save Sinclair); A LETTER FROM MRS THATCHER TO ROBERT MAXWELL (about football violence); I'LL SUE, SAYS MAXWELL (I forget whom); and so on, as no other newspaper proprietor has done in my know-ledge of Fleet Street.

20
FAREWELL

I remained editor of the *Sunday Mirror* for only five months after Maxwell took over. I did not fancy having to submit to his views on policy and the constant involvement with him this would entail after thirteen years of freedom. He had as rapidly forgotten his promise not to interfere in the editorial side of his papers as he did the pledge to offer Mirror employees shares in the company 'as soon as possible'. Perhaps, like me, he regarded these promises as mere face-savers for Reed International when they bowed to institutional pressure and sold out. He had already, in addition to my editing the *Sunday Mirror*, appointed me to the curious title of senior group editor a few weeks after his coup, when I reminded him of his unasked for pledge to make me editorial chief. He did this a little reluctantly I thought, because he likes to be the sole boss. We were having coffee on a Saturday morning in December when he said, 'You can be editor of the *Sunday Mirror* for as long as you like, but when do you want to give it up?' 'January the first,' I replied shrewdly. I continued, 'May I suggest you make me deputy chairman so that no one will suspect you have pushed me out? You don't need to give me any more money because of the rise you gave me as senior group editor.' He agreed to the title immediately and increased my salary by £5000. All very fair, I thought, and I was greatly relieved that under him I no longer had the best executive job in journalism, that of an editor.

Years earlier I had decided to retire, as Hugh Cudlipp did more sensationally, at sixty which was the following October. Les Carpenter, then chief executive of Reed International, had made this possible by reducing my pensionable age from the curious one of 62½ years that applied to Mirror Group directors. It was not that I was tired of editing. That never palled with me, but the idea of someone over sixty editing the *Sunday Mirror* struck me as both ludicrous and greedy. Happily for my pride, but not for my unquestionably able successor, Peter Thompson, the circulation plunged after I left. This may have proved something about my editorship, or about Maxwell's grip on the newspapers, since both the *People* and the *Daily Mirror* also lost many readers. There had been a slight decline in sales before I left the *Sunday Mirror*, which I attributed largely to Maxwell's mishandling of promotions, too much space devoted to them, and too much time devoted to endless meetings with Maxwell instead of editing the paper.

I quite enjoyed doing for ten months what I always thought was the prerogative of editorial directors and such-like, which was very little. On Saturdays I would visit Peter Thompson, who spent at least ten hours every working day in his office, and out of the politeness invariably shown to editorial directors who did not make a nuisance of themselves he would open a bottle of wine for me. Then I would go across what was inevitably known as the bridge of sighs for a similar visit to Richard Stott, then editor of the *People*. His particular concoction for me was Irish whiskey and ginger ale. I would look at their layouts, read their leaders, and occasionally make suitable cautionary noises about contempt of court or libel. They treated me with the respect due to someone who had edited both their papers for much longer than most editorial directors. We would all meet later for lunch in the executive dining club with the top brass on the papers. Maxwell, in a typically generous gesture to journalists, had laid on a free lunch every Saturday including wine after I had told him that the club was kept closed on Saturdays by the previous management because none of them came in on that day. His personal staff came to look after us. I did not think so much of Maxwell's generosity to me, his foul-weather friend. When I pointed out that the car the company was allowing me to keep on my retirement was four years old and due for replacement, he declined to do so. This was after he had won a superb vintage Bentley convertible, worth far more, in a raffle. He did eventually make the ex-gratia payment traditionally awarded to retiring Mirror Group directors. However, I do not view him with a jaundiced eye. His personal menu card was different from everyone else's in his private dining-room. It had a calorie count against each course, and his guests had to eat the same bland food in the fight against his flab. Yet I had seen him eat mountains of cottage cheese before going out to dinner. He is a character, and at least that is in the best and worst traditions of Fleet Street.

At this time in 1985 there was little more than a rustle in the wind to indicate the hurricane that was to engulf the national newspapers.

Today was due shortly, but by some sound instinct Fleet Street sensed that it and Eddie Shah would be a flop and colour pictures a disappointment. Maxwell called in all the hundreds of so-called managers one Sunday morning and said that half of them would have to go. The threat that they would be fired, if necessary, was suddenly withdrawn, no doubt when Maxwell recalled that he had promised Reed, in their unctuous concern for the staff they were deserting, that there would be no compulsory redundancies. Then he had an extraordinary piece of good fortune. The auditors drew attention to a massive surplus in the Mirror Group pension fund inherited from Reed. £34 million of it could legitimately be used for generous voluntary redundancy payments and the company could take what is called a holiday from paying pension contributions for several years. Reed, apparently, had no idea this huge sum was available in the kitty. It was a windfall that staggered even Maxwell. He had always boasted that because of the value of the property he had acquired the papers for nothing. Now he was actually being paid to own them. He had been undercharged and he was overjoyed. Armed with the money, and threatening to close down the papers if he did not succeed, he and his managers persuaded one third of the staff to leave. Many did so gladly. A large number approaching their retirement age were able to go on full pension. Only relatively few had the distinct impression they had been fired, contrary to Maxwell's pledge of no compulsory redundancies, but most of the arm-twisting was done by chapels concerned to preserve jobs for the majority. It was a bloodless revolution without precedent in Fleet Street. Maxwell had achieved something beyond the wit of any previous managements. He had more than compensated for his early blunders.

All this happened within a few months of my retirement. The loss-making Mirror papers were put dramatically into profit, as instantly as a cup of Maxwell House coffee. Maxwell was able to launch the *London Daily News*, with direct input by journalists and few of the restrictive practices that had crippled the industry. It was printed at three centres away from Fleet Street. The great exodus in fact began when Maxwell succeeded in transferring the production of the *Sporting Life* after tumultuous rows with the printing chapels as early as 1985. It was followed by Rupert Murdoch's stunning, and in my opinion justified, overnight flit to Fortress Wapping, at which the newest production techniques replaced the oldest, without restrictive practices, and with no more than a couple of issues wholly lost. The other papers had to follow or face ruin. The *Daily Mail* and the *Mail on Sunday* planned to move their editorial teams to Barker's in Kensington High Street, which would have been unthinkable three years ago, and their printing to dockland. The *Daily* and *Sunday Telegraphs*, already printing on the Isle of Dogs, decided to shift their journalists and management to South Plaza Quay, also in dockland. The *Observer* headed for Battersea, with regional printing, and the *Financial Times* to its new print works near the Blackwall Tunnel. Only the Express papers seemed to linger. They followed Maxwell's example and shed many staff at great cost, unassisted by the pension fund. The manager responsible was later fired.

It's still the same old story, really. Fleet Street as it was known may have gone, but the usual rules apply. A paper can have a superlative general manager (no journalist has yet met one). It can have a circulation or sales director known and respected by even the humblest wholesaler, which is supposed by some alchemy, never understood outside circulation departments, to lead to the paper in question being given pride of place at local newsagents owned by retailers. It can have a publicity director like the *Mirror*'s John Jenkinson who, at the behest of an insane proprietor, could fill Wembley Stadium for a log-sawing contest. (One of his notable achievements was to organise a motor race around Mexico, which some crazed person thought would promote sales of the *Mirror*.) It can have the cream (if that is the right word) of advertising bosses, who smokes huge cigars and is given the table next to Jeffrey Archer's in the Savoy Grill, and a direct input, high technology satellite printing process that would have imbued a sense of failure in Caxton himself. But if the paper is wrong not even bingo and its up-market variations can provide more than a remission from eventual doom.

This statement of the blazingly obvious is not understood by many managers of my acquaintance. They tend to regard journalists and their curious habits, such as extremely expensive lunches with each other that are claimed on expense chits to be with the Archbishop of Canterbury or the head of MI5, with open contempt. Down the years I have seen them take one decision after another that damages the only part of the paper that sells it, the editorial matter that, as my former deputy Joe Grizzard says, 'keeps the rules apart'. When I first became editor of the *Sunday Mirror* in 1972 we had 210 columns of editorial in a 48-page paper and 126 columns of advertising. When I left it for the (under Maxwell) ludicrous post of deputy chairman we had only 177 columns of editorial and 159 of advertising. Hugh

Cudlipp's successors had filched nearly five pages from our readers. Worse than that, because of the initial ludicrous failure of managers to make the very simple new technology work, coupled, of course, with the bloody-mindedness of the print union chapel officials, whereas previously we had twelve news pages starting from scratch on Saturday, we were reduced to five, and after I left fewer than that. All manner of good stories that came in on Saturday were cut to shorts or held, in the often forlorn hope that we would get enough pages changed later in the run to do them justice. The later journalists can bring out a paper, the better it is: another obvious truth. The sports editor and I had a steady mail from aggrieved readers asking why we did not carry the dog results, why Ipswich Town received such scant coverage, and why half the paper was advertising. Everything must be geared to getting the paper to bed as late as possible. I remember during the war the *Star* was the only one of the three London evening newspapers on sale in Reading with the news in a headline that looked a foot deep GHANDI IS SLAIN. The others did not even have it in the stop press. I had a healthy respect for the *Star* from that moment on.

A training course is required for Britain's new breed of press baron. Far more important than appearing as a guest star on a chat show is getting the editorial into shape. This was demonstrated in textbook style with the launch of *Today*, which in nautical terms was nearly the equivalent of the captain sinking the Titanic without even leaving the Clyde. No newspaper, probably, was more eagerly awaited. It had goodwill that the divine blessing of the Pope or the combined millions of Murdoch, Maxwell and Tiny Rowland could not begin to bestow. The public had at last got the message about the tyrannical power and outrageous exploitation of the public by the print union czars. Eddie Shah was a national hero. But the paper flopped. It was a disaster, and not merely because the blurred printing of the colour pictures gave the nation double vision and became a national joke. It failed simply because the paper was bad. The editor, a good man, was the wrong man. That was evident to any competent journalist merely by looking at his product. It would have been evident to a Beaverbrook or a Murdoch from the dummy runs that preceded publication. Eddie (as all Fleet Street called him) did not know what was wrong. If he did, he did not know how to put it right. Full marks for valour, but both had to go.

Most of the papers that have died since my first cycle ride to the *Reading Mercury* were a loss only to the hordes of workers and relatively few journalists who worked on them. I doubt if the ghost of Lord Kemsley himself, the most depressing of press proprietors, would have shed a phantasmal tear at the closure in swift succession of the *Empire News*, the *Sunday Chronicle* and the *Sunday Graphic*. It was an editor of the last of these whose one moment of fame was when he had the testicles of a prize bull painted out of a photograph to avoid offending Lady Kemsley. The apocryphal postscript to this Fleet Street story is that the owner of the bull then sued.

The closure of the *News Chronicle* was a grievous loss to decent journalism, brought about by the unhappy coincidence of a weak proprietor and bad editor in office at the same time. If some press barons are guilty of outrageous excesses, Laurence Cadbury and Norman Kersley were guilty of something far worse in Fleet Street's eyes, failure. It was a feat without parallel to have killed off the paper that in post-war years had the greatest cartoonist, Vicky; one of the most respected political commentators, A. J. Cummings (never mind that I heard Tom Baistow, a founder of the Socialist Journalists Society, crying in despair in El Vino's 'I can't think of a headline for his damned column'); the best genuine diarist, Ian Mackay; plus Robert Lynd; and the most talented of all film critics, Richard Winnington. Terence Lancaster reminds me of a story told about the *Chronicle*, formerly the *Daily News*, in its final days. Someone said what a pity that Charles Dickens, who edited the *Daily News* for a brief period, was not still alive to save the paper, to which his companion replied: 'What a pity Norman Kersley is not alive.' To my surprise, Beaverbrook asked me to take on several *News Chronicle* journalists as an act of charity and advised me to seek Kersley's advice. After we had lunched at the Savoy, he and I strolled along the Embankment and stood talking for a moment or two outside his former office. The building was closed. There was litter in the doorway through which journalists all Fleet Street revered had walked or staggered. I was deeply moved. Kersley prattled on, seemingly unaware of the extent of the catastrophe that had befallen our profession and himself.

Part of the curriculum of a school for proprietors should be to study the successful launch of the *Independent*. It had no colourful figure like Eddie Shah to excite public interest. Its editor and creator Andreas Whittam Smith rated just above nil on the charismatic scale. Few potential readers knew his face, voice or background. Despite his convictions to the contrary, the *Independent* had no obvious spot in the market place. *The Times, Guardian* and *Telegraph* are all excellent newspapers. But with no Maxwell money (or very little, as it turned out, since he had bought some shares secretly), and without the vast managerial/editorial experience of a

Murdoch, the *Independent* is the most startlingly brilliant new newspaper probably since Northcliffe's *Daily Mail*. Because, of course,
the editorial is right. The editor is right. He has proved at last that
journalists can actually do it on their own without a proprietor
whose ego will not be sated until he rules the world. The *Independent* could not have been conceived, let alone survived, without the
new technology to which Fleet Street was the last newspaper printing centre in the world to succumb.

Sadly another vast change has occurred. When ships sank, planes
crashed, presidents were shot and politicians were found to sin as
grievously as the rest of us, it was to newspapers like the *Daily
Express* and the *Daily Mail* that readers turned for the ultimate in
news coverage. Now it is the newspapers formerly known as the
'heavies', like *The Times, Guardian* and *Observer* plus the new
Independent that have adopted the best characteristics of the
popular press. Their sales have risen accordingly. The *Daily Mail*
has neither gone up or down, which is quite enough for Sir David
English to deserve his respected niche in Fleet Street history as its
editor. The sales of the *Daily Express* remain halved. Richard Stott,
the bravely independent new editor of the *Daily Mirror*, is clawing
back some of the readers lost in the exultant excesses of Maxwell's
takeover. I heard him say to the man who may yet become a great
proprietor, 'Page two is yours, Bob. The rest is no go.' Generally
Maxwell has learned, or been taught, a great deal since my period
with him. He must take the main responsibility for the failure of the
London Daily News. If he had asked me I would have advised
against his confusing, fatal idea of a 24-hour paper, but the *London
Daily News* was a good try. Maxwell's name now appears in-
frequently and he no longer feels personally responsible, complete
with pictures of himself, for resolving every problem that besets the
human race. Among the popular papers, only the *Sun* and the *News
of the World* have triumphed over all the trends, selling nearly 4 and
5 million copies respectively; the milch cow that has financed Murdoch's huge success and, serving their more snobbish readers right,
enabled him to save *The Times* and *Sunday Times*.

The micro-chip, replacing the evocative hot-metal smell and the
clamour of the old composing rooms with the silent wizardry of
computer technology, has made it far easier for the good, bad and
indifferent to survive. These are golden years for journalists. There
will be other new newspapers and great opportunities. How ironical
that this has come about because the place journalists loved most no
longer exists. Goodbye Fleet Street. It had to die.

INDEX

Agate, James, 90–1
Ainsworth, Harry, 40, 41, 47, 49
Aitken, Ian, 3, 6, 75, 88, 148, 153
Aitken, Max, 1, 21, 54, 61, 67, 72, 75, 90, 94, 98, 99, 105, 119, 120, 139, 140, 143, 148, 151–2; relationship with, 114–16, 123–6, 141, 150, 155–6; with Giles, 73–4
Anderson, Evelyn, 33, 34
Archer, Jeffrey, 251
Armstrong-Jones, Anthony see Lord Snowdon
Astor, David, 82
Atkins, Tommy, 203
Attlee, Clement (Lord), 33, 35–6, 42

Baddeley, Jean, 224
Bailey, Steve, 173
Baistow, Tom, 253
Baker, Peter, 67–8, 74–5, 129–30, 151–2
Banks, John, 234
Barkley, William, 75
Barnes, Clive, 104, 144–5
Bartholomew, Harry Guy, 201, 202
Basham, Bertie, 49–51
Baxter, Beverley, 5, 115, 130
Bean, Mr Justice, 195
Beatles, the, 103
Beavan, John, 203
Beaverbrook, Lady, 91, 92, 139, 142, 148–9
Beaverbrook, Lord, 1, 35, 40, 54, 55, 56, 64, 65, 66, 67, 68, 70, 71, 78, 84, 85–6, 87, 88–90, 92–3, 95, 96, 102, 104, 107, 108, 111, 126, 128, 129; on articles by: Barnes, 144–5; Fairlie, 145–6; Forster, 91–2; Winn, 132–3;
attitude to: black Africa, 79–81; Commonwealth, 82–3; Royal Family, 76–7; Blumenfeld letter, 116–17; death of, 148–9; Eden, support for, 60–2; Edwards's resignation, 189; first meeting, 2–6; Gale interview, 146–7; illness, 141–3; influence on *Daily Express*, 97–100, 115–16; last birthday, 147; memos from, 118–25, 130, 133–4, 136–7, 143–4; rift in relationship, 138–40; staff relations, 73–5
Beeston, Richard, 30
Bellisario, R., 169–70
Benson, Harry, 148–9
Berman, Monty, 206
Berry, Lady Pamela, 155
Bevan, Aneurin, 35, 36, 37–8, 39, 61, 154; resignation, 46
Beyfus, Drusilla, 22
Biggs, Ronald, 167
Birkin, Vic, 241
Black, Bob, 28–9
Black, Conrad, 130, 228
Black, Peter, 144
Blackburn, Tom, 1, 86, 87, 88, 93, 99, 105, 106, 114, 120, 126, 140, 147–8, 156, 188
Block, Leslie, 161
Blumenfeld, R. D., 79, 130; letter from Beaverbrook, 116–17
Blyth, Chay, 161
Boothby, Robert (Lord), 33
Bowes, Roger, 225
Braine, John, 160
Brenard, Arthur, 66
Brittenden, Arthur, 77
Brodie, Peter, 160

Brown, George (Lord), 216
Buchanan, Stanley, 47–8
Buckton, Ray, 216
Burnet, Alistair, 109
Burrington, Ernie, 237
Butler, R. A., 145, 154–5
Butterfield, Jill, 144

Cadbury, Laurence, 253
Callaghan, James, 164, 183
Campbell, Sam, 35, 40–9, 51, 53, 157,
    159, 161, 167, 170, 173, 184–5, 187,
    198–9
Carpenter, Les, 218–19, 248
Carr, William, 129
Cassidy, Dennis, 193–4
Chamberlain, Neville, 117
Chambers, Peter, 124
Chapman, Brian, 95
Chapple, Frank, 181
Christiansen, Arthur, 6, 55, 85, 94, 97,
    115, 116, 118, 123, 130, 138, 141;
    Headlines All My Life, 117
Christiansen, Michael, 167, 200, 205
Christopher, John, 132
Churchill, Randolph, 70; attacks Eden,
    57–9; libel cases: Campbell, 187–8;
    Edwards, 188–91; on NATO article, 61
Churchill, Sir Winston, 3, 4, 33, 58, 95,
    141, 201; relationship with
    Beaverbrook, 60, 153; support for
    Randolph, 188–9; Tories regain
    office, 42
Clark, Douglas, 65, 69
Clarkson, Wensley, 173, 176–7
Cleare, Bill, 21
Colville, Richard, 169–70
Comyn, James, 186
Connor, Bill (Cassandra), 103, 201
Connor, Lady Megan, 201
Cook, Gerry, 100, 105
Cook, James Stewart, 52–3
Cotton, Billy, 111, 232
Cousins, Frank, 92
Crone, Tom, 174, 178–81, 183
Crossman, Richard, 38–9
Cudlipp, Hugh, 40, 42, 65, 98, 114,
    116, 146, 151, 154, 158–9, 165, 167,
    196, 198–200, 248, 252; appointed
    editorial director *Daily Mirror*, 202;

consultant to Maxwell, 246; IPC
    chairman, 204–5; leaves *Sunday
    Pictorial*, 201; Reed's takeover, 209;
    retires from IPC, 210; working with,
    206–8
Cummings, A. J., 253
Cummings, Michael, 34

Dalton, Hugh, 172
Davidson, Hugh, 160, 184, 185–6
Deakin, Arthur, 36
Dean, Brenda, 218
Deedes, William (Lord), 129
Delfont, Bernard (Lord), 133
Delmer, Sefton (Tom), 120–1
Dempster, Nigel, 174
Denning, (Lord), 134
Diamond, Jack, 216
Dinsdale, Dick, 42
Dobson, Christopher, 75
Donnelly, Desmond, 35
Donoughue, Bernard (Lord), 217
Dorran, Bill, 164
Douglas, Torrington, 43
Downing, Brian, 213
Drake, Peter, 119
Driberg, Tom, 75, 95, 160
Drury, Frank, 166, 171

Eade, Charlie, 187
Earle, Peter, 166
Eden, Sir Anthony, 3, 58, 60, 61; Suez,
    62
Edwards, Brigid, 110, 208, 215, 216,
    223
Edwards, Jimmy, 191
Elland, Percy, 54, 56, 58, 62, 70, 72, 96
Ellis, Frederick, 68–9, 163
Ellwood, Laura, 2, 34, 37, 48–50, 51,
    90–1, 92, 126, 206
Elmer, 'Gus', 22–5, 28
English, David, 30, 140, 143, 169, 254
Esser, Robin, 152
Evans, Harold, 65, 68, 128
Evans, Trevor, 75, 148, 155

Fairlie, Henry, 145
Farmer, Hugh, 193–5
Farr, David, 161
Findlater, Richard, 34

Foot, Michael, 2, 3, 5, 32–3, 35–6, 37, 39, 46, 55, 61, 65, 75, 92, 210–11, 216; publishes Randolph Churchill's *Tribune* article, 187
Foot, Paul, 114, 194
Foran, Major, 20, 23
Formby, George, 42–3
Forster, Peter, 90–2, 124; Edwards's writ against, 191–3
Foster, Roy, 214
Francis-Williams, Lord, 95, 188
Freeman, John, 35
Fyvel, Tosco, 32, 34

Gadd, Graham, 167, 171
Gaitskell, Hugh, 35–6, 38, 153
Gale, George, 2, 145, 146, 154–5
Gardner, Ken, 160, 164
George (driver for *Daily Express*), 112–13
Giles, Carl, 72, 73–4, 102
Goodman, Arnold (Lord), 156, 168, 191, 193
Goodman, Geoffrey, 231
Goodwin, Noel, 104, 145
Gordon, John, 40, 64, 202
Gourlay, Logan, 232
Grade, Lew, 206
Graham, Clive, 102
Graham, John, 168
Green, Felicity, 212
Grimsditch, Peter, 129
Grizzard, Joe, 198, 251
Gubbins, Nathaniel, 90
Gunn, Bert, 54

Hackett, Denis, 100, 151, 208, 209
Haines, Joe, 60, 78, 154, 217, 229–30, 231–2, 243
Hamilton, Denis, 159
Hardcastle, William, 123
Harding, Gilbert, 41
Harper, Stephen, 146
Haswell, Robert, 170
Hayes, Walter, 187
Head, Bob, 213
Healey, Denis, 165
Heath, Edward, 78, 152, 155, 161
Helliwell, Arthur, 165
Hennessy, Patrick, 92

Hipwell, W. R., 202
Hirst, Mr Justice, 245–6
Hoare, John, 161
Hogg, Quintin (Lord Hailsham), 155
Home, Alec Douglas (Lord), 145, 155
Hope, Anne, 183
Horwood, Vic, 226–7
Hoskins, Percy, 75, 148
Howard, Keith, 84, 108, 132, 156, 157
Howard, Lee, 42, 208, 211
Hudgell, Ken, 222–3, 226
Humphreys, James, 166–7

Ingrams, Richard, 194, 235
Investigative stories: animal charities, 48–9; black market steel, 47; Hull fish cartel, 52–3; Malayan massacre, 164–5; Messina brothers, 45; Mitcham bank raid, 162–3; pornography, 166–7; Rotherham post office raid, 163–4; Royal train, 171–83; spiritualists, 49–51
Irving, Clive, 100, 104, 124

Jackson, Martin, 145
Jacobson, Sydney, 167, 206–7, 209, 217
Jagger, Mick, 160
Jameson, Derek, 129, 191
Jarratt, Alex, 116, 182, 197, 209, 210, 211, 220, 222; managing director IPC, 196
Jay, Douglas, 33
Jenkins, Alan, 25
Jenkins, Clive, 216
Jenkinson, John, 240, 251
Johnson, Paul, 145
Johnson, Peter, 112
Johnstone, David, 161
Jones, Elwyn (Lord), 216
Junor, John, 1–3, 30, 40, 55, 64–8, 71, 90, 100, 102, 115, 130, 138, 139, 150, 156, 157, 169, 170, 188–90, 219, 235

Keeble, Harold, 76, 100, 102–3, 106, 152
Keeler, Christine, 134, 160
Kemsley, Lord, 252
Kendall, Kenneth, 157–8
Kennedy, Jackie, 99
Kennedy, John F., 140

Kersh, Cyril, 41, 188
Kersley, Norman, 253
Keys, Bill, 218–19
Killian, Richard, 75
King, Cecil, 42, 82, 196, 198, 199, 200, 205, 209, 211, 213, 233; Café Royal conferences, 202–3; reinstates Cudlipp, 202
King, Stella, 66
Kinnock, Neil, 38, 235, 244
Klein, Rudolph, 56, 62
Knight, John, 101
Kruschev, 59, 106

Labour Party: 1951 election defeat, 42; Maxwell proposes new paper, 216; *Tribune*'s Bevanite policy statement, 46
Lamb, Larry, 169, 201
Lancaster, Osbert, 72, 75, 102, 151
Lancaster, Terence, 98, 140, 154, 159, 165, 229–30, 231, 253
Lane, Harold, 28–9
Lawther, William, 36, 38
Lee, Jennie, 37, 39
Legum, Colin, 82
Leslie, Ann, 144
Levin, Bernard, 104, 152
Lewin, David, 133
Lloyd, Nick, 168, 174
Long, Douglas, 212–13, 224, 226
Low, 4
Lowe, Shirley, 124
Lucas, Norman, 168
Lucas, Ted, 204–5
Luckett, Frank, 21, 22, 24
Ludlow, Robin, 178

McCaffery, Tom, 235
McCarthy, Bill, 30
McColl, René, 74, 76, 104, 106, 148
MacGregor, Ian, 232
Mackay, Ian, 253
McKay, Peter, 182
MacKenzie, Kelvin, 245–6
Macmillan, Harold, 139, 145, 153, 155
McMillan, Jimmy, 78, 79
MacSharry, Deirdre, 144, 152
Mallalieu, ('Curly') J. P. W., 38, 40
Manifold, Laurie, 159, 167, 171, 194

Marchant, Hilde, 51
Marks, Derek, 139, 155–6
Matthews, Bruce, 240, 246
Matthews (Lord), 128
Maugham, Somerset, 91
Maule, Henry, 28
Maxwell, Elisabeth, 220
Maxwell, Ghislaine, 217, 238
Maxwell, Robert, 4, 5, 60, 98, 99, 107, 116, 138, 139, 146, 168, 191, 199, 201, 213, 214, 215, 219, 220–1, 225, 229, 243, 244, 245, 247, 249, 250, 252; BPCC buys Odhams plant, 218; bids for Mirror Group, 222; *Daily Record* ultimatum, 226; Ethiopian appeal, 241–2; launches campaigns, 231–3; new jobs for all, 225–6; Pergamon bids for *Observer*, 218; press conference, 227; proposes new Labour paper, 216; Snowball bonanza, 241; *Sun*, case against, 246; wartime experiences, 217; 'Win-a-million' game, 236–41
Mead (Beaverbrook's butler), 4, 77, 89, 91, 127, 141, 142, 148–9
Messina brothers, the, 45
Mikardo, Ian, 32, 36, 47
Miles, Tony, 128, 177–8, 180, 182, 211, 212, 213, 214, 218, 221, 224, 225, 226, 230, 236
Millar, George, 90, 133
Milligan, Spike, 160
Molloy, Mike, 103, 201, 224, 229, 231, 242, 243, 244, 245
Montgomery, David, 168
Morison, Stanley, 81
Morrison, Herbert, 33
Morrison, Lionel, 185–6
Morton, J. B. (Beachcomber), 74
Mosley, Leonard, 85–6, 145
Mossman, Jim, 30
Mossman, John, 29
Mountbatten, Edwina (Countess), 101
Muggeridge, Malcolm, 188
Murdoch, Rupert, 97, 99, 107, 109, 128, 129, 202, 209, 227, 240, 243, 252, 254; Fortress Wapping, 250
Murray, George, 78
Murray, Len, 232

Neale, Frank, 20–1, 22, 23, 24, 26, 33
Needham, Bill, 109
Neill, Brian, 186–7
Nener, Jack, 198–9
Newberry, Mike, 30
Newman, Jim, 172–3, 178
Norfolk, Duke of, 74
North, Rex, 40
Northcliffe, (Lord), 254
Nudd, Eric, 46

O'Sullevan, Peter, 102
Owen, Frank, 75

Parker Bowles, Colonel and Mrs, 174, 181–2
Patrick, Victor, 1, 67
Payne, Reg, 42, 203, 205
Pettingell, Frank, 23
Pickering, Edward, 84, 85, 90, 94, 96, 97, 98, 100, 102, 103, 106–8, 110, 111–13, 115, 124, 126, 128, 130, 148, 153, 158, 208, 211; knighthood, 116
Pincher, Chapman, 75
Pinnington, Geoffrey, 178, 201
Pitman, Robert, 65, 78, 91
Plesch, Arpad 92–3
Poole, Oliver (Lord), 61, 68–9, 155
Powell, Enoch, 26, 162
Profumo, John, 129, 134, 155
Profumo, Valerie, 129
Proops, Marjorie, 207, 240, 242
Pulley, Frank, 185–6

Radford, Fred, 28
Ramsey, Dr Michael, 207
Raybould, Eric, 72, 101, 111, 112, 151, 152, 155
Raymond (Beaverbrook's valet), 80–1, 89, 92, 94, 140
Rayner, Claire, 242
Reece, Gordon, 235
Reed International, 208, 209, 213, 218, 220, 227, 248, 250
Rees-Mogg, William, 107
Reid, Jimmy, 244
Rice-Davies, Mandy, 134
Richard, Keith, 160
Richards, Morley, 120–1
Ridgway, John, 161

Roberts, Percy, 202, 208, 209, 211, 212, 213
Rochez, Harry, 197
Rogers, Frank, 202
Rook, Jean, 144
Rosenberg, Josephine, 88–90, 93–4
Rothermere, (Lord), 187
Rothman, Nat, 46
Rowe, Charles, 47, 52
Rowland, 'Tiny', 218, 252
Royal Family, the: Beaverbrook's attitude to, 76–7; engagement of Princess Elizabeth and Lieutenant Philip Mountbatten, 28; death of King George VI, 51–2; pursuit by 'paparazzi', 169–71; Royal Train story: correspondence with Shea, 177–80; official denial, 177; press reaction, 182; publication of correspondence, 181; Snowdon divorce, 207
Ryder, Don (Lord), 196, 198, 208, 211
Rydon, John, 104

St John Stevas, Norman, 181
Samuel, Howard, 36–7
Sanders, Terry, 240
Savile, Jimmy, 41
Scargill, Arthur, 232
Scott, George, 188
Scott, Norman, 129, 164, 171
Shah, Eddie, 250, 252–3
Shand-Kydd, Frances (Lady), 174
Sharpley, Anne, 54, 62
Shaw, Dorothy, 126
Shea, Michael, 174, 177–8, 180–1, 183
Shepherd, Ross, 45
Shinwell, 'Manny', 164
Shulman, Milton, 22
Simpson, Joseph, 166
Sissons, Peter, 222
Snagge, John, 157–8
Snowdon, Lord, 76, 207, 215
Somerfield, Stafford, 65, 129
Soutar, Willie, 115
Spain, Nancy, 104, 109
Spooner, Frank, 171
Spooner, Pamela, 85, 109
Sprinzel, Pam, 140
Stevens, David, 99, 130, 228

Stevens, Jocelyn, 151
Stott, Richard, 249, 254
'Strong, Richard', 58–61
Swaffer, Hannen, 51, 131

Taylor, A. J. P., 3, 117; Blumenfeld's
   letter in *Beaverbrook*,
   116
Taylor, Bob, 161
Thatcher, Margaret, 3, 42, 183, 235
Thompson, John, 129
Thompson, Peter, 214, 248–9
Thomson, D. C., 238
Thomson, George Malcolm, 74, 78, 83,
   138, 148–9, 153
Thomson, Roy (Lord), 89, 147, 198,
   218
Thornton, Clive, 128, 213–14, 220, 221,
   222, 236
Thorpe, Jeremy, 129, 164, 171
Tory, Peter, 242
Trelford, Donald, 218
Trevelyan, John, 166
Tull, 'Mickey', 24
Tween, Roy, 225

Vicky, 4, 253

Walledge, Len, 199
Waterhouse, Keith, 230
Waterman, Jack, 56
Webb, Duncan, 44–5, 51
Weston, Garfield, 147–8
Westover, Anne, 115
Westropp, Edward, 65, 66
Whittam Smith, Andreas, 253
Wigg, George, 38
Williams, David, 55
Wilson, Harold, 3, 35, 36, 82, 138, 145,
   154, 165, 168, 199–200, 205, 211, 216
Wilson, P. J., 171–4, 177
Winn, Godfrey, 109, 130–3
Winn, Roger (Lord Justice), 69, 163
Winnington, Richard, 253
Wintour, Charles, 55, 58, 61–2, 72, 85,
   155, 183
Wolff, Michael, 78
Wood, Roger, 97, 124, 126, 130
Worsthorne, Peregrine, 145
Wyatt, Woodrow, 127, 187

Yates, Ivan, 93, 193
Young & Rubicam, 234, 236, 239

Zec, Donald, 168, 201, 207